# Sodium Girl's LIMITLESS Low-Sodium COOKBOOK

+

This book is printed on acid-free paper. ♾

Food styling by Adam Pearson
Cover design by Jeff Faust
Interior design by Joline Rivera
Published by John Wiley & Sons, Inc., Hoboken, New Jersey
Published simultaneously in Canada.



Library of Congress Cataloging-in-Publication Data

Goldman Foung, Jessica, 1982-
Sodium girls limitless low-sodium cookbook/Jessica Goldman Foung; photography by Matt Armendariz.
p. cm.
Includes index.
978-1-118-12377-5 (pbk.); 978-1-118-26044-9 (ebk.); 978-1-118-26593-2 (ebk.); 978-1-118-26040-1 (ebk.)
1. Salt-free diet--Recipes. I. Armendariz, Matt. II. Title.
RM237.8.G65 2012
641.5'6323--dc23

Printed in China

10 9 8 7 6 5 4 3 2 1

# SODIUM GIRL'S LIMITLESS LOW-SODIUM COOKBOOK

JESSICA GOLDMAN FOUNG

PHOTOGRAPHY BY MATT ARMENDARIZ

JOHN WILEY & SONS, INC.

# CONTENTS

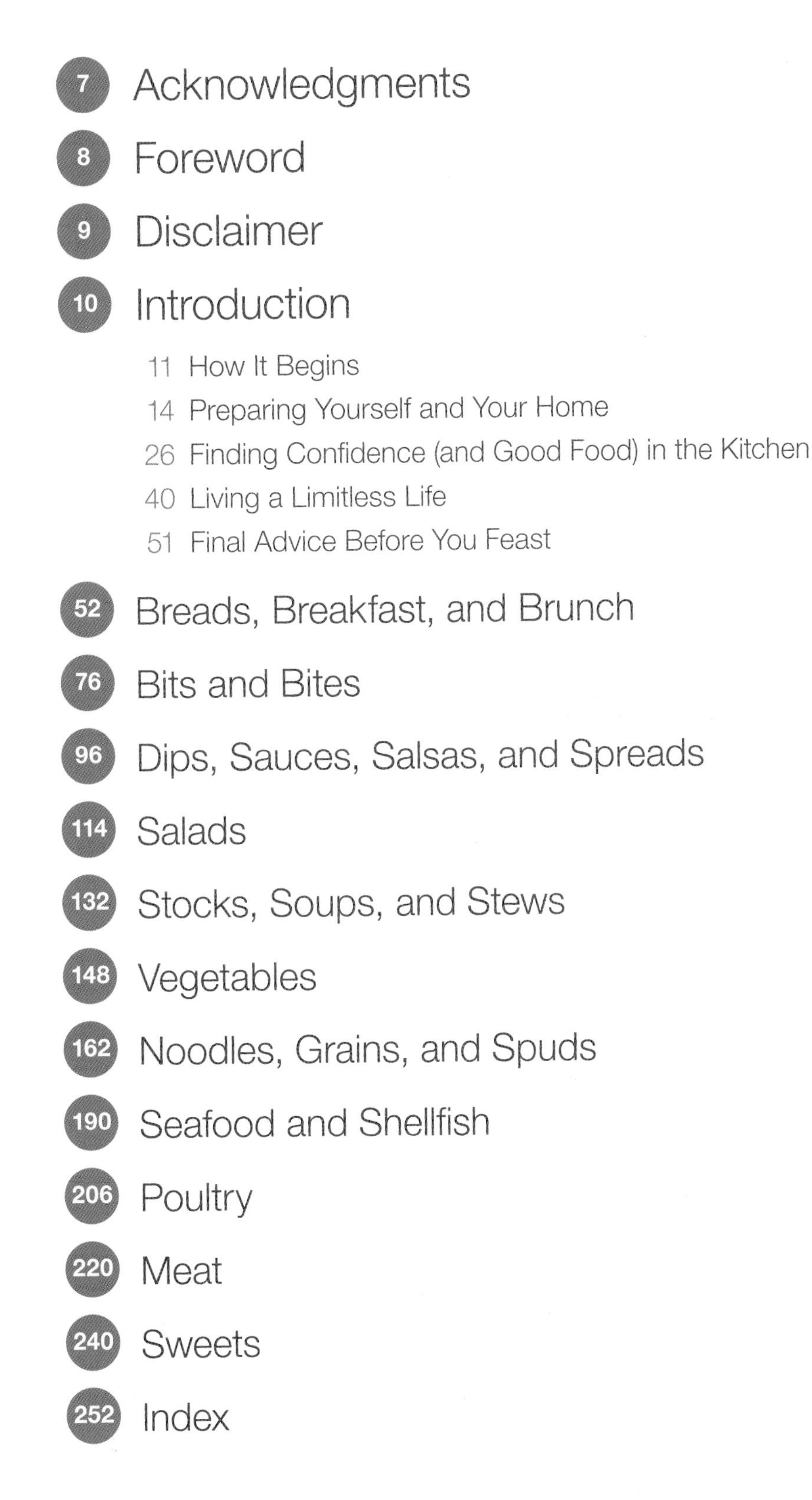

"Laughter is the best medicine. Food is a close second. And when you have both, it makes a killer dinner party."

—*Me*

# ACKNOWLEDGMENTS

Endless words of gratitude go to...

My personal chef, my best buddy, and my husband, who introduced me to bok choy and believes in me more than I ever could;

My brave parents, who continue to selflessly offer their love, support, kitchen, and kidneys;

My brother, who inspires me always and motivated me to teach myself to cook;

My FIL, MILs, SILs, GIL, and BIL who take on this diet with gusto and (over)feed me often;

**The Creative Team:** Matt Armendariz, Adam Pearson, Gaby Dalkin, Glen Coco (Teri Lyn Fisher), Alexis Hartman, Jenni Ferrari-Adler, Justin Schwartz and the Wiley Publishing team, Karsha Chang, Heather Bandura, Adelaide Mueller, and the crew at Bernie's Coffee Shop for the workspace and endless caffeine;

**The Pros:** Chef Ethan Howard, Karen Solomon, Chef Traci Des Jardins, Chef Amaryll Schwertner, Chef Hubert Keller, Amanda Hesser and Merrill Stubbs (Food52.com), Jennifer Engle, Chef Josip Martinovic and McCalls Catering & Events, Chef Scott Youkilis, Michael Pierce, Cathy Barrow, Chef Alan Carter, and the helpful folks at the Nutrient Data Laboratory;

**The Mentors:** Jess Thomson, Cheryl Sternman Rule, Christine Van DeVelde, Twilight Greenaway and the team at CUESA (for my first food writing gig), and Donald Gazzaniga;

**The Doctors:** Bunting, Lambert, Ng, Fraze, Westphal, Phelan, Wu, and everyone at Stanford Hospital who keep me ticking and kicking;

The countless friends and family (personal insert-name-here: ____________) who buy salt-free spices and slave away in the kitchen all in the name of perfected low-sodium recipes;

And last but not least, Frank and Stein (my two resilient kidneys), without whom this book would not exist.

# FOREWORD

When life gave Jessica Goldman Foung lemons, she didn't make lemonade. She made hollandaise sauce, and low-sodium enchiladas, pot stickers, and all the foods she was told would be off-limits on her new low-sodium, no-salt diet.

Her passion for life included eating well, and rather than compromise, Jessica became an expert about her own health conditions and then the sodium content in nearly every food and its ingredients. She set about on an adventurous culinary journey back to her favorite foods.

The result was her energetic, flavor-packed food blog, *SodiumGirl.com*, and now this guide, where she brings readers to a new way of thinking about preparing food that is delicious, beautiful on the plate, and always low sodium. This is no ersatz cookbook, but rather a savvy primer on reeducating your palate, developing creative techniques for sleuthing out new tastes and celebrating the complex and diverse world of flavors beyond the salt shaker.

*—Nora Cain, Director Stanford Hospital Health Library*

*She brings readers to a new way of thinking about and preparing food that is delicious, beautiful on the plate, and always low sodium.*

# DISCLAIMER

I am not a dietitian, nor a nutritionist, nor a professionally trained chef—and most definitely not a doctor. Although, at this point, from the number of appointments and trips to the hospital I've had, I could play a pretty convincing one on television. By Malcolm Gladwell's calculations, it takes approximately 10,000 hours to become an expert in a particular field. So when it comes to keeping a low-sodium diet, I definitely consider myself a reliable resource.

After eight-plus years (or over 70,000 hours), I understand the ins, the outs, and the middles of cutting salt from food while keeping flavor and spontaneity in one's life. I have been on this journey for almost a decade, at first feeling alone, uninspired, and confused. But once I figured out how to master this diet, and do it in a way that felt effortless and fun, I began to get excited. I began to feel full. And I became more creative and capable than ever before.

But before we dive into the good stuff, let me stress one more, very important point: everybody and every body is different, especially when it comes to salt. The recipes and advice I am sharing in this book are what works for me. I cannot promise any specific health results (sorry, folks—no money-back guarantee). But I can promise that by being proactive about your health and adding nonmedical approaches to your medical care—whether it is following a low-sodium diet, doing yoga, or meditating before bed—you will most definitely feel empowered. In the sometimes unpredictable world of health, your effort to eat, live, and breathe as fully as possible will result in a sense of control.

So if you're ready to change your diet, remember to make it personal. Figure out what works best for you and be sure to talk to your dietitian and your doctors (the real ones with the certificates on their walls) to create the best health and diet plan for your needs.

With every plate of food you create and share from this book, we will (together!) prove that being on a low-sodium diet does not have to keep anyone from being totally satisfied. And most importantly, that you can greatly contribute to your health care with your own two hands.

PS: More than 55 salt-loving friends tested each and every dish in this book. None of them were on, nor needed to be on, a low-sodium diet, and only three qualified themselves as preferring pepper over salt. The rest said they would dump salt directly in their mouths if it were socially acceptable. And only two of the testers had to order last-minute pizza due to flavor-lacking results. Those recipes have since been revised.

PPS: A special note of gratitude to the recipe testers for their time, trust, honesty, and waistlines.

# INTRODUCTION

# HOW IT BEGINS

## SOME PEOPLE LIVE TO EAT.

## OTHERS EAT TO LIVE.

## + THEN THERE ARE THOSE OF US WHO ASPIRE TO DO BOTH.

If you're holding this book, I think it is safe to say you fall into the third category. You love food. Your pointer finger doubles as a sponge. Your bookshelves are filled with Ina Garten, Bobby Flay, and Thomas Keller—not Chaucer, Shakespeare, or J. K. Rowling. And your chin is not just a part of your face, but a safety net for catching aimless drips of sloppy sauces—it would be a shame to lose them to a napkin.

Point is, food is something you enjoy. So when your doctor told you to limit what you consume for health's sake, you most likely entered a state of shock. The diet sounded less like a fun challenge and more like a culinary death sentence.

But before you think your relationship with food is over (or you completely ignore your doctor's advice), let me say this: you've been given a gift. Not just because you may be able to improve your health with recipes rather than pills, but also because you may begin to enjoy and appreciate food more than you ever did before.

Trust me, I've been there. I was also told to cut out salt. I was handed the DASH guide to a low-sodium diet. I stared blankly at my kitchen pantry, thinking, "What the hell am I going to eat?" and felt like my diet and life were suddenly limited to the bland basics. So, yes, I understand what you're feeling. Overwhelmed, unsure, and certainly uninspired. But after I adjusted my perspective, tied on an apron, and decided to write my own rules about low-sodium cooking, I found that the diet was not the end of a flavorful, spontaneous life; it was the beginning of one. And you'll have to just trust me on that, too.

Today, I aim to consume between 500 and 1,000mg of sodium a day—less than half a teaspoon of salt. I rarely eat processed foods, I never use the salt shaker, and yet I manage to eat well. Really well. And it is because of my dietary restrictions that I now do more, pursue more, and never take "no" for an answer.

Before I had limits, I rarely ate beyond my comfort zone, which was typically American fare of fried chicken and mac 'n' cheese. I hated the idea of pastas and stews (I'm still confused as to why), I pushed aside vegetables, and I was never interested in trying anything authentic, foreign, or complex. I wasn't a picky eater; I was just dull. Turns out that I was actually more limited before sodium was an issue.

In removing the salt from my kitchen, though, I was forced to be more daring and creative with my food and my activities. I became "culinary curious," metaphorically jet-setting all over the world to find new spices, food combinations, and ingredients that would surprise my palate. I was hands-on with my food and with the people who cooked for me, whether it was my best friends, my parents, or my favorite local chefs.

I turned the challenge of a low-sodium diet into a game, like many of my favorite food shows, inviting people to play along—a challenge that even those without health needs conquered with equal enthusiasm and success. And with the right approach, my low-sodium diet not only made me feel better, but I think it actually made me (and the food I ate) more interesting, too. Staying on the diet felt more like an ongoing dinner party than a chore, and it proved to be far from colorless or boring.

So that's the positive spin, the ultimate goal, the final results. And here's the reality: adjusting to the diet does take time, effort, and enthusiasm. It takes failures and slip-ups, messes and extreme patience. It doesn't happen overnight, because your taste buds need to mend from oversalted processed foods. But I promise that you'll get there. You'll start to notice the natural flavors of ingredients again. You'll taste a bell pepper and go bonkers over its sweetness. You'll find that turnips and radishes are spicy; meat, chard, and beets taste a bit salty; and even Brussels sprouts have a sugary essence. And once you hit a low-sodium dish out of the ballpark, you'll be addicted to creating home runs from then on, knowing that you never have to settle for less.

I DECIDED I WOULD DO WHATEVER I COULD, ON TOP OF MY WONDERFUL MEDICAL CARE, TO GIVE MY BODY AND THE MEDICINE THE BEST CHANCE TO WORK.

Before moving on to the rest of my story (and goodness, there's so much to cover), it is important that I confess one final truth: I've had practice at this whole limited-diet thing, long before salt was a problem. Low-sodium foods were not my first foray into a restricted diet; four years prior to my kidney failure, I had been diagnosed with a gluten allergy. This was in 2001, before markets, restaurants, bakeries, and the world really knew what that meant. Before there was a "Gluten-Free Girl" or any websites or magazines dedicated to the subject. When the only gluten-free products one could order (online) still tasted like bricks. And bookstores only carried a handful of guides, none of which were colorful, personal, or exciting. I learned then that much of my dietary success and satisfaction would have to come from my own experimentation and exploration.

I hit the Internet, I played with my food at home, and I even managed to eat well in college (reserving a gluten-free space within my dorm kitchen). I traveled to Italy for a semester, safely feasting on Parmesan cheese, prosciutto, and melon. Yes, the irony of this last sentence is not lost on me either. But the point is, I made the diet work. I educated my peers and myself, and eating without wheat or casein did not stop me from enjoying food or the adventures of life.

I was prepped to be proactive, and that's a good thing, because only a few weeks after I returned from the land of slow food and pizza, having not touched a single thread of salt-free handmade pasta, I found out that gluten was not the issue. Lupus was. And this autoimmune disease was attacking my kidneys and my brain. Aggressively.

Instead of returning to my college dorm room, I spent my winter quarter housed in many of Stanford Hospital's units. I was given chemotherapy treatments; I was on apheresis; I was on dialysis; and I was on the kidney transplant list. After three months of incredible medical care and an enormous amount of support from family and friends, I eventually stabilized. I was able to move out of the hospital and back home. I even started taking college courses again, trying to get my life—a new life—back on track, fully aware that I had survived. But my kidneys had not.

Now, I could have functioned as a 21-year-old, on dialysis, waiting on the transplant list. But that wasn't the kind of life I wanted to live. I was attached to machines every three days for three to four hours at a time, and while I was happy to be alive, I longed to be free.

I decided I would do whatever I could, on top of my wonderful medical care, to give my body and the medicine the best chance to work. And since my kidneys were declared in absolute renal failure, I decided to give them a much-deserved vacation. That's when I began my strict low-sodium diet, hoping that, with a little relaxation, they might decide to come back, bored from all the rest, excited to work again.

And over the next year, my kidneys began regenerating, a feat my doctors still cannot fully explain. I was taken off dialysis, I've been officially kicked off the kidney transplant list for eight years, and I've simply stayed healthy, active, and alive with my diet and medications alone.

That's how this journey began. That's how we land back at the beginning of this chapter, when I was told to go on a low-sodium diet and I decided to take it very seriously. I was determined to do what I could to strengthen and nourish my body, and, as a stubborn young person, I was equally resolute to eat and drink up all that life had to offer me. Just because my food was now limited, my life did not have to be.

Like gluten-free cooking in its younger years, low-sodium cooking and living is still wildly misrepresented. The rules often state that a low-sodium diet means no salt shaker; no convenience foods; nothing canned or processed; no salty dips, sauces, or broths; no eating out, or at least not eating anything exciting; no fun. But I wanted to go out and play with my friends. I wanted to travel. I wanted to go to restaurants at the last minute and actually get something good (and low-sodium) to eat. I wanted exceptional food at my wedding. I wanted to go to and eat at potlucks. And I wanted to bring a salt-free potato salad that others would rave about too. So I quickly decided that the old rules were not going to work for me. I did away with "nos" and began to search for the "yesses."

That's what this book is about. It is filled with the cans and coulds and shoulds of keeping a low-sodium diet. Not only will it give you all of the tools to make over your favorite salty foods, but it will also help you create new recipes of your own. You will learn how to make low-sodium versions of the classics you crave; how to make satisfying low-sodium meals quickly and with a sense of whimsy and fun; how to impress your palate and your friends; and how to overcome low-sodium obstacles both on your plate and in your life.

And you will learn how to eat to live, live to eat, and of course, enjoy everything in between.

# PREPARING YOURSELF + YOUR HOME

## IF YOU'RE READY FOR IT, THERE ARE THREE SIMPLE STEPS YOU NEED TO TAKE IN ORDER TO TURN A LOW-SODIUM DIET INTO AN EXCITING ADVENTURE.

### 1 Change Your Perspective

First, you have to adjust your perspective from feeling limited to limit*less*. Let's face it, food tastes good with salt: French fries, pasta water, even chocolate. Salt is everywhere. And you rightly feel restricted by your low-sodium diet because flavor has become synonymous with the taste of salt. How many times do you hear judges on cooking shows say that the food lacks taste and needs more salt? We have become a salt-obsessed culture. And often, when we eat, the flavor we look for is no longer just the taste of food enhanced by salt, but the salt itself. This is why products that try to mimic or simply eliminate the unmatchable taste of salt end up flat and unsatisfying.

But what happens if we shift our focus? What if we stop trying to recreate the taste of salt and, with an array of thoughtful techniques and spices, we turn our attention back to the food itself—the true star of the meal? The answer is good food made with less sodium and more imagination. In looking for flavor beyond salt, you will begin to play with a fresh palette of tastes and textures, and ultimately reintroduce your palate to a new definition of flavor.

As soon as you start thinking about the ingredients you can use, instead of what you cannot, low-sodium cooking will transform into an adventure rather than an afterthought. And when judges (friends, family, Tom Colicchio) taste this food, they'll search for the warmth of nutmeg, the artichoke essence of salsify, or the numbing fire of a Fresno pepper. Not the salt.

As soon as you start thinking about the ingredients you can use, instead of what you cannot, low-sodium cooking will transform into an adventure rather than an afterthought.

# THE LITTLE BLACK DRESS THEORY

Grab a cup of tea and ponder this hypothetical situation: what if someone told you that you couldn't wear black anymore? No really, take a sip from that steaming cup and think about it for a second.

I love wearing black. It's my go-to color. It's slimming, it's professional, it's easy. I count on my little black dress and my killer "I'm going to nail this meeting" black suit to make getting ready quick and easy. In my opinion, having to clear my closet of every black item would feel like a horrible joke. And having to replace my favorite clothes with other things (what could those even be?) and restyle my wardrobe (what would I wear?) would be an expensive and time-consuming undertaking.

But then, a moment of brilliance. If I really had to get rid of the black, a nice navy suit wouldn't look half bad and it is just as snappy for business meetings. Actually, there's that gold metallic number, the one I've had my eye on for a while but didn't have the guts to pull off, that turns out to be more striking than the cliché (and face it, fading) black dress in my closet. And when the next formal event rolls around and I can't fall back on the standard black outfit, I'll just have to rock that hot number instead. Maybe trying something new and standing out isn't such a bad thing after all.

Now, take another sip of your morning brew and imagine applying this same theory to your cooking. Salt is like that little black dress (or suit). And just like your once-monotone closet, it is merely one of the many ways to coax color and good taste from fresh ingredients. By looking beyond the salt, you're only trading simple food statements for dishes with more personal flair.

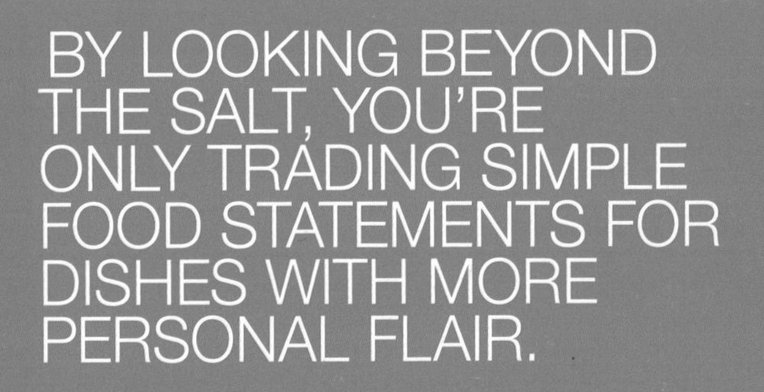


Unsalted butter, when browned, adds a nutty, earthy note to recipes. Vinegars lend a tang to meats, greens, and even ice cream. Spices like cumin, curry, fennel seed, and mustard bring robust flavor. Wine reductions and beer baths, molasses marinades and citrus dressings add complexity. Choices abound; salt-free meals don't have to fade into the background.

## Get Educated

The next step in achieving a successful diet is to educate yourself. If you don't know where sodium hides, it will be pretty difficult to avoid. And more importantly, if you don't know which foods are naturally low in sodium, your pantry will remain unnecessarily sparse.

For years, I'd been mistakenly eating many foods that were packed with sodium while avoiding others that were exceptionally low. For a quick lunch, I regularly filled up on tuna fish sandwiches without mayo (because I thought I was being sodium-smart), not even realizing that the bread alone—due to baking powder, baking soda, and yes, salt—accounted for 200mg of sodium per slice. Adding another 400mg to 500mg from the tuna, I easily hit my maximum daily allotment in a single lunch. In addition, I had cut out all seafood and pork, thinking that anything from the ocean or related to a Christmas ham was too high in sodium for my body. In reality, certain fish have some of the lowest sodium numbers of all the proteins. And as for pork, unless it has been brined, salted, or cured, it too falls in the low-sodium category and brings terrific savory flavor to the table. I clearly failed my intro to low-sodium studies.

But once I actually did some research, using resources like the USDA National Nutrient Database for Standard Reference and Bobbie Mostyn's *Pocket Guide to Low Sodium Foods*, I found that most fish has less sodium per serving than chicken and beef. And even some clams and oysters are fairly low in sodium (depending on how they're treated and packaged) and can add a natural salty taste to soups and stocks—something unexpected in a low-sodium diet. To this day, I continue to brush up on the sodium contents of natural foods—everything from eggs to celery to eel—and I constantly hunt grocery stores and the Internet for new low-sodium products like pickles, yogurt, and mustard. In writing this book, I've come to learn that even cantaloupe and artichokes contain a decent amount of natural sodium, a fact that I use to boost the flavor of blander dishes.

Beyond ingredients, it is also important to understand how much sodium you consume on a daily basis. The 2010 Dietary Guidelines for Americans state that people should eat less than 2,300mg of sodium a day and that 50 percent of the population, especially those with certain medical conditions, should eat 1,500mg of sodium a day or less. To put that in perspective, 1 teaspoon of salt has 2,300mg. Go measure it—you'll see how shockingly small it is.

1 TEASPOON

½ TEASPOON

## + YOU MAY KNOW HOW MUCH SODIUM YOU SHOULD EAT, BUT WHAT DOES THAT LOOK LIKE?

1 teaspoon of Morton Iodized Salt contains 2,360mg of sodium, which is barely higher than the 2010 USDA recommended daily intake for most Americans (2,300mg a day). And ½ teaspoon contains 1,200mg of sodium, which is slightly less than the recommended daily intake for over 50 percent of Americans (1,500mg a day).

It's easy to see how pinches and dashes can add up. And why, with the sodium in natural and processed food, most of us eat beyond the recommended amount, without even knowing it. But now that you know how much sodium you can consume, and where that sodium is coming from, you can make smart (and delicious) decisions that keep you full and healthy.

And while more than 75 percent of the sodium Americans consume is, on average, from packaged goods, most whole ingredients contain sodium as well. As you start realizing how much sodium is in that steak dinner or homemade sweet potato pie—even without the bottled sauce or reconstituted gravy—you'll see just how easily you can reach the 1,500mg limit without even touching the canned goods.

It is important to know these numbers because, whether you are counting calories or sodium, the last thing you want to do is sit at a table with a reference book and a calculator. You want to know the information well; you want to memorize it; you want it at your fingertips. That way, you can design a diet and boundaries for yourself that will help you make quick, smart, low-sodium choices. Without a second thought.

YOU WANT TO KNOW THE INFORMATION WELL; YOU WANT TO MEMORIZE IT; YOU WANT IT AT YOUR FINGERTIPS.

Now, let's pause for a moment to test your low-sodium IQ. Try to guess which items have the higher amount of sodium. And keep the answers to yourself.

+ **4 ounces of ground pork versus 1 raw artichoke**
+ **1 teaspoon of baking soda versus 1 large egg**
+ **1 cup of 2% milk versus 3 ounces of monkfish**

Do you have your guesses locked in? Are they your final answers? Well here are the shocking results:

+ **A 4-ounce portion of ground pork has around 60mg of sodium, whereas an uncooked, medium artichoke has 120mg.**
+ **A single teaspoon of baking soda has over 1,200mg of sodium, while a large egg has just over 70mg.**
+ **1 cup of 2% milk contains around 115mg of sodium, whereas the monkfish has only 15mg. Not that you would pour pureed monkfish over a bowl of cereal. But it's just an example of the surprising sodium information you'll start to learn.**

Once you know where ingredients fall on the sodium spectrum, you can decide which things you'll keep in your diet and which you'll ditch in order to stay within your safe zone. I personally avoid any whole ingredients that naturally have more than 100mg of sodium per serving. That means all meat, vegetables, and fruit are okay and most shellfish are out. And when it comes to canned goods, I use only those products that have 20mg of sodium per serving or less, depending on how much I need in a recipe.

# IN LABELS WE TRUST?

Some people love shopping for clothes. I love getting lost in grocery stores. Even when I only mean to pick up a bundle of asparagus, I can spend a good hour (or, truthfully, more) at the market. I often find myself wandering down the aisles, all of them, turning packages, bags, and cans around to study the nutrition labels. I look at products that are salt-free or sodium-free, and even those that are not, because you never know what you'll find. That's the trick to being a good grocery store detective.

Without fail, every trip leads me to discover a new low-sodium product, like a jar of salt-free salsa or a box of lemon and green tea–flavored rice cakes. Or it will alert me to the fact that my favorite salt-free chips now have triple the amount of sodium, nixing them from my go-to shopping list.

Even if you still prefer looking at clothing or car magazines, if you use prepared products in your diet, you must read labels constantly. It is a part of your continued low-sodium education, and not only will it keep your diet on track, it may also take you places you never thought you'd go. Like the deli section, where you might just discover no-salt-added sliced turkey breast.

Like no-salt-added tomato paste, for example. I use a lot of it in this book as it has a rich, umami flavor—a savory taste most commonly associated with soy sauce. The particular brand of tomato paste I use has only 10mg per 2 tablespoons, which is perfect for recipes that call for 2 tablespoons or less. But if a recipe were to use a larger amount of canned tomato paste, like 4 cups, then that ingredient would add up to too much sodium for my body, especially if there are other naturally high-sodium ingredients like chicken or beef in the dish. It's all about context and balance.
By creating these personal guidelines, I know

**While more than 75 percent of the sodium Americans consume is, on average, from packaged goods, most whole ingredients contain sodium as well.**

my daily totals will generally fall somewhere in my range of 500 to 1000mg of sodium a day. And I can effortlessly cook, eat, order, and enjoy my food without having to think about it too much.

### 3 Get Creative

Finally, to make really outstanding food, you have to get creative.

I read, eat, and breathe food. I watch cooking shows and food competitions daily and I flip through a lot of non-sodium-related cookbooks to learn new cooking techniques, flavor combinations, and genres of cuisines. Alice Waters's cookbooks taught me how to poach, dice, and chiffonade. Mark Bittman's articles taught me that I could cook anything. The "Serious Eats" columns constantly enlighten me about new spices and DIY versions of condiments, takeout meals to make at home, and crazy riffs on classics (like their Food Lab's Buffalo Fried Turkey for Thanksgiving). These resources taught me to trust my two hands and my whimsical ideas and that, if there was something I wanted to make, with a flip of a page or a Google search, I could figure out how.

Think of a low-sodium diet as the ultimate exercise in creativity and risk-taking. Isn't that what every good cook is after? Whenever I come up against a sodium stumbling block, I immediately think of ways to overcome it. I focus on the salty ingredients and imagine how to mimic them in look, taste, feel, or flavor. And this is where the fun starts.

By being innovative, your low-sodium cooking automatically becomes different and impressive. If you can surprise yourself and your palate, the level of satisfaction will have nothing to do with salt anymore. Use spices and herbs in unusual ways; explore new flavor combinations and ingredients that you hadn't tried before; add untraditional textures—with seeds, nuts, or dried fruit—to traditional dishes; and coax out the natural sweetness, saltiness, and spiciness found in whole foods.

Successful low-sodium cooking means taking an innovative approach to making standard dishes. It often takes time and thought, and is best enjoyed with others. And food made this way—with love and delight—will impress even those guests and friends who use salt. They might even ask for seconds.

*By being innovative, low-sodium food automatically becomes different and impressive.*

# EMBRACING YOUR DIET:

## + A NOTE FROM DONALD GAZZANIGA, THE ORIGINAL MASTER OF NO-SALT COOKING

When I began my strict, no-salt diet, my wife and I had about six spice bottles on the kitchen shelf. Now it looks like we have six hundred.

Taking on this diet was an easy choice, as I hoped it would keep me off the heart transplant list. But enjoying it took time. My taste buds slowly adjusted over a couple of months. I found it most difficult to find quick snacks. But while I was out one day, I remember buying a bag of baby carrots, my only choice, and realizing that, wow, these taste really good. Pretty soon, I began to notice that everything had its own flavor and I could taste more nuanced differences in various foods. Before, with salt, I had never caught those subtleties.

The biggest surprise of all, though, wasn't just the change in my taste buds, but the fact that I could cook successfully without salty, processed ingredients. Before my diagnosis and dietary changes, we already cooked without added salt. But we ate the standard Italian dishes and, occasionally, takeout. And I couldn't believe how easily I could replicate those meals at home, without salt or too much frustration. Once you start doing it, once you really start living it, this diet just becomes habit. Now, I can simply look at a plate of food and know (within a few points) how much sodium is in it. Without having to look anything up.

THE BIGGEST SURPRISE OF ALL, THOUGH, WASN'T JUST THE CHANGE IN MY TASTE BUDS, BUT THE FACT THAT I COULD COOK, SUCCESSFULLY, WITHOUT SALTY, PROCESSED INGREDIENTS.

# LOW-SODIUM ADJUSTMENTS

ACCEPTING, ENJOYING, AND EMBRACING YOUR LOW-SODIUM DIET WILL NOT HAPPEN OVERNIGHT. AND LET'S BE FRANK, NOT MUCH IN LIFE EVER HAPPENS WHILE YOU SLEEP, EXCEPT FOR GETTING GRAY HAIRS, WRINKLES, AND ZITS, AND THOSE THINGS AREN'T MUCH FUN. SO LET'S JUST AGREE TO AGREE THAT GETTING USED TO YOUR NEW LOW-SODIUM DIET WILL REQUIRE YOU TO BE A BIT PATIENT AND MAKE SOME CHANGES.
THREE SIMPLE CHANGES, IN FACT.

IN ORDER TO GET YOUR LOW-SODIUM DIET STARTED ON THE RIGHT NOTE, YOU ARE GOING TO NEED TO GIVE A LITTLE EXTRA OF THE FOLLOWING:

+ MONEY

+ EFFORT

+ TIME

### 1 Money

Before we start the cooking, we have to do a little house cleaning. Some primping and preening. Because your kitchen is about to become the most cherished room in your home. Forget your comfy spring-foam mattress or your brand new flat screen. They can't make you a crispy-skinned chicken, now can they? No they can't. But your oven sure can.

Since you are going to be spending a lot of time with your kitchen, let's begin by getting to know it well. Turn the broiler on "high" and say hello; take a good look around; take stock of what you already own (stove, pots, refrigerator—check), and what you don't (food processor, baking sheets, blender—to be acquired). Most importantly, start imagining what additions will make this space, and cooking in general, feel luxurious and exciting.

When I say that you are going to have to use a bit more money, I'm not talking about the food you are eating. Yes, you may shell out more dough for seasonal, fresh ingredients. And I am aware that—especially in some parts of the country—good produce and meat can be expensive and sometimes difficult to find. This, of course, is a much larger subject, bigger than this book's pages can rightly explore. But be aware that a percentage of proceeds from this book will go to an organization that is helping address the problem.

But in my experience in the Bay Area, the "full meals" that come wrapped in plastic can cost more than a basket of what is in season. According to the American Heart Association, processed foods make up over 75 percent of an average American's daily sodium intake and as such, using whole ingredients is an essential part of a successful low-sodium diet. Do what you can to eat fresh and use websites like LocalHarvest.org and Eatwellguide.org to find farmers' markets near you. It's just one way you can find good deals on good food and discover an array of products you won't normally find in a grocery store.

The cash you spend on your ingredients, however, is not the money I want to talk to you about. The initial budget-stretcher that may come as a surprise is the cash you'll spend on your kitchen, turning it into a personal oasis for delicious low-sodium food. That means outfitting it with all the spices used in this book and any others that strike your fancy. It means buying vinegars with fun names (like champagne, balsamic, and red wine) and oils with unique flavors (grape seed, coconut, and even avocado). And treating yourself to the kitchen accoutrements that make you excited to cook.

You also want to eliminate any roadblocks or obstacles that might keep you from loving time in your kitchen. I'm talking about being too tired to take the heavy stand mixer from the top shelf or the hatred of having to clean up. Don't avoid these issues. Solve them. Buy utensils—like a food processor, a dough cutter, a handheld blender, and most definitely a rice cooker—that are easy to clean and cut down on cooking time. Make sure the hard-to-handle equipment is in easy-to-reach spaces so that you'll actually use it.

And remember to add things to the list that make cleaning up fast and efficient, like chemical-free cleaners (so you can wipe off the counter while you cook), a small vacuum, broom, sponges, gloves, or Sham Wows. Messes and spills will happen. A lot. But you can be prepared to tackle them, without getting (too) stressed.

Finally, don't forget about the little non-food-related touches. Do you like working with coworkers or noise? Then put a stereo in the kitchen so you can listen to the news or your favorite artist and never feel alone. Does color lift your mood? Then stock up on plates, pots, cloths, and pictures that are bright and wildly patterned. Is your kitchen space limited? Check out small-space design books and blogs for ideas on how to craftily store your gear.

Don't feel like you have to spend a ton of money on these items, either. Check newspapers, flea markets, garage sales, Craigslist, and eBay to find slightly used cooking equipment. Ask your family, friends, and even your local restaurant to see if they have any orphaned tools that need a loving home. And most definitely put items you crave on your birthday or holiday wish lists. There is no better present than the gift of health, or the tools that will get you there.

---

*Messes and spills will happen. A lot. But you can be prepared to tackle them, without getting (too) stressed.*

## NOT ALL SPICES ARE CREATED EQUAL

When filling up your spice rack, make sure you buy curries, powders, and any other seasonings that say they are "salt-free" on the packaging. Often, salt is used as a flavor enhancer or filler in spices, especially in mixes and rubs. So before you buy, read the label carefully and make sure you are getting one without any sodium.

### 2 Effort

There's no way around it; healthy and tasty low-sodium food generally needs to be cooked from scratch—at least for now. There are a few salt-free items on the grocery shelves these days. But be aware that many "low-sodium," "heart-healthy," and "sodium-smart" products are merely a lower-percentage version of the high-sodium originals.

Even though cooking from scratch takes more time, it is actually much healthier for you. And by making your favorite meals at home, you can eat your favorite convenience items while easily eliminating a huge chunk of sodium—not to mention sugar, calories, and other nasty additives. Buffalo wings from the local joint will skyrocket your sodium intake, but in making them yourself, you can keep your numbers low and cravings satisfied. With savvy substitutions, a bit of humor, and the willingness to experiment, there isn't much you can't re-create without salt. (Except for bacon. I'm still working on that.)

And when you come across recipes that don't fit in your schedule, save them for a special occasion when you have a few extra hours, like a rainy day, a dear one's birthday, or when all you want is a steamy stove facial as you lovingly stir your risotto. The point is, with some effort, you can make and eat almost anything you want on a low-sodium diet.

### 3 Time

Finally, let's talk about the minutes, hours, days, and years you will devote to your food and your health. With good habits and care, you'll have many to use.

In keeping a low-sodium diet, you will not only have to spend more time in the kitchen, you will also have to spend time letting your taste buds adjust to food without salt. I tread carefully in what I'm about to say, as I never want to seem like I'm attacking salt—ever. It has an important place in food, in cooking, in history, and on the kitchen table. But in many ways, salt has become an addiction.

With our affection for convenience foods, we've become addicted to the taste of salt. When you think about soup from a can, you aren't really thinking about roasted chicken or tomatoes—you're thinking of the salt. That's what your mouth, your brain, and your palate is expecting. And that's why, when beginning a low-sodium diet, they may be a bit disappointed. At first.

Find a trustworthy low-sodium sponsor and be patient as your taste buds and expectations adjust. It may take a couple of months or longer, but keep at it. And when you feel weak, think of roasted red peppers. For years I didn't know that they were sweet. But I will always remember the moment, weeks after I had started my new diet, when I ate a forkful of them and experienced an explosion of flavor. I realized, all this time, I'd tasted food covered in salt and not actually the food itself. I was suddenly aware of the natural spice in plain ingredients. I even sent a good number of dishes back to the kitchen when dining out because a simple seared steak or wilted greens tasted so darn good on their own. And I realized that when the food itself is the center of attention, it doesn't need much else to be satisfying. Though using some of those new spices and sauces you bought won't hurt either.

*Even though cooking from scratch takes more time, it is actually much healthier for you. And by making your favorite meals at home, you can eat your favorite convenience items while easily eliminating a huge chunk of sodium—not to mention sugar, calories, and other nasty additives.*

# FINDING CONFIDENCE (AND GOOD FOOD) IN THE KITCHEN

## THERE ARE TWO KINDS OF COOKS IN THE WORLD: THOSE WHO LOVE TO COOK AND THOSE WHO FEAR IT.

At this point in the book, some of you have already flipped past my words of wisdom and headed straight for the recipes, eager to get your eat on. Don't worry—I often do that, too.

Then there are those of you who have read the first section three times and are clinging to this sentence for dear life, hoping to delay the inevitable reality that you will have to cut an onion and turn on your stove.

Either way, you're still here, because (a) you think I'm funny, (b) you're excited about trying this diet, or (c) you are putting off doing your laundry or taxes. And I commend you for your commitment, whatever the reason. But let's take a moment to work on that kitchen confidence. You'll need it.

If you're timid about the upcoming pages of measurements and lamb shanks, kale, and roasting pans, let me assure you that everyone has a cook inside of them. You just need to trust your instincts, remember to use common sense, and encourage that whisk-wielding warrior to come out. You'll be surprised at who emerges.

Take my lovely mother, for example. While everything about food excites me, my mother has to remind herself to eat lunch. I usually manage to eat two. While I find the kitchen and creating new dishes a relaxing, invigorating experience, she finds it intimidating and would rather shrivel her greens in the microwave than awaken them with garlic and hot oil. And while I search and scavenge to put as much flavor into my cooking as possible, she is perfectly content with a piece of chicken breast and a side of broccoli. With nothing on it. (Read: cooking in microwave.)

But that was then. Turns out you can teach a mom new tricks. As my right-hand superwoman throughout the process of writing this book, she transformed from a timid novice to a kitchen tornado. She now dices, slices, and even knows what a turnip is. She cooks quickly and confidently and isn't afraid to experiment, or offer me advice on how to improve my recipes. No, really. She now calls in the morning to tell me that, overnight, she realized the green bean casserole would be better with mushrooms instead of sweet potato chips. How quickly things change.

My mom is truly a cooking caterpillar that metamorphosed into a fearless food butterfly. She is proof that, even if you don't think you belong in the kitchen, you do, and with time, you'll become passionate and proud of the meals you create. And you'll probably start calling me to tell me how to make mine better.

So when you get anxious about melting your first tablespoon of butter, just remember this story. And that like you and my mom, there was a time when I too had no idea how to julienne or braise, or what either of those words meant. But in a short while, I learned how to cut vegetables into different shapes. I learned to trust my own taste buds and culinary judgment; to be confident in trying new combinations of flavors (maybe blueberries will go well with steak?); to enjoy the process of experimenting and making mistakes, and then, with a sprinkle of sugar or spice, to make the meal right again.

# A LETTER FROM MY MOM, EXPERT NERVOUS COOK

"Chef" would not be a word used to describe me. I can cook, but it was never something I loved to do or found relaxing or fun. I did as little as possible in the kitchen. And when my darling daughter suggested that I be one of her recipe testers, I was not only aghast, but also intimidated.

*Me? Are you sure?* She explained that I would be the perfect tester, because if I could follow the recipe and actually produce the desired dish, then she would be confident that just about anyone else could. (Note from author: Sorry about the backhanded compliment, Mom.)

With that "empowering" sentiment, I decided to embrace my new title and job with enthusiasm. My first attempts went slowly, and I realized that I was not only unfamiliar with my kitchen, but unfamiliar with the grocery aisles as well. I realized I had to slow down, take my time reading the recipe, and learn to navigate the produce section. I felt like I was on a scavenger hunt, often resorting to seeking out a kindly clerk to guide me to my item.

After a few testing trials, I took my mentor's advice and went to the nearest kitchen store and outfitted myself with a few new pans and improved utensils. I also found that hidden in my own kitchen drawers were never-before-used items such as a mandoline, a garlic press, and a zester. I was on a great adventure and having fun.

I can now say some twenty recipes later (note from author: she's being modest; she's probably made all of them) that I love cooking. I am excited about each new recipe and can now even multitask my way through more than one at a time. I love buying the fresh ingredients, assembling all the items on my kitchen counter, and then making my way through a recipe, from the first chop to the final bite.

# DIRECTIONS ON HOW TO IGNORE DIRECTIONS

**True confession:** When I found out that I would be writing a cookbook (hooray, pop the champagne!), I had to go out and buy measuring spoons (sudden moment of anxiety and concern, and another glass, please). That's because, when I cook, I merely dash and drizzle, taste and adjust as I go. I approximate, I substitute, I ad-lib, and I follow my impulses, not directions.

Of course, when I first started cooking, I relied heavily on recipes for instruction. I followed them carefully, calculating each pinch of spice and drop of liquid. And I panicked when an ingredient was followed by the words "to taste." Williams-Sonoma doesn't carry that measuring spoon.

Even to this day, when I try an ingredient or genre of cuisine that is unfamiliar, I still rely on recipes to learn what I am supposed to do and how I'm supposed to do it. After that initial lesson, though, I allow myself to draw wildly outside the lines. I pour and sprinkle freely, approximating the suggested amounts, adding more chili or using white pepper instead of black, simply because I can. And this is what I love most about cooking: the complete freedom to try new things. I've found that the more I trust myself and the less I follow recipes, the better the food tastes (to my palate) and the more fun I have in my kitchen.

Since this book is intended to be a trustworthy guide, though, I certainly went out and bought measuring cups and spoons, cute ones, which I used and liked to use. I measured everything I made. I was as exact as possible. I tested and retested until I was certain that what ends up on your plate is the same thing that was on mine. And I'm so glad I did.

But once you have built up your kitchen confidence, please, by all means, feel free to use these recipes as merely a canvas for your own masterpieces. And change things according to your own preferences. Too spicy? Take the pepper down a notch. Missing something with oomph? Try a sprinkle of that new rub you just picked up. Prefer to cook your veggies in butter instead of oil, or vice versa, or in some other newfangled liquid that I don't even know about? Be my guest and let me know how it goes. I'm making new mistakes and new discoveries every day, too. It's all a part of this crazy low-sodium adventure.

**Simply Put, Honor Thy Palate.**

Yours is different than mine and while I may be having a torrid affair with cumin and smoked paprika, you may be getting serious with curry and coriander. You may also have to cut down on other nutrients, like phosphorous, potassium, and certain proteins, depending on your specific health needs, which eliminates tomatoes, beef, and many of the other ingredients in this book. So use these recipes as a mere starting point to get ideas, to get excited, and to get inspired. And then add and subtract as you like. Make these recipes yours; scratch out ingredients and add your own twists. If I could attach a pen to every copy of my cookbook, I would, because your brain should be tingling with new ideas so ferociously that you just have to write them down.

And to show you how serious I am, I want to lend you three simple meals that are perfect for building your kitchen confidence and discovering your own taste preferences: **1.** Beer Butt Chicken; **2.** Refrigerator Frittata; and **3.** my weeknight favorite, the Rice Bowl. Each one is simple in preparation and plain enough that any flavors, ingredients, or other means of spice will produce satisfying results without measuring spoons or strict instructions.

# BEER BUTT CHICKEN

This is one of the easiest and most delicious ways to roast a chicken. By balancing the whole bird on an open can of beer (or really any can of liquid), you infuse the meat with moisture and allow the fat to drip off, leaving a crispy outer shell. As for the rub, the world of spices is open to you. Chicken is a very friendly medium when it comes to pairing flavors, so pick two or twenty to massage on the skin. No matter what you use, the final product will be quite gorgeous. And as it is also simple to prepare, it makes a great meal for one or many.

**Suggested salt-free blends to start:**

**Tried and True:** 1 teaspoon lemon pepper seasoning + ½ teaspoon garlic powder + ½ teaspoon dried dill

**Smoky Spice:** 1 teaspoon smoked paprika + ½ teaspoon freshly ground black pepper + ¼ teaspoon chili powder

**Moroccan Adventure:** 1 teaspoon ground cumin + ½ teaspoon curry powder + pinch of ground cinnamon

**Serves 4 to 6**

1 (12-ounce) can of beer

1 (4-pound) fryer chicken, washed and patted dry with paper towel

Your salt-free spice rub creation

+ Preheat the oven to 450°F. Rearrange your oven racks so only one remains at the very bottom. Pour out half of the beer and use a sharp knife to carefully poke holes in the can near the top. Make at least 4 to 5 slashes.
+ Take your bird, name it (I called mine Trixie), and make sure the giblets and other innards are removed from the cavity. With your fingers, gently separate the skin from the meat. Use the natural entry points at the behind and the neck, and work your way around Trixie the best you can.
+ In a small bowl, mix your spices and then, using your hand, rub them all over Trixie—front and back and legs and wings. Feel free to double the suggested spice measurements if it seems you need extra rub.
+ Place the beer can in the middle of a baking pan and gently set your bird on top of it, placing the can up its can. Trixie should now be standing upright.
+ Place the baking pan on the lowest rack, holding the bird so that it doesn't tip over. Cook for 15 to 20 minutes, until the skin has started to turn brown and crispy. It may smoke a little, but don't be alarmed. Just open a window. Then lower the heat to 325°F and cook for an additional 45 minutes to 1 hour.
+ When the time is up, the skin should be golden brown and crackling. Carefully remove your bird from the oven, holding it again so it doesn't tip over. Do not cut yet! Let the meat rest until it is cool enough to touch, about 10 minutes, a perfect amount of time to cook some side vegetables. Then carefully remove the chicken from the can onto a carving board. Slice and serve.

# REFRIGERATOR FRITTATA

This recipe is simply the result of what was in my crisper the day I made it, which was: kale, new potatoes, eggs, a quarter of a white onion, and garlic. As most of these ingredients had been in the refrigerator for a while, I needed a quick way to use them up, and making a frittata was the perfect solution. I've put the vegetables I used on the ingredient list, but just as you should play with the spices in this dish, also feel free to play with your produce choices. Frittatas are a great way to extend those dollars you've spent on groceries, keeping as much as possible from the trash or compost. And if you have leftover proteins or grains, go ahead and throw them in too. I've even put cooked noodles on top, flipping it over once it had cooked, making a quick pasta crust. Plainly stated, there's no wrong way to dress up this dish.

**Suggested salt-free flavors to start:**

**Garden Fresh:** ¼ teaspoon dry mustard powder + ¼ teaspoon honey + dash of apple cider vinegar

**Hint of Heat:** ¼ teaspoon paprika + pinch of freshly ground black pepper + pinch of red chili pepper flakes

**Trusty Italian:** ¼ teaspoon dried oregano + ¼ teaspoon dried parsley + dash of balsamic vinegar

**Serves 4**

- 1 tablespoon olive oil
- ¼ white onion, sliced
- 3 garlic cloves, diced
- 1 cup thinly sliced new potatoes
- 1 cup thinly sliced kale leaves, stems diced as well
- 2 large eggs
- Any salt-free spices or sauces you have on hand

+ Preheat the oven to 400°F.
+ Add the olive oil to a medium, oven-safe skillet over medium-high heat. Add the onion and garlic and cook, stirring, until softened, 2 to 3 minutes. Add the potatoes and diced kale stems and cook, stirring occasionally, allowing them to soften, about 10 minutes. Finally, add the kale leaves and mix the ingredients, continuing to cook until the leaves become vibrant and soft, 5 minutes.
+ Meanwhile, in a small bowl, beat the eggs with about 2 tablespoons of water and your seasonings until well combined. Then, back at the stovetop, reduce the heat to low. On one side of the pan, lift up as many vegetables as possible with a wide spatula and pour in one third of the egg mixture. Repeat this step on the other side of the pan with another third of the egg mixture, then pour the remaining egg mixture on top.
+ Press down with your spatula so that all of the vegetables are covered in liquid.
+ Place the pan into the oven and cook for 12 to 15 minutes. When ready, give the pan a good shake. If the eggs stay put without shimmying, then the frittata is ready to eat.

# RICE BOWL

The first step in this recipe is to get a rice cooker. Besides a handheld immersion blender, this is my favorite kitchen tool. It saves me a lot of time and effort, and I can make cups of steaming rice without having to carefully watch my pot. I create the main course while my rice cooker makes the grains. It's a wonderful relationship.

And when a day has run long or I'm exhausted, a simple rice bowl is a quick and filling meal to fall back on. As you'll see, the dish is more of an equation than a recipe, allowing you to use whatever ingredients you have, you crave, or are on sale at the store. So turn on that rice cooker and have dinner or lunch on the table in minutes.

**Suggested salt-free rice bowl combinations to start:**

white rice + leftover chicken thigh + sugar snap peas + 3 cloves sliced garlic + sprinkling of black sesame seeds as garnish

brown rice + skillet-fried tofu + grilled or oven-roasted zucchini and eggplant + curry powder + ground cardamom

black rice + fried egg + sautéed red cabbage + dash of sesame oil + dash of rice vinegar + red chili pepper flakes

unseasoned wild rice mix + browned ground pork + panfried asparagus + jalapeño pepper + fresh lime juice

**Serves 4**

- 2 cups rice
- 4 servings protein
- 3 cups vegetables
- Seasonings, your choice

+ It all begins the same way: place your rice in the rice cooker and add the amount of water indicated on the back of the rice package or cooker directions—the amount will vary depending on the type of rice you choose to use. Turn on the rice cooker and watch it make perfectly fluffy rice. Aren't you glad you bought it?
+ Then, this is where the fun starts. As the rice cooks, steam, brown, grill, roast, or fry the proteins and vegetables you picked from the list above (or your own imagination). In general, it is best to cook each ingredient individually as they tend to cook at different speeds and temperatures. For example, if you are using the first suggested combination, add 2 teaspoons oil to a skillet and begin by cooking the snap peas over medium-high heat, stirring, until they are vibrant in color, about 5 minutes. Remove the snap peas from the skillet, add the garlic and cook, stirring, until golden brown and crispy, 2 to 3 minutes. Remove the garlic and finish by heating up those leftover chicken thighs for 6 to 8 minutes.
+ Once all the toppings have been prepared, spoon even portions of rice into the bowls and layer your protein, vegetables, and any sauces or garnishes over the top. Serve warm.

# HOW TO READ THE RECIPES

I KNOW YOU'VE SEEN A RECIPE BEFORE. YOU'VE PROBABLY USED A FEW ALREADY IN YOUR LIFETIME. BUT FOR THE SAKE OF REVIEW, LET'S GO OVER SOME BASICS. WHEN YOU FLIP TO THE NEXT SECTION, EACH RECIPE WILL INCLUDE THE TITLE OF THE MEAL (WHAT YOU'LL EAT), THE INGREDIENT LIST (WHAT YOU'LL USE), THE DIRECTIONS (HOW TO USE THEM), AND A PICTURE TO GET YOU DROOLING.

Now that you have those pointers down, there are a few other things that are unique to the recipes in this book. So let's go over those details.

## 1 What We're Making

There is already a handful of wonderful low-sodium cookbooks. I wouldn't be where I am today without them. From *The No-Salt Cookbook*, I learned to make a basic tomato sauce. From *The Complete Idiot's Guide to Low-Sodium Meals*, I learned to make onion-smothered pork chops. And from *The No-Salt, Lowest-Sodium Cookbook*, I learned how to whip up kung pao tofu and several BBQ sauces. I mean to honor these wonderful guides with my own addition to the growing low-sodium library, and I highly recommend that if you don't own them yet, grab them for your own home. The more information and recipes you have, the better your food will be.

But this book is not just about the fundamentals of low-sodium cooking; it is also about taking on the ultimate challenges of making over high-sodium favorites. It is about finding creative substitutions for the saltiest ingredients, giving you low-sodium versions of your favorite meals that meet your taste expectations. It is about proving that you can eat (and do) anything on a low-sodium diet. And with each slurp of salt-free pad Thai, I hope you are reminded that there is a solution to every obstacle. Even getting that pad Thai sauce stain out of your pants.

*It is about proving that you can eat (and do) anything on a low-sodium diet.*

## 2 How Long Until We Eat?

As for giving you time demarcations for each recipe, I don't. That's because the first time you cook something, even if it only requires you to blend three ingredients together, it will most likely take a while, and I don't want you to feel pressured to go faster or feel like you are doing something wrong. You may be just getting used to your kitchen, handling a peeler, and watching two pots boil at once, which, if you stare at them, could take a really long time. So don't stress over the clock; instead enjoy your time with your food.

Just remember that the more you cook, the faster and more fluid you'll become. Soon, you'll cook your veggies while simultaneously roasting a lamb, cleaning last night's dishes, and sneaking a few bicep curls in between. You'll get there. In the meantime, I'll let you know if a recipe requires you to start a day ahead ("Plan Ahead") or set several hours aside ("Got Time to Spare"), so that you have an idea of the effort level involved, rather than just the minutes.

## 3 Extra Advice

As you dig into the recipes, you'll begin to notice some extra names gracing the pages in this book. That is because a handful of well-known tastemakers and chefs, whom I've met through my culinary adventuring, offered to create low-sodium dishes. Just. For. You. Which seriously puts the "special" in special diet. I mean, who else can say two Top Chef Masters made them a potato pie and a grapefruit salad?

Their contributions are edible testimony that even with a restricted diet, you can eat just as well as anyone else; that you are not alone in your low-sodium adventuring; and that the people in your life, without dietary health needs, are willing to cook salt-free meals for you—and cook them with care and flavor.

So when you think you are bothering your friend or the chef at your favorite restaurant with a low-sodium request, think of these recipes. They are proof that you are not. Go ahead and ask them to hold the salt.

## 3 Making Sense of the Sodium

You'll see that each recipe is followed by something titled "sodium count." These numbers will not tell you the total amount of sodium in the recipe or in a single serving of the dish; instead, the numbers represent the approximate amount of sodium you'll find in individual ingredients.

Why is this helpful? Well, while I'm sure there is some neat iPhone app or sodium mathematician that can quickly figure out the amount of sodium per bowl of yakisoba or plate of pumpkin pasta, that's not how I approach my low-sodium diet.

When I sit down to a meal, I don't have a fork in one hand and a calculator in the other. That would be distracting and exhausting. Instead, I have memorized the amount of sodium that exists in typical portions or serving sizes of individual ingredients. And with this information,

I am able to roughly estimate how much sodium is in each dish, where that falls within my sodium boundaries (remember when we talked about that?), and how that fits within the context of what I've eaten that day. I know which meats, vegetables, and products are low enough for me to consume anytime in any portion size; which ingredients are too high in sodium and I should avoid; and which ones are higher in sodium but are still low enough to use when the rest of the dish is practically sodium-free.

Personally, I think this is a realistic approach to understanding your sodium intake. I find it makes cooking and eating easier and more enjoyable, and I want to give you the tools to create your own sodium boundaries. Of course, if you still want to know the total amount of sodium in that pasta, by all means, take out that calculator. Now you have the numbers.

Also note that some ingredients, like flour, have no sodium in them at all and will not appear in the sodium count. Some ingredients, like shiitake mushrooms, have so little sodium (2mg per mushroom) that I did not include them in the counts either. But any ingredient with 10mg of sodium or more per typical serving—the big hitters, if you will—will be listed, as will the occasional super-low-sodium ingredient, if it is the star of the dish.

All the sodium amounts for whole, fresh ingredients are based on numbers provided by the USDA National Nutrient Database for Standard Reference. This database is updated annually and the numbers referenced in this book come from the Standard Reference, Release 24 (September, 2011). As many sodium counts changed in the process of writing this guide, I'm certain more will shift by the time it reaches your shelves. So whether you download the entire database or use the online site, keep yourself updated on the latest information. Freely search for nutritional information in pretty much any ingredient, whenever you want. And if there is something you cannot find, you can also email the Nutrient Data Laboratory (currently at NDLInfo@ars.usda.gov) and an appropriate food specialist will respond quickly to your query.

The sodium counts for processed ingredients (like canned tomato puree or low-sodium ricotta) are based on the lowest-sodium items I have found on grocery store shelves. Please use them as sodium guides when going on your own market hunts. And most brand names and links for these products can also be found on the Sodium Girl website (www.sodiumgirl.com).

---

*Personally, I think this is a realistic approach to understanding your sodium intake. I find it makes cooking and eating easier and more enjoyable, and I want to give you the tools to create your own sodium boundaries.*

## LOST? ASK FOR HELP

I've done my best to include descriptions that make every step as clear as possible. But if there is a direction, an ingredient, a cut of meat, or even a kind of cooking utensil used in this book that you do not understand or are not familiar with, get on that computer and look it up. If you are still not sure what turnips look like, then browse some images. And if there is confusion between a saucepan and a skillet, ask a friend or someone at your local kitchen supply store. The more information you have, the more excited you'll be to get in your kitchen, and the less likely you are to come home with a yam (which might work just as well as that turnip).

# HOW TO SALT-FREE YOUR OWN RECIPE

Let me guess—there are still some foods that you dearly miss eating (your grandmother's spanakopita) and you feel a bit dismayed that there is no low-sodium recipe for them in this book. Don't be deterred, because even though I may have left out instructions for your favorite spinach pie, I have given you all the tools you need to make it yourself.

Just as I have altered shrimp cocktails, Greek salads, and cream cheese frostings with low-sodium stand-ins, you too can master low-sodium makeovers for any food, no matter how salty the recipe is to begin with, even phyllo-covered, feta-filled spanakopita.

To salt-free a recipe, you simply need to follow these steps:

+ First, pick a recipe.
+ Then, spot all the ingredients that are the big sodium contributors.
+ Describe those ingredients by the qualities they bring to a dish—their color, flavor, and texture.
+ Next, brainstorm ingredients that can mimic those same qualities. What could stand in for the flaky phyllo? Would a butter-based dough, although thicker, add enough of a crunch? What is creamy like feta? Could low-sodium ricotta or mascarpone cheese mixed with lemon zest work?
+ Most likely your substitutes will not be exact replicas of the original, nor will they always be similar in color, flavor, and texture, but you can get close to imitating at least one part of the dish, and I still consider that a successful swap. If a certain ingredient does stump you, browse other cookbooks and the Internet to see ways in which other cooks have taken creative liberties with the same recipe. It will inspire you to make uncommon associations and to think beyond the obvious.
+ Finally, try it out. Worst-case scenario is that your low-sodium makeover doesn't work and you have to make a rice bowl (page 33) for dinner. But don't give up. Return to your kitchen and continue to experiment and revise until you have that spinach pie you crave.

"We are in the business of taking care of people and we're always being thrown curveballs. When we receive a special request, it forces us to actually stop and think, look at our ingredients, and make sense of the products we have. It is in these moments that you turn off the robot and really start to create things."

*—Scott Youkilis, Owner and Executive Chef of Maverick and Hog & Rocks*

# LIVING A LIMITLESS LIFE

At some point, your kitchen will become your low-sodium sanctuary. With your own hands (and pots and pans), you can rest assured that every meal you make will be low in sodium, safe to eat, and most importantly, good. With a dice, slice, braise, or roast, you will create exciting food without the salt. And with the trusty salt-free substitutes you'll learn about in this book, you can even make salt-dependent dishes you thought you would never eat again. In the comfort of your home, you never have to worry about the food or mourn the loss of salt. Instead, you can embrace all the other flavors, foods, tastes, and experiences at your fingertips. And that is a relief.

But there comes a time when you have to leave the kitchen, the proverbial culinary nest, and explore a whole low-sodium life that awaits you, right outside your doors. This can be a seriously frightening concept.

Once you have become a fearless low-sodium cook, the idea of trusting someone else with your food is completely daunting. It isn't just your hunger that hangs in their hands; now, it is your safety and health too.

## 1 Salt-Free Dining

For almost seven years, I have enjoyed phenomenal food at some of the most happening restaurants in the Bay Area. I have been served chilled corn gazpacho; pea shoot risotto; Japanese izakaya (we're not talking simple sashimi); Korean noodles; and even a fennel seed ricotta, created especially for me. All without salt.

Even though many books, articles, and other low-sodium resources advised me to not eat out, I completely ignored them. I figured, if I could make great-tasting food at home, then someone with more gadgets and gizmos in a professional kitchen could do equally as well, if not better. And with time, I realized that not only could I successfully dine out on a low-sodium diet—on the cheap or for a special occasion—but that I could receive some really memorable meals.

I was not always so confident about dining out, though. When it came to venturing beyond my spice rack, I initially felt like my needs were too complicated for others to take on. I thought my dietary limits would be a nuisance to busy kitchens. And I figured if someone was willing to make a salt-free meal for me, it would probably be very simple, maybe bland, and not worth the money.

My husband, however, was not satisfied with the idea of simply watching me drink my water while he devoured his meal. He loves food. He knows I love food. And he wanted us to be able to share in the joys of a dining experience, spending the hours after a meal reliving the delicate orange sauce or perfectly seared fish skin.

For our maiden voyage, he chose Maverick, a small restaurant where the co-owner was also the executive chef. My husband (barely boyfriend at the time) called the day ahead to warn of my restrictions and that evening, I was greeted by pan-seared duck breast nestled in homemade gnocchi, made all the richer by a reduction of red wine and butter. Oh hello, delicious.

It was a simple but carefully crafted meal and with enough lead time and information, Scott Youkilis, the master of the food, was able not only to make adjustments, but to enjoy the challenge as well. His enthusiasm gave me the confidence and the proof that I could eat well beyond my kitchen. It is also how I knew I needed to lock this guy up stat. My husband, that is, not Scott.

As I ate out more often, I noted what worked and what did not. And soon, I had a list of dining rules that guaranteed a successful, low-sodium experience. The key was to be creative, communicative, and educated. And above all else, it required teamwork between me and the kitchen. Great low-sodium meals are almost guaranteed when the diner is proactive and the chef is prepared and willing to take on a challenge.

By taking a few simple steps, it is easy to order low-sodium meals that not only meet your needs, but also exceed your expectations.

## 2 Five Essential Dining Tips

- **The more communication, the better.** Let the restaurant know about your restrictions before you arrive and provide a copy of your dietary needs that can be passed back to the kitchen.
- **Be clear on what you cannot eat and more importantly, what you *can* eat.** If you offer suggestions on how to safely spice up your dish, chefs will take that as a cue to be creative.
- **Be loyal and build relationships.** The more you frequent a restaurant, the more the kitchen will understand you and your needs.
- **Educate yourself.** Be aware of the techniques, products, and menu items that are likely to contain sodium and which are easy to make salt-free. Words like **cured, brined, smoked, and braised** generally mean ingredients have been salted. So avoid these items. Be aware that many times, vegetables and meats get blanched in salted water or marinated in salty sauces earlier in the day. If you call ahead, though, you can ask for fresh produce and protein to be put aside for you, without the salty bath.
- **Be grateful.** Be sure to tell the kitchen how much you appreciate the effort. While you and your dietary needs are not a nuisance, a simple thank you goes a long way and ensures great care and effort the next time around.

# LOW-SODIUM DINING CARD

I have a small laminated card that I bring with me everywhere I go. It's in my purse pocket at all times and, when I am dining on the fly, it helps to effectively communicate my needs to the kitchen so neither I nor the waiter or waitress have to.

Every time I give the card to a waiter or chef, it is greeted with enthusiasm. It makes everyone's life easier: the server's, the kitchen staff's, and definitely the diner's. I know I can get tired of rattling off all those ingredients I can't eat and this little card gives me a much-needed break.

So copy the following list, make adjustments according to your diet, and cover it in plastic. Put it in your bag, wallet, or clutch and never leave home without it. It is your ticket to a savory, salt-free meal.

## LOW-SODIUM DINING CARD

**WHAT I CANNOT EAT**

1) No salt
2) No salt-blanched vegetables or grains
3) No salted stocks or broths
4) No salted or premarinated, pre-seasoned meats
5) No dairy (except for those listed on the right)
6) No shellfish
7) Nothing with soy sauce, fish sauce, or other heavily salted sauces
8) No vegetables or beans from cans, bottles, or bags (unless label reads 0mg Sodium)

**WHAT I CAN HAVE**

1) All meat and fish
2) Garlic, onions, sesame oil, ginger, unseasoned vinegars
3) Any grains that have not been cooked in salted water or salted broths
4) All fresh vegetables and fruits
5) Unsalted butter, heavy cream, half-and-half, crème fraîche, and some mascarpone (with 15mg or less per serving)
6) Citrus, chile peppers, herbs, and salt-free seasonings

### Dining on Someone Else's Bill

Whether it is a wedding, a dinner party, or some other occasion beyond your home, there are moments when you suddenly find yourself eating on someone else's tab. Which either leaves you hungry, salted, or feeling nervous about asking for a special meal.

But let me tell you this: Get over it. Really. Think of all the people without dietary needs who don't think twice about being picky eaters. You know that person who orders a BLT without the lettuce, with turkey instead of tomato, and all the condiments on the side? Yeah, we all know those people. Just think of them when you feel like your needs are a nuisance. Then think about why you are asking for special accommodations—your health. Now do you feel better? Never be afraid or ashamed to be up front with your needs. Own it. Your body and your stomach will thank you.

And if you are still bashful, just think about how you would feel if someone came to your home and, for whatever reason, couldn't enjoy the meal you made. You would feel horrible and I bet your friends and loved ones would too. Because when you gather around a communal table—whether it is yours or someone else's—it is about sharing. And you want everyone to participate. So share your needs with your hosts so they can share their love-filled food with you.

Of course, there are those situations where the person paying is not someone you know very well. If you feel uncomfortable passing along your eating guidelines to them, you always have two other options: eat before you go or bring a snack pack. I have to admit, even when I am told there will be low-sodium goodies for me, I often stock up on fuel just in case. By preparing for the worst-case scenario, I never go hungry or succumb to eating something that is salty. And when the host or hostess asks about the food, I just say it was lovely and then I give my leftovers to someone else at the table. In taking these precautions, not only will you avoid sodium, you'll stay full, and you may also make a new friend. It's a win-win situation.

---

*Never be afraid or ashamed to be up front with your needs. Own it. Your body and your stomach will thank you.*

# LOW-SODIUM TRAVELS

WHETHER YOU ARE STAYING IN YOUR COUNTRY OR CROSSING BORDERS, TRAVELING ON A LOW-SODIUM DIET IS CHALLENGING, BUT ENTIRELY POSSIBLE. I'VE NOW SUCCESSFULLY ENJOYED COUNTLESS ROAD TRIPS, TOURED SEVERAL STATES, BACKPACKED FOR WEEKS IN THE WILDERNESS, AND EXPLORED FOREIGN NATIONS WHILE EATING SALT-FREE. AND I'D LIKE TO PASS MY TRAVEL TIPS ONTO YOU.

### Eating on the Go

As soon as you step out that door with your luggage, you forgo the guarantee of fresh, healthy food, and are often left with fast-food options that are loaded with sodium. And while gummy peaches and lemonade are delicious, they are not enough to sustain you over a long trip.

Even in these limited situations, though, it is still possible to find food that fits within your sodium guidelines. Airports, gas stations, and even the corner drugstore all carry staple, low-sodium treats that you can safely nibble on. They are far from gourmet, but they will assuredly keep you satiated as you get from point A to point B.

### Airports and Pit Stops

**Fruit:** Most coffee shops, cafés, and breakfast establishments are bound to have whole fruit (bananas, apples, oranges) or cups of fruit (think grapes, cantaloupes, and pineapple) that will be salt-free.

**Baked potato:** This low-sodium starch can be found at some airport food courts, most restaurant menus, and even at Wendy's. Yep, low-sodium fast food exists.

**Hard-boiled eggs:** Another easy find at coffee shops or even gas stations. If you are hankering for a protein fix, this is a great option.

**Yogurt:** Most yogurts land in the 100mg per serving range, which is a lot if you are snacking on them all day long. But if you haven't had anything to eat or have skipped one or several meals during travel, go ahead and dig in. One container has less sodium than a three-egg omelet, so it won't cut too deeply into your sodium allotment.

**Steamed rice:** If there is a Japanese or Chinese restaurant in the airport food court, chances are they have steamed rice on the menu. Just make sure it is not sushi rice, which typically contains salt and seasoned vinegar.

**Frosted Mini-Wheats:** Believe it or not, this cereal has only 5mg of sodium per serving and makes a really filling snack. Keep your eye out for this one. I've found them literally all over the world. Even in Belize.

To ensure that you always have something to eat, make room in your luggage for low-sodium snacks. Lightweight, flat, and easy to pack, these products are perfect stuffers for you and your carry-on.

**Low-Sodium Packing List**

**Baby food:** When you're in a pinch for something low-sodium, head straight to the pacifiers and the diapers. Baby food tends to have little to no salt in it. And while a spoonful of Gerber pureed peas will not be of the same caliber as a slowly stewed pea soup, when you're hungry, it's something. And I have to admit, the latest lines of baby food don't actually taste half bad. You can eat them hot or cold, and they are nutritious to boot.

**Corn tortillas:** Most corn tortillas (not wheat or flour) are low in sodium, and because of their flat shape, they pack well and can add substance to a simple breakfast (scrambled eggs) or lunch (salads). Who knows, you may even be lucky enough to stumble upon some sliced tomatoes or an avocado, and then you'll be delighted you brought those doughy disks with you.

**Canned fish:** It can be smelly, but for a guaranteed protein fix, a can of low-sodium tuna or salmon will get the job done. There are several low-sodium canned fish products available, even smoked kipper. Just remember to pack a can opener. And some breath mints.

**Dried fruit, vegetables, nuts, and seeds:** Before I leave for a trip, I hit the bulk bins and fill up on dried strawberries, figs, apple rings, and sunflower seeds. Eat them to curb midday rumblings or use them to brighten up blander menu options, like a simple green salad.

**Salt-free peanut and nut butter packets:** There are several lines of individual servings of peanut butter, tahini (sesame butter—great for those with nut allergies), and even chocolate-covered coconut butter, all which do not require refrigeration and do not contain sodium. Filled with protein, energy, and great flavors, these little packets are a packing must. The tahini also works well as an S.O.S. salt-free dressing for salads.

**Salt-free popcorn:** This snack is dependent on availability of a microwave and finding a version without the sodium (they do exist). But popcorn is really filling and when not popped, it is completely flat and perfect for your suitcase.

TO ENSURE THAT YOU ALWAYS HAVE SOMETHING TO EAT, MAKE ROOM IN YOUR LUGGAGE FOR LOW-SODIUM SNACKS.

### Going Abroad

One travel challenge that gave me major pause was leaving the country. In voyaging abroad, not only must one face finding low-sodium food in a totally foreign place, but suddenly there is also a language barrier to deal with. As if getting your passport wasn't trouble enough. But don't worry about your needs getting lost in translation. You can use the same tools you use at home, like your dining card, to guarantee safe eating. They'll just be written in an unfamiliar dialect.

While preparing for a friend's wedding in France (ooh la la!), it dawned on me to give my hospital a call. I asked to be connected to their patient services office, I told them about my upcoming trip, and they immediately put me in touch with a translator.

As easy as *un, deux, trois*, I had a fully Frenchified transcript of my dietary needs. They also translated all of my medical information. With these documents in hand, finding low-sodium meals was easier than finding a Métro stop. It may take extra preparation, but after going to Brazil, Belize, New Zealand (okay, they speak English there), and even Thailand, I can assure you that no low-sodium border is too difficult to cross.

# IDENTIFYING AND OVERCOMING SNEAKIER SODIUM CHALLENGES

## OF COURSE, LIVING LIFE TO THE FULLEST IS ABOUT MORE THAN JUST DINING OUT AND TRAVELING, ALTHOUGH THOSE TWO THINGS ALONE WOULD MAKE FOR A PRETTY GOOD EXISTENCE.

Beyond the kitchen and the table, there are baseball games (ones you watch and ones you play in). There is college. There are oceans and swimming pools. There are even unexpected events, like having to take medicine and undergo medical procedures. All events, places, and things that may cause you to come in contact with extra sodium.

Whether or not the following concerns specifically affect you, they are all good reminders that low-sodium diet challenges exist in more than just food. And that, as we've already proven, they are easily overcome. You just might need to buy a snorkel.

### Racing and Fueling

For the last few months, you have been training for (insert here—a triathlon, aquathon, marathon, or any activity that brings you farther than the walk from your refrigerator to your couch), and your muscles, mind, and spirit are set to crush the course.

In the last few hours before the start whistle blows, you gather all the tools you need to finish this test of physical endurance. You've packed the tennis shoes, the padded shorts, the swim goggles, and an extra pair of socks. But don't forget one of the most important items you need to keep your body moving: fuel.

The majority of sports snacks and drinks are very high in sodium. A vanilla Power Bar? 200mg of sodium. Chocolate CLIF Bar? 140mg of sodium. And the old standard, orange Gatorade? 270mg of sodium. Which is perfectly fine and important for most people, but might be too much for your body.

Avoiding the high-sodium energy snack issue may seem like an impossible feat, worse than climbing an 11 percent incline. (If you don't know what that means, your thighs thank you.) Packing a bag full of granola isn't very practical or aerodynamic, and you don't really want to tuck other low-sodium snacks into your shorts. But here's the great news: For effective, low-sodium race snacking, there are a few brands of sports gels that do a great job of keeping you energized without overloading you with salt. You can also replace that Gatorade with a bottle of coconut water, which is bursting with natural electrolytes (especially potassium) and tends to be under 40mg of sodium per serving. These products will refresh your body and keep your muscles from cramping, without all the extra sugar or salt. And as always, consult your doctor and dietitian to make sure you're giving your body what it needs for a top performance.

### Skip the Peanuts and Cracker Jacks: Eating at the Ball Park

Hot dogs, burgers, and garlic fries: these were the treats that lured me to stadium seats when I was younger. I longed for the processed and salty flavors of the ballpark, and I happily joined my father at any event that came with a side of ketchup and nacho "cheese." My affair with these lip-smacking snacks, however, did not last forever. When my kidneys quit, so did my fast-food addiction. But my love for a sports outing on a sunny day remained strong.

In order to go out to the ball game and not have to leave by the third inning to get sustenance, I forgot about the peanuts and caramel corn and started bringing my own low-sodium snacks. I now fill my bag with low-sodium sandwiches, made from no-salt-added bread and low-sodium deli meat. And because I'm in charge of the food, I don't have to settle for simple offerings. I can bring anything that fits into a plastic container. I've packed pasta, hummus, chicken wings, and even homemade sushi. I just think of it as a personal tailgate, in my purse, where any craving can be met. And with this food, I have enough energy to keep cheering through the fourth quarter, that shoot-out, or a nail-biting 12th inning.

### Medicine and Medical Procedures

While medicine can often be, well, your best medicine, be aware that many pills, vitamins, and other products used in medical procedures can contain high amounts of sodium. As with everything else, be sure to consult your doctor first on what is best for your body. But also be an advocate for your needs and ask them to help you find lower-sodium solutions.

When buying over-the-counter pills, always check the labels and packaging as you would with spices and prepared foods. Also, for many surgical procedures, doctors require you to take certain precautions to—I'll gently put it this way—clean out your system. Laxatives are often saline-based and thus high in sodium, so consult your doctor to see if you can use sodium-free alternatives instead.

Use a keen sodium-curious eye with your medical care just as you would with your food. In talking to caretakers, I have avoided extra sodium from treatments, saline drips, and medications. Sometimes I have to be a bit pushy to be heard. But the more knowledgeable I am about the numbers and the options, the more easily my request and concerns are honored.

### Water

Remember that snorkel I mentioned before? I swim with one. It's not the kind you use with flippers, but an official, lap-swimming snorkel that comes straight up my face and out of the water. I have made quite a fashion statement at my pool, especially with the addition of my blue nose plugs.

But more important than my reputation is the fact that this little contraption keeps me from getting sodium during my workouts. A few years ago, my blood pressure started to climb. Nothing about my diet changed and my kidneys were still chugging along nicely, working even better than they had in the past. The sudden jump in my diastolic and systolic numbers didn't make sense and before going on extra medication, I took a close look at my routine. It was summer, I was training for a triathlon, and I was swimming at least once a week, if not more. It made me wonder, could the pool be the problem?

Turns out, one of the active ingredients in chlorine is sodium chloride, and in my hood, many pools have moved to a salt water solution to keep the waters clean. Every time I turned my head to gulp for air, I was swallowing extra sodium. And that's where the snorkel comes in. It may look goofy, but it lets me freestyle without worry.

As for drinking water, the information is a bit murky. Let's begin a few hundred years ago, when old beer legend says that Napoleon, so taken by the taste of England's Bass Ale, attempted to build an exact replica of the brewery in France. However, without the chemistry of the Burton water (which contained higher levels of dissolved salts due to the presence of gypsum), the beer just never tasted the same. So Napoleon didn't get his ale. But due to his mistrials, we get a reminder that sodium does exist in our drinking water.

According to the EPA's last assessment, they found that most drinking water contains 20mg of sodium per liter, which is considered low-sodium. They do note, however, that if they did a recalculation today, it might result in higher numbers, but not necessarily anything that is a health concern. If you are worried, though, you can always contact your local health department, water supplier, or check out the EPA website for the Safe Drinking Water Hotline to find out more on what's coming out of your tap.

Also, be aware that water softeners do contain sodium ions, and the harder the water, the more water softener will be used, which means added sodium. But before you start only drinking bottled water, if you're truly concerned, consult professionals or get your water tested by a lab or an at-home kit.

### College and Cafeterias

Oh hey, campus cuties! Let me just say this up front, I'm jealous. It has been over six years since I graduated from my alma mater. And while a few things have changed, I know one thing remains true: being in college with an eating restriction can seem like a totally uncool, time-sucking task.

Although my graduation cap is a bit dusty, I remember the challenges of being on a campus, without my own kitchen, navigating a strict diet. I understand that food, especially in college, is about more than sustenance. It is about being social, gathering with friends, making memories, and not feeling different. And after successfully living low-sodium (as well as gluten and nut-free!) as an undergrad and beyond, I can promise you that, with a few simple tips, you can take on your food limitations without ever feeling limited.

**The Dining Hall:** The cafeteria's daily offerings most likely do not meet your food needs, but it isn't difficult to make adjustments. Talk to the Disability Resource

Center and find out who runs the campus kitchen. Ask if you can store perishables in a corner of their refrigerators and see if you can use their stoves and ovens to make your own food. Better yet, provide the staff with recipes, ideas, and a list of what you can and cannot have, and see if they will make special dishes for you at every meal. I'd bet there are more people than just you on campus who share in your need. So take it one step further and start an eating club online or a Facebook group. Band together with your fellow special eaters and make your meals a social and educational experience.

**Restaurants:** The gang is gathering at the local Tex-Mex restaurant for So-and-So's birthday fiesta and you'd love to order more than a margarita. If you know where the party is going down, then give the restaurant a call a few hours or even a day ahead of the reservation. Provide the staff with a list of your dietary requirements and offer suggestions of which dishes from the menu you think are easiest to adjust. Chances are there is something they can whip up and, with enough notice, they'll most likely be able to set aside ingredients and give your diet a good-old college try.

**Snack Attacks and Late-Night Cravings:** They are unavoidable and especially strong during deadlines and finals when you have limited time to get to a store. And since your taste buds often desire something hearty, full of carbs, and let's face it, sweet, keep your dorm room stocked with quick-cooking and microwavable grains (oatmeal, instant rice, couscous, and quinoa) and tasty toppings (jam, dried fruit, nuts, honey, and salt-free peanut butter). This will make refueling easy.

**Dating:** While most people think only about what jeans they'll wear on that first meet-up, you worry about ordering a meal without breaking out the meds. But it is really easy to eat well and eat safely on a date. There's only one thing you need to do: be honest. I know, it's scary. But remember, relationships are built on honesty. So are good meals. And when you tell someone up front about your needs, you are not only guaranteed a safe dining experience, but you also have a quick way of weeding the studs from the duds. If your date understands your diet and takes on your health obstacles with enthusiasm, then you know you've found a winner. And if not, on to the next one.

*Remember: relationships are built on honesty. So are good meals.*

# FINAL ADVICE BEFORE YOU FEAST

## AT THIS POINT, I HOPE YOU'RE EAGER TO CLOSE THIS BOOK, READY TO THROW THESE PAGES AND MY ADVICE ASIDE IN ORDER TO START YOUR OWN LOW-SODIUM ADVENTURES. SILLY, SATISFYING, NON-SALTY ADVENTURES.

Like that moment when Dorothy arrives in Oz, I hope this guide returns the color to your food and your outlook on a salt-free life. After taking charge of what's possible, you'll discover experiences and opportunities that you never dreamed were possible. And most importantly, you will discover a world where a part of your healthcare is in your own hands. Where your diet isn't exhausting, but fulfilling. Where owning your needs will not impede your life, but improve it. And where salt-free food is not only good for you, but impressive and pleasurable for your friends too.

You have the power to make your low-sodium life exciting and if you take away nothing else from this guide, please remember that anything is possible. Nothing can stop you from living the most limitless life. And even wearing a snorkel to the pool can be cool.

Be full, be creative, be daring. Now close this book and get started.

Chow on.

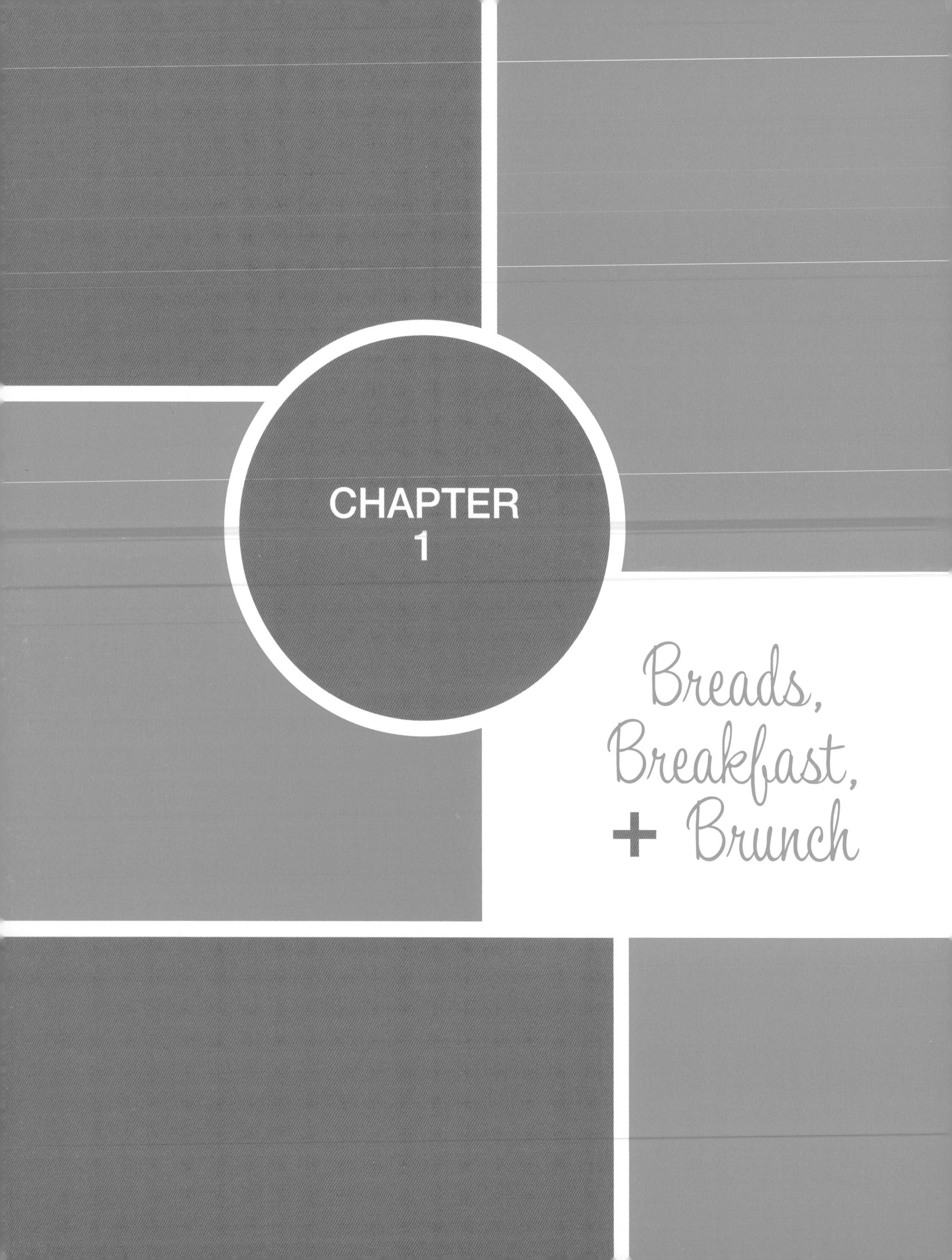

# CHAPTER 1

# Breads, Breakfast, + Brunch

If you know me, then you already know that I love breakfast and brunch more than any other meal of the day. And since I just told you that, we can now be best friends.

But back to my favorite subject. All week long, I wait for the weekend, when life slows down, and I get to break fast leisurely. Steaming cups of coffee flanked by crispy hash browns, fluffy scrambles, syrupy pancakes, and a bagel covered in a schmear with smoked salmon—this is what my breakfast dreams are made of. Add in a bevy of friends sitting on a sunny patio, gabbing about the week's events, and you have a recipe for a perfect morning. Simply put, everything about breakfast and brunch is great; the drinks, the company, and most definitely the food.

Here's the tricky part, though. While egg dishes can easily be made without added salt, other breakfast and brunch staples, like preseasoned home fries, baked goods, French toast, and, of course, Bloody Marys, are usually loaded with it. The culprits are salty spice mixes, salted butter, baking powder, baking soda, ketchup, Tabasco, Worcestershire, cured meats, and the salt shaker itself.

But don't swear off breakfast just yet, because even the saltiest of morning favorites can be made low-sodium. And by applying creative salt-free substitutes, your potatoes, pastries, and even those Bloodies will easily stand up to the originals, if not prove more impressive. Who wants a normal stack of pancakes when you can slice through a pile of zucchini flapjacks? Or a breakfast sandwich stacked with homemade chorizo and butter rolls?

Gather your pals, brew the coffee, and be sure to invite the sun. This weekend, you'll be serving up morning classics with all the runny, oozy, sweet, and savory flavors you can dream of.

*Simply put, everything about breakfast and brunch is great: the drinks, the company, and most definitely the food.*

## **QUICK TIP:** BREAKFAST ON THE GO

For many, preparing a hearty breakfast is as easy as snap, crackle, and pop. But for those on a low-sodium diet, achieving a balanced morning meal poses a bit more of a challenge. As a society of busy commuters, we want food that is both nutritious and convenient. But most prepared items, such as bagels and cereal, are brimming with hidden sodium. Ingredients like baking powder, baking soda, dairy, and added salt can make the first meal of your day close to 50 percent of your daily allowance.

Before you reach for your skillet, though, take another stroll down the grocery store aisles. The trick to finding convenient low-sodium breakfasts lies in brand-hunting and savvy substitutions. And with a keen eye for reduced sodium products, it is easy to satiate your early morning cravings, on-the-go, while avoiding the extra salt.

SALT CAN MAKE THE FIRST MEAL OF YOUR DAY CLOSE TO **50%** OF YOUR DAILY ALLOWANCE.

*(Sodium numbers were taken from popular supermarket products, not USDA averages)

**Typical Choice:**
A bowl of berry-flavored cereal (280mg per 1 cup) with 1% milk (160mg per 1 cup)
Total: 440mg of sodium
**Low-sodium Alternative:**
A bowl of shredded wheat or puffed rice cereal (5mg per 1 cup) with soy or coconut milk (15mg per 1 cup)
+ Total: 20mg of sodium

**Typical Choice:**
1 packet of maple and brown sugar instant oatmeal
Total: 260mg of sodium
**Low-sodium Alternative:**
1 cup quick-cooking oats with 2 teaspoons brown sugar and ¼ teaspoon cinnamon (pack it in a plastic bag to take to work)
+ Total: 0mg of sodium

**Typical Choice:**
Plain bagel (490mg of sodium) with cream cheese (125mg per 2 tbsp) and smoked fish (223mg per ounce)
Total: 838mg of sodium
**Low-sodium Alternative:**
Corn tortilla (0mg of sodium) with farmer's cheese (10mg per ounce) or no-salt-added mustard (0mg of sodium) and no-salt-added deli turkey meat (30mg per ounce)
+ Total: 40mg of sodium

**Typical Choice:**
Strawberry yogurt (95mg of sodium) and fruit and nut granola (80mg per ¾ cup)
Total: 175mg of sodium
**Low-sodium Alternative:**
No-salt-added soy strawberry yogurt (20mg) and no-salt-added fruit and nut granola (0mg per ¾ cup)
+ Total: 20mg of sodium

**Typical Choice:**
Ready-to-bake, seasoned hash browns (⅔ cup)
Total: 300mg of sodium
**Low-sodium Alternative:**
Ready-to-bake, no-salt-added hash browns (1 cup)
+ Total: 10mg of sodium

**Typical Choice:**
Wild blueberry muffin
Total: 440mg of sodium
**Low-sodium Alternative:**
Apple and blueberry wheat-free cereal bar
+ Total: 45mg of sodium

**Typical Choice:**
Chocolate Croissant
Total: 220mg of sodium
**Low-sodium Alternative:**
Toasted, no-salt-added bread (10mg per slice) with hazelnut spread (15mg per 2 tbsp)
+ Total: 25mg of sodium

**Typical Choice:**
Packaged cottage cheese and strawberry snack cup
Total: 390mg of sodium
**Low-sodium Alternative:**
No-salt-added cottage cheese (45mg per ¼ cup) with fresh strawberries or 2 tablespoons of strawberry jam (0mg of sodium)
+ Total: 45mg of sodium

# MURRAY CIRCLE BUTTER ROLLS

How do you make salt-free bread? When I asked Chef Ethan Howard that question, his answer awaited me in the Michelin-starred Murray Circle restaurant kitchen. At 5:00 a.m.

After twenty-four hours of bread boot camp, five trial versions at home, a few pinches of mace and, of course, Chef Howard's blessing, these salt-free rolls are now ready for you. To make any time of the day.

**Makes 16 rolls**

**Effort Level: Got time to spare**

- ¾ cup warm water + plus 2 tablespoons if dough looks dry
- 1 (¼-ounce) packet rapid active dry yeast
- 2½ teaspoons granulated white sugar
- 2 large eggs, at room temperature
- 6 tablespoons (¾ stick) unsalted butter, melted
- ½ teaspoon ground mace
- 2 cups bread flour
- ½ cup all-purpose flour, for kneading and rolling

+ In a stand mixer fitted with the dough hook attachment, combine the water, yeast, and sugar. Stir and let it rest for 5 minutes. The mixture will become foamy and this means that the yeast is alive and ready.
+ Add 1 egg, the butter, and mace to the bowl and turn the mixer to low speed. When the ingredients are well combined, increase the mixing speed to medium and slowly add the bread flour ¼ cup at a time. Continue until the dough forms a ball, 5 to 8 minutes. If the dough looks too dry (i.e., the dough starts creeping up the kneading hook), add a touch of water. If it is too sticky, add a bit more flour. The dough is ready when it feels soft and pillowy and doesn't stick to your hands. Shape the dough into a ball, return it to the mixing bowl, and cover the bowl with plastic wrap. Allow the dough to rise for 1 hour. Note: Bread rises best in warm environments. So if your stove or heater is on, this will provide a perfect amount of heat. If not, just know that the dough may need a little extra time to rise.
+ When the dough has doubled in size, cover a baking sheet with parchment paper and lightly flour your work surface. Then with a dough cutter or a knife, separate the dough into 4 even portions and separate those into 4 even portions again. Quick math: You now have 16 portions.
+ Roll each portion into a smooth ball and place on the parchment paper, with the seams or cracks on the bottom. Repeat until all the portions have been rolled then line the dough balls side by side, touching one another, in 4 even rows of 4 rolls. Cover them with a cloth and let them rise again, 45 minutes. This is a great time to fold laundry.
+ When the rolls are almost risen, preheat the oven to 400°F and beat the remaining egg in a bowl. Using a pastry brush or your hand, gently coat the tops of the rolls with just a little bit of the beaten egg wash. When the oven comes to temperature, place the rolls on the middle rack of the oven. Bake until the tops are golden, 12 to 14 minutes.
+ Remove the rolls from the oven and allow them to cool for 3 to 5 minutes. The rolls will have a honey-colored, crisp crust, with a soft buttery crumb. And as one tester commented, they are cute and delicious. Serve warm with unsalted butter or jam.

### + sodium count:

Eggs: 71mg per large egg

## + note

Feel free to reshape the dough according to your bread needs. Make the rolls long and thin for hot dog buns or large and round for hamburgers.

# KOREAN ZUCCHINI FLAPJACKS

Based on the Korean *hobak jeon*, these vegetable pancakes are simple, healthy, and made to order. I really encourage you to experiment with other types of summer squash. And, as for the flavor profile, you can stick to the Asian spices suggested below or forget the sesame oil and add herbs and citrus for a garden-fresh twist. Or throw in shredded nori, jalapeños, and sesame seeds to the batter to add color and unexpected spice.

**Makes 4 large pancakes (or 12 small pancakes)**

- 1 large zucchini, washed
- ⅔ cup all-purpose flour
- 1 cup water
- 1 large egg
- ¼ teaspoon dry mustard powder
- ¼ teaspoon freshly ground black pepper
- ¼ teaspoon ground turmeric
- ⅛ teaspoon cayenne pepper
- 1 green onion, thinly sliced
- Sesame oil, for frying
- Low-sodium plain Greek yogurt or dash white vinegar

+ Using the largest holes of a box grater, grate the zucchini.
+ In a medium bowl, mix the flour, the water, and egg until it forms a smooth batter. Mix in the mustard, black pepper, turmeric, and cayenne. Add the grated zucchini and green onion, and mix again until everything is well combined.
+ Pour 2 teaspoons of sesame oil into a medium skillet and twist the handle back and forth so the oil rolls around the pan, giving it an even coating. Cook over high heat for 1 to 1½ minutes. Drop in a small amount of batter to see if the oil is hot; if it hisses, you're ready to go.
+ Lower heat to medium-high and pour about one-fourth of the batter into the pan, using a spatula to spread it into a thin circle. Allow the pancake to set and brown, about 3 minutes on one side. Then flip it, cooking the other side for another 3 minutes. The pancake will crackle and pop in the oil and if you have any trouble, try using two spatulas to turn it. When both sides have turned golden brown and crisp, transfer the pancake onto a paper towel–lined plate. Repeat to make the remaining pancakes, adding more oil to the pan each time.
+ Serve warm with a dollop of Greek yogurt for dipping or a drizzle of vinegar if you like tang, and repeat until all the batter is gone.

### + sodium count:

Zucchini: 26mg per large zucchini; Egg: 71mg per large egg; Plain Greek yogurt: 60mg per 6-ounce container depending on brand

# SWEET POTATO "BACON PATTIES" + EGGS BENEDICT

Bacon is one of the few foods that may be impossible to make without salt. According to Cathy Barrow, one of the cofounders of Charcutepalooza (an online cooking community centered around monthly homemade charcuterie challenges), the salt is the essential ingredient in the curing process, penetrating the cells to tenderize the meat. And while I've tried to make low-sodium bacon by wrapping pork belly in nori and bonito flakes—hoping the natural salt in these ingredients would do the trick—my experiments only resulted in fatty pieces of meat and stomachaches.

Since then, I turned my attention to a new tactic. Instead of breaking down pork belly without salt, I decided to break down the qualities one looks for in bacon-heavy dishes, using those descriptions as clues to discover adequate (and safe) non-bacon substitutions.

For my virgin attempt, I chose to make over Eggs Benedict, a classic bacon-centric brunch dish. I began the challenge by defining my nemesis's purpose: the round cut of Canadian bacon adds a firm texture to contrast with the silkiness of the egg and sauce. The bacon's smoky and savory bite counters the sweeter notes of the buttery hollandaise and runny yolk. And finally, for looks, the bacon is a juicy, sunburned circle of yum that adds color to the plate.

With those descriptors in hand, I realized that a sweet potato, covered in savory spices, was the perfect stand-in for the salty pork, providing a similar texture, taste, and color. It is a cheeky, low-sodium, and vegetarian-friendly play on the classic that could fool your most observant friends. And it is a great example of how you can overcome even the saltiest barriers with your imagination.

**Makes 6 to 8 servings**

Eggs Benedict

- 8 tablespoons (1 stick) unsalted butter
- 8 large eggs (for poaching) + 3 large egg yolks (for hollandaise sauce)
- 1½ tablespoons fresh lemon juice
- ⅛ teaspoon cayenne pepper

Sweet Potato "Bacon" Patties

- 1 teaspoon smoked paprika
- 1 teaspoon ground cumin
- 1 teaspoon ground turmeric
- Pinch of ground white pepper
- 1 tablespoon olive oil
- 2 medium sweet potatoes, peeled and sliced into ¼-inch rounds
- ¼ teaspoon white vinegar
- Fresh tarragon leaves, for garnish (optional)

+ Preheat the oven to 400°F.
+ This dish is all about timing, so you may have a hard time keeping all the elements hot on the first try. But read through the directions, breathe, and get ready to be a bit of a whirlwind in the kitchen.
+ First, let's prepare the homemade hollandaise. Bring a small pot of water to a boil. Then, in a small saucepan, melt the butter over very low heat. As it melts, prepare a double boiler by filling a pot with a few cups of water and placing a smaller heat-proof bowl or pot over it. The water should not touch the bottom of the bowl. Over medium heat, bring the water in the bottom pot to a rolling boil and then lower to a simmer. Then place the 3 egg yolks in the top bowl of the double boiler and whisk until they begin to thicken, 1 to 2 minutes. Add 1 tablespoon of the boiling water (from your first small pot) and continue to whisk until it thickens. Repeat, adding 1 tablespoon of water at a time, until you have added a total of 4 tablespoons of boiling water, whisking the mixture after each addition.

+ Add the lemon juice to the thickened mixture and remove the bowl from the double boiler. Briskly whisk the sauce as you slowly pour in the melted butter. Add the cayenne and continue to beat the sauce until it is thick. Cover with a lid or aluminum foil to keep the sauce warm.
+ Place the paprika, cumin, turmeric, white pepper, and olive oil in a large bowl and mix until combined. This is your wet rub. One by one, dip the sweet potato rounds into the bowl and, using your hands, rub in the spice and olive oil mixture. Then place the spiced sweet potatoes in an even layer on a greased baking sheet (you may need to use two). Repeat until all the sweet potatoes are covered with the wet rub.
+ Put the sweet potatoes on the middle rack in the oven and roast for 5 minutes on one side. Flip the patties and cook for 5 minutes on the opposite side. Remove from the oven and cover with foil to keep warm.
+ Now, let's finish the dish by poaching our eggs. Prepare to poach by filling a tall, heavy-bottomed pot halfway with water and bring to a rolling boil over medium-high heat. Crack each egg into a separate bowl and fill another, larger bowl with warm water. If you are making several poached eggs at one time, you can hold the finished eggs in the warm water bath while you make the others.
+ Once the water in your tall, heavy-bottomed pot has started to boil, lower the heat so that little bubbles gently crack on the surface. Add the vinegar and gently stir it in with a spoon. As you are stirring, slide the egg into the water being careful not to touch it with your spoon. The stirring action, or vortex, will wrap the egg white around the yolk and it will also keep the egg from settling and sticking to the bottom of the pot. If your egg came straight from the refrigerator, it should take 2 to 3 minutes to cook.
+ Remove the egg with a slotted spoon and test if it is done by gently pressing on the yolk. If the egg pushes back against your touch, it is ready. Place the poached egg into the bowl of warm water and repeat.
+ Preheat the broiler.
+ When all the eggs are poached, warm the sauce by placing the uncovered bowl or pot of hollandaise back on the double boiler. Heat over medium, whisking to reconstitute. Then place the sweet potato patties back in the oven on the middle rack with the broiler on high. Cook until the tops are crisp, 1 to 2 minutes.
+ To serve, put 2 to 3 patties next to each other on each plate. With a slotted spoon remove an egg from its water bath, jiggling it a bit to get rid of the liquid, and lay it over the patties. Drizzle with a healthy helping of hollandaise sauce and, if you have fresh tarragon lying around, sprinkle a few leaves on top for color as well. Dig in.

**+ sodium count:**

Egg yolks: 8mg per large egg; Egg: 71mg per large egg; Sweet potato: 72mg per medium sweet potato

# ISLAND BREAKFAST BREAD PUDDING

Excellent French toast recipes consist of sweet bread, soaked in dairy and egg, fried to golden perfection. Soft on the inside, toasted on the outside, it is a rich treat. And it can often land you upwards of 500mg of sodium for two slices.

To keep the decadence but lower the salt, I decided to take the elements of French toast and turn them into individual cups of bread pudding. I swapped the high-sodium dairy for low-sodium coconut milk and added other sweet, island-inspired flavors like warm cinnamon, ginger, star anise, bruléed pineapple, and tart apple to enhance and balance the sugar notes bubbling in the dish. If you wish to add a savory twist, continue to play on the tropical theme and add lemongrass pieces to the custard as it heats, removing it before adding the milk to the bread.

Because all the ramekins bake at the same time, this dish is great for entertaining large groups since you don't have to man the skillet for each serving. And if you have leftover coconut milk and pineapple, pair your pudding with a frothy piña colada smoothie.

**Serves 6 to 8**

- 6 to 8 oven-proof ramekins
- 10 slices of no-salt-added bread, crust removed and cut into 1-inch cubes
- 3 cups coconut milk (the kind in the carton)
- 1 cinnamon stick
- 1 (1-inch) piece fresh ginger, peeled
- 1 whole star anise
- 4 large eggs
- Zest and juice of 1 large orange
- 6 tablespoons light brown sugar
- 2 teaspoons ground cinnamon
- 1½ teaspoons vanilla extract
- ¼ teaspoon peeled and grated fresh ginger
- 2 large Granny Smith apples, peeled and diced into ½-inch cubes
- 1 cup diced pineapple, cut into ½-inch cubes
- 1 cup thinly sliced pineapple rectangles

+ Preheat the oven to 350°F. Grease the ramekins and set aside.
+ Put the bread in a 9 x 11-inch baking pan. Bake until it is crisp, 20 to 25 minutes, turning the bread chunks every 5 to 8 minutes to make sure they toast evenly and don't burn.
+ While you're waiting, place the coconut milk, cinnamon stick, fresh ginger piece, and star anise in a small pot and warm over low heat. Crack the eggs into a medium bowl and whisk until the yolk and white are combined. Add the orange zest, orange juice, 4 tablespoons of brown sugar, ground cinnamon, vanilla extract, and grated ginger to the eggs and whisk again. It will look like melted cinnamon ice cream.
+ When the milk is warm, remove the cinnamon stick, ginger piece, and star anise. Slowly add ½ cup of the milk into your cool egg mixture, whisking as you pour. This technique is referred to as tempering your eggs, which warms them slowly so they don't curdle. When the eggs are mixed with the milk, return them to the pot with the milk, continuing to whisk as you pour. Cook the mixture over medium heat for 3 to 5 minutes more. Test to see if the custard is thick enough by dipping a spoon into the mixture. If you can draw a clean line across the back of the spoon with your finger, then it's ready to be taken off the heat.

+ When your bread is toasted, transfer it to a large bowl. Add the diced apple and diced pineapple to the bread, as well as the warm custard, and mix well. Let the bread soak up the custard for 15 minutes. Distribute even amounts of the mixture into the greased ramekins.
+ Wipe off any bread crumbs from the baking pan and place the ramekins on it. Return the pan to the oven and set your timer for 30 minutes. While you're waiting, slice up the rest of your pineapple triangles.
+ Remove the baking pan from the oven, place 3 or 4 slices of pineapple flat on the top of each bread pudding dish, and sprinkle with the remaining 2 tablespoons brown sugar. Return the baking pan back to the oven and cook until the egg is set, 15 minutes. Test if it is ready by shaking the dishes. If the custard doesn't shimmy, it is time to eat.

### + sodium count:

No-salt-added bread: 10mg per slice; Coconut milk, carton: 15mg per cup; Eggs: 71mg per large egg

## ANY WAY YOU SLICE IT: HOW TO CUT A FRESH PINEAPPLE

I once received a very large, very fresh pineapple as a present. And I nervously left it, untouched, on my counter for days. I stared at it, the pineapple stared back at me, and it was like a Western showdown (woman versus fruit) where eventually, one of us was going to have to give in. As the stubborn pineapple stood its ground, ripening with time and releasing sweet smells from its prickly shell, I got over my nerves, got on my computer, and finally learned a skill that every guy or gal should pick up at some point in his or her life. I conquered that pineapple, and now I'm going to teach you how to slice one up, too.

To start, get a trusty serrated knife. Then, to see if your pineapple is fresh enough to eat, gently tug at one of its leaves. If it pops out without too much pulling, it is time to cut it open. Lay the pineapple on its side and slice off the very top. Do the same to the bottom and then stand it upright on its sturdiest end.

Hold the pineapple with one hand and slice off the rind, working from top to bottom like cutting kernels off a very large, sugary piece of corn. You may have to go around the pineapple two times as the first layer of the flesh is usually a bit hard and not very pleasant to chew on. Once you get to the juicy part, though, you're free to slice and dice however you want. Cut the pineapple into spears, circles, stars, or artistic renditions of your pet. And the next time you receive a pineapple as a gift, you'll know exactly what to do.

# POMEGRANATE GRANOLA FRUIT CHUNKS

I love to hike. I love to backpack. I don't mind not showering for days on end or getting really close (you know what I mean) to Mother Nature. But one thing I will not stand for is feeling hungry, even if it is between breakfast and lunch, and that's why I made this granola.

Many mixes on the market contain salt to balance the sweetness of the other ingredients. And while products without sodium do exist—and they are delicious and welcome additions to the aisles—they lack a savory element that makes granola a tasty afternoon snack, and not just a sugary dessert.

To fix the problem, I made a version of my own with oats, dried fruit, sugar, and one added surprise: pomegranate molasses. Its fruitiness allows it to blend well with the other sweet flavors, while its unexpected tartness adds some savory contrast. It has less sodium than normal molasses, it provides a pleasant pucker, and it helps clump the ingredients together: a combination of achievements that will have your hands quickly dipping back in for more.

**Makes 5 cups chunks**

- 2 cups rolled oats
- ½ cup diced dried apricots
- ½ cup chopped dried figs (or prunes)
- 2 tablespoons unsalted butter
- ¼ cup packed light or dark brown sugar
- 3 tablespoons honey
- 2 tablespoons pomegranate molasses
- ¼ cup grated orange zest
- Juice of 1 orange
- ½ cup dried cranberries

+ Preheat the oven to 350°F.
+ Place the oats in a 9 x 12-inch baking pan and into the oven. Toast the oats until they get a golden glow and begin to smell oaty, 10 to 12 minutes. Take the pan out of the oven and place the oats in a large mixing bowl. Lower the oven to 300°F.
+ While the oats are toasting, chop the dried apricots and figs with a knife, or give them a quick pulse in the food processor.
+ Place the butter in a medium pot over medium heat and cook until it begins to brown and smell nutty, about 5 minutes. In a separate bowl, whisk together the brown sugar, honey, pomegranate molasses, orange zest, and orange juice. Add to the brown butter and bring the mixture to a boil over medium-high heat. Cook for 2 minutes and then pour immediately into your mixing bowl with the oates, chopped fruit, and cranberries.
+ Wipe any crumbs off the cooled baking pan, and line it with parchment paper. Stir the contents in the bowl until well combined and pour the mixture onto your parchment paper-lines baking pan, spreading it evenly with a spatula.
+ Bake for 25 to 30 minutes. The granola is ready when it has turned a darker shade of brown, but is still soft to the touch. Allow it to cool and harden at least 45 minutes before cutting or breaking into chunks.

**+ sodium count:**

Dried fruit: look for products that have 10mg or less per serving

# BREAKFAST IN BRUSSELS

If you told me when I was ten that I would say what I am about to say, I would have told you that your pants were on fire. But here goes nothing. I love Brussels sprouts. You may have started to realize that I am really emphatic about a lot of things, especially food. But in all seriousness, I really love these vegetables.

After having a salad made from sprout leaves, you'll never want lettuce again. Shredded or simply pulled apart, they serve as a unique and tasty canvas for dressings and creamy sauces. And by giving them a quick sear in nutty browned butter, you will bring out the Brussels sprouts' natural sweetness and give them a bit of crunch as well. It is a combination that is so dreamy, you'll want to keep the dressing simple, which is why we'll top these leaves with a delicate, oversized poached egg hat and call it a day.

**Makes 4 small servings**

2 pounds Brussels sprouts, washed
4 large eggs
¼ teaspoon white or champagne vinegar
2 tablespoons unsalted butter

+ Cut the nubby ends off the sprouts and then separate the leaves with your hands. It will take about 10 minutes to get through the pile, so try to lure some help with the promise of a delicious meal. When you've finished, set all the leaves aside in a bowl.
+ Prepare to poach your eggs by filling a tall, heavy-bottomed pot halfway with water and bring it to a rolling boil over medium-high heat. Crack each egg into a separate bowl and fill another, larger bowl with warm water. If you are making several poached eggs at one time, you can hold the finished eggs in the warm water bath while you make the others.
+ Once the water in your tall, heavy-bottomed pot has started to boil, lower the heat so that little bubbles gently crack on the surface. Add the vinegar and gently stir it with a spoon. As you are stirring, slide the egg into the water, being careful not to touch it with your spoon. The stirring action, or vortex, will wrap the white around the yolk and will also keep the egg from settling and sticking to the bottom of the pot. If your egg came straight from the refrigerator, it should take 2 to 3 minutes to cook.
+ Remove the egg with a slotted spoon and test if it is done by gently pressing on the yolk part. If the egg pushes back against your touch, it is ready. Place the poached egg into the bowl of warm water and repeat to poach the remaining eggs.
+ Melt 1 tablespoon of the butter in a large pan over medium heat and allow the butter to brown, 2 to 3 minutes. Add half of the Brussels sprouts to the pan, increase the heat to medium-high heat, and cook the leaves, without stirring, for 3 minutes. They will crackle and pop in the butter and start to turn brown on their edges or where they are touching the pan. Stir the leaves and cook for 3 minutes more. Transfer them to a plate and set aside. Heat the remaining 1 tablespoon butter. Allow it to melt and brown again, another 2 to 3 minutes. Add the other half of the Brussels sprouts to the pan and repeat the same steps as before.
+ When all the sprouts have been cooked, lay a nest of the crispy leaves on a plate and top with a poached egg. Serve, crack that yolk, and enjoy.

**+ sodium count:**

Brussels sprouts: 22mg per cup; Eggs: 71mg per large egg

# OYSTER PO' BOY POPS

I know you're thinking, oysters? Has this gal gone loco? I, too, thought the succulent candies of the sea were out of the question for my no-salt diet, but the real surprise is that oysters from the Pacific are 90mg per 3 ounces and wild oysters from the East only are 72mg per 3 ounces. Which means, yes, they are naturally saltier than a pear, but not much more than a hard-boiled egg.

If you miss the taste of Oyster Po' Boy sandwiches—a seaside comfort food that stirs up memories of overcast bay weather, a cold brew, and a bonfire—I have found a way to turn this classic sandwich into a one-bite, low-sodium wonder. I took all of the original ingredients, shrunk them down, and turned them inside out.

They are the perfect size for a brunch appetizer—a spicy, fried treat on a toothpick that's bound to be a crowd-pleaser. And while they are quick to fry up, the most time-consuming part of the recipe will definitely be shucking the oysters. So either ask the guy or gal at the fish counter to shuck them for you, or get an oyster knife, a towel, and a lesson on YouTube and do it yourself, adding yet another cool skill to your low-sodium tool belt.

**Makes 12 pops**

- 1 cup canola oil, or enough so that the pops are more than halfway submerged
- 12 oysters, shucked (see note)
- 3 teaspoons prepared low-sodium horseradish
- Juice from 1 tangerine or small orange
- ½ jalapeño, finely diced
- 1 cup yellow cornmeal
- ½ cup all-purpose flour
- 1 tablespoon dried parsley
- 2 teaspoons ground cumin
- 2 teaspoons smoked paprika
- 2 teaspoons garlic powder
- 2 teaspoons chili powder
- 1 large egg
- ½ cup low-sodium plain Greek yogurt
- 1 lemon, cut into wedges

+ In a high-sided skillet or wok, warm the oil over high heat.
+ While the oil is heating, mix the shucked whole oysters with 2 teaspoons of the horseradish, the tangerine juice, and diced jalapeño in a small bowl and let marinate for 10 minutes. Then, in another bowl, mix the cornmeal, flour, dried parsley, cumin, paprika, garlic powder, and chili powder. This is your coating. In a third bowl, whisk your egg.
+ Take an oyster and a handful of the jalapeño marinade and roll them in the dry ingredients until you have a chunky oyster-jalapeño nugget. Dip the nugget into the egg mixture, and finally give it a second dip into the cornmeal coating mixture. Set aside on a plate and repeat until all of the oysters have been coated.
+ Before frying your pops, test the oil to make sure it is ready. The oil should be 330°F, but if you do not have a thermometer, throw in a little of the cornmeal to see if the oil hisses. When it does, you're good to go. Then, before dipping any pops, cover a plate or cookie sheet with some paper towels so your fried oysters have a place to drain.
+ Using a slotted spoon or a spider, carefully lower the pops (2 or 3 at a time) into the pan. Let them fry and crisp until they turn golden brown, about 2 minutes, then use the spoon to flip them onto their other side, cooking 1 minute more. Remove the pops from the oil and let them drain on the paper towels. Repeat with the remaining oysters.
+ To serve, skewer the warm pops with toothpicks. Mix the remaining 1 teaspoon of horseradish with the Greek yogurt in a small serving bowl. Serve with lemon wedges for your guests to squeeze, and watch those pops disappear.

## + note

Farmed Eastern oysters tend to be saltier than wild ones, landing around 150mg per 3 ounces. Much like shrimp (and now clams and finfish too), the sodium content for any type of oyster can be higher depending on whether they were treated with sodium solutions during their trip from the shore to the store. Talk to your fishmonger or butcher in order to make sure your oysters fit within your sodium limits. Or buy frozen or canned products that come with a nutritional label.

### + sodium count:

Pacific oysters: 90mg per 3 ounces; Eastern wild oysters: 72mg per 3 ounces; Prepared low-sodium horseradish: 20mg per 1 teaspoon depending on brand; Egg: 71mg per large egg; Plain Greek yogurt: 60mg per 6-ounce container depending on brand

# ROASTED ROOT HASH WITH LEMON PEPPERCORN SAUCE

When buying packaged breakfast potatoes or ordering them from a menu, beware that most are salted and seasoned. Of course, they don't have to be so high in sodium and it is easy to make a tasty salt-free version at home. You can use any spices to give low-sodium spuds some kick. Hot spices. Savory spices. Herb spices. But for this recipe, I figured we would go a different route and use the natural flavors found in whole ingredients. And since we are forgetting about the spices, let's forget about the potatoes too and give unexpected root vegetables a chance at the starring role. Radishes and turnips, this is your big break.

When roasted, these veggies become juicy and sweet, adding complexity to the common spud. And to keep it savory, drench them with the creamy lemon sauce. Those whole peppercorns will add a pleasant pucker and pop.

**Serves 4**

Roasted Root Hash

- 1 pound radishes, well washed and trimmed
- 1 pound turnips, well washed and trimmed
- 1 pound small potatoes
- 1 leek, well washed
- 1 tablespoon olive oil
- ¼ teaspoon ground white pepper

Lemon Peppercorn Sauce

- 2 tablespoons unsalted butter
- 1 tablespoon all-purpose flour
- ¾ cup heavy cream
- 1 garlic clove, smashed in a garlic press
- 1 shallot, minced
- 1 tablespoon whole black peppercorns
- 2 tablespoons fresh lemon juice

+ Preheat the oven to 400°F.
+ To prep your roots, cut the radishes, turnips, and potatoes into ¾- to 1-inch cubes. Put them all into a large baking pan.
+ Now for the leek, here's a tip—leeks hide a lot of dirt between their leaves. So to properly wash them, cut the leek in half lengthwise, and then wash well in between each leaf, ensuring no grit ends up in your food. Then set both leek halves side by side, flat side down, and cut the white and green parts horizontally into thin slices. They will look like half circles. Cut them vertically in half and set aside.
+ Add the olive oil and white pepper to the vegetables in the baking pan and mix with a spoon or your hand. Place the baking pan in the oven and cook until the vegetables begin to soften, 45 minutes, taking the pan out at the 20-minute mark. Add the leeks and mix everything until combined. Place the baking pan back into oven for the remaining 25 minutes.
+ Right before the hash is done, place the butter in a small saucepan or pot over medium heat. When the butter has melted, add the flour, whisking constantly for 2 minutes. Add the cream and whisk until well combined, 2 minutes more. Add the garlic, shallot, and peppercorns and cook, still stirring, for 5 minutes. The sauce will start getting thick at this point. Stir in the lemon juice and whisk until the sauce is smooth and creamy, and remove from the heat. The sauce may separate when you initially add the lemon juice, but vigorous whisking for 30 seconds to 1 minute will be enough to bring it back to its thick consistency.
+ To serve, place the hash into a large serving bowl. Immediately add the sauce to the vegetables, mix, and dig in while it's warm. Leftovers are equally delicious the next day. Just reheat and eat.

### + sodium count:

Radishes: 45mg per cup; Turnips: 88mg per cup (about 1 medium turnip); Potatoes: 10mg per small potato; Leek: 18mg per leek; Heavy cream: 5mg per 1 tablespoon

# HOMEMADE CHORIZO PATTIES

You've most likely met chorizo in its traditional form: ground, cured, and sometimes smoked pork that has been seasoned chili, smoked paprika, and salt, covered in sausage casing, and used in everything from scrambled eggs to Jambalaya. The bad news is that, for most products, one link can land you around 750mg of sodium. But the good news is that many countries have their own versions, so I decided that low-sodium eaters could have one of their own, too. And while I can't use sausage casing (often made from brined intestines), I could use a similar mix of traditional spices to mimic the taste of that spicy pork treat.

As usual, feel free to experiment with the spices you use. In Toluca, Mexico, they specialize in a green chorizo made with tomatillo, cilantro, chilies, and garlic. And sometimes, the ground pork is even "cured" overnight in vinegar and more chili powder. So use the recipe below as a starting point and then experiment with your own breakfast sausage creations at home. Serve along with eggs, or even inside one of your Murray Circle Butter Rolls (page 56) for a complete breakfast sandwich.

**Makes 8 to 10 small patties**

- ½ pound ground pork
- 6 garlic cloves, smashed in a garlic press
- 2 teaspoons chili powder
- 2 teaspoons onion powder
- 2 teaspoons smoked paprika
- 2 teaspoons ground cumin
- 1 teaspoon dried oregano
- 1 teaspoon freshly ground black pepper
- ⅛ teaspoon ground cloves
- 2 tablespoons canola oil

+ In a small bowl, mix all of the ingredients (except for the canola oil) with your hands or a fork. You want the bounty of spices to disappear into your pork to keep them from burning in the pan. So don't be afraid to really get in there and work that meat. Then cover a large plate with a paper towel for your chorizo patties to drain after their quick dip in the oil.
+ Now it's sausage time. Heat the canola oil over medium heat in a high-sided pan. Test the oil with a small piece of pork and if it hisses it is ready. Form balls that are slightly bigger than the circle formed by your fingers when you make an "okay" sign. Okay? Okay! Flatten them slightly into patties—they should be about 3 inches in diameter and about ½ inch thick—and without overcrowding the pan, place 4 to 6 patties in the oil. Cook until the meat is browned, 4 to 6 minutes. Lower the heat a bit if they begin to burn.
+ Use a spatula to flip the patties and brown for another 4 to 6 minutes on the other side. Take the patties out of the pan and place them on the plate covered in a paper towel. Repeat until all the meat is used.
+ Serve while hot.

**+ sodium count:**

Pork: 63mg per ¼ pound

## + note

If you are using the chorizo for the Cast-Iron Herb Pizza recipe (page 188), skip making the chorizo into patties and place the seasoned meat directly into a skillet over medium-high heat. Stir with a spoon and break up the meat into chunks, and cook until it turns brown and a bit crispy, 8 to 10 minutes. If the meat sticks to the pan, add a touch more oil or lower the heat.

# FRAÎCHE START CARROT QUICHE

Quiches are made of flaky crust, creamy custard filling, and a cheesy top, which means one slice will get you high marks on your sodium counter. But making a quiche at home, salt-free, is entirely possible. It just takes a bit of work since you have to make the crust from scratch. Get out your food processor and set aside a bit of time, because this dish is worth the effort. You'll be too busy licking the buttery crumbs from the empty pan to even remember the work that went into rolling your own dough.

To make up for a lack of salt, I wanted to fill this quiche with color and bright flavors. Remember, you eat with your eyes as much as you do with your mouth. I used grated purple, white, and orange heirloom carrots to achieve goal one, and as for flavor, I complemented their sweetness with fresh dill, one of my favorite herbs. To make up for the typical cheese topping, I filled my quiche with crème fraîche instead. It adds a creamy, dairy quality and it makes the custard superlight, so you can eat more without feeling heavy.

**Makes 1 delicious 9-inch quiche**
**Effort Level: Got Time to Spare**

Crust

- 10 tablespoons (1¼ sticks) unsalted butter
- 1¼ cups all-purpose flour
- ¼ teaspoon garlic powder
- ¼ teaspoon onion powder
- 4 to 6 tablespoons ice water

Filling

- 1 teaspoon safflower or vegetable oil
- 2 medium shallots, thinly sliced
- 4 medium carrots, peeled
- 5 large eggs
- 3 tablespoons all-purpose flour
- 1 cup crème fraîche
- 1 cup half-and-half
- ½ teaspoon freshly ground black pepper
- ½ teaspoon dried dill
- ½ teaspoon dry mustard powder
- 1 teaspoon chopped fresh dill

+ Generously grease a 9-inch pie plate and set aside. Then cut the butter into cubes and place them in the freezer to chill for at least 20 minutes.
+ Put 1¼ cups of the flour, the chilled butter, garlic powder, and onion powder into a food processor and pulse until combined. The flour will begin to look grainy and crumbly. Then add 1 tablespoon of ice water at a time, continuing to pulse until the dough forms a ball. Remove the dough, wrap it in wax paper, and place in the refrigerator for 1 hour.
+ While the dough is chilling, prepare the other ingredients for the tart. Heat the teaspoon of oil in a small skillet over medium-low heat. Add the shallots to the pan and cook, stirring, until they have softened and let off a sweet aroma, about 5 minutes. Set aside.
+ Use a box grater or food processor to grate the carrots—the finer the grate, the better. You should have about 2 cups of grated carrots. Place them and the shallots into a clean dish towel or cheesecloth and squeeze out all the extra liquid. Remove them from the towel or cheesecloth and set aside.
+ When the dough is chilled, remove it from the refrigerator. Let it warm to room temperature, about 5 minutes. Preheat the oven to 350°F.
+ Right on top of the wax paper you used to wrap the dough, roll out the dough into a 12-inch circle about ⅛ inch thick. Transfer the dough to your pie dish by simply putting your well-greased, 9-inch pie dish upside down over the center of the dough, leaving a 1- to 2-inch overhang on every side. Gently, with one hand on the pie plate and one under the wax paper, turn the whole thing right side up and use your hands to press the dough into place. Remove the wax paper and fold the overhanging dough gently under itself. Using the tips of your fingers or

fork tines, press down on the dough along the rim of the pie plate, forming decorative indents or a nubby-looking edge. Either way it will be buttery and delicious. Trim away any excess dough.

+ Use a fork to prick a few holes through the bottom of the dough—this will keep the dough from bubbling as it bakes. Put a piece of parchment paper (not wax paper!) on top of the dough and fill the bottom with dried beans or peas or whatever you have to act as an oven-safe weight. Place the pie dish into the oven and bake the dough for 15 minutes. Take the pie dish out and remove the parchment paper and weights, then put the pie dish back into the oven until the crust begins to turn a golden hue, 15 minutes. Remove the pie dish from the oven and allow the crust to cool, about 10 minutes.
+ While the crust rests, continue to prepare the filling. Place 1 egg and the remaining 3 tablespoons of flour in a mixing bowl, and using an electric mixer, mix at high speed for 30 seconds. Add the other 4 eggs and mix until well combined, another 30 seconds
+ In another bowl, whisk together the crème fraîche and the half-and-half until smooth. Slowly pour in the egg mixture, whisking in one third at a time. When well combined, add the black pepper, dried dill, dry mustard, and fresh dill. Stir until blended.
+ Pour the shallot and carrot mixture onto the bottom of your crust and then pour in the egg and crème fraîche mixture until it reaches just ¼ inch below the edge of the crust. Place the pie dish on a baking sheet and into the oven. Bake until the custard sets, 35 minutes. Remove the quiche from the oven and allow it to cool at least 5 minutes before slicing and serving.

### + sodium count:

Carrots: 42mg per medium carrot; Eggs: 71mg per large egg; Crème fraîche: 10mg per 1 tablespoon; Half-and-half: 15mg per 2 tablespoons

## + note

If you don't have the time for or interest in making a crust, you can easily prepare this quiche without one it. Simply pour the carrots and custard straight into a greased pie plate and bake for the same amount of time. You can use this technique for any leftover filling as well.

Remember, you eat with your eyes as much as you do with your mouth.

# A CLASSIC BLOODY MARY

Bloodies are usually made with prepared vegetable juice, Tabasco, Worcestershire sauce, horseradish, pepper, and lemon. Bottled low-sodium tomato and vegetable juice can run as high as 170mg of sodium per cup, and Tabasco and Worcestershire can add another 200mg to the total with just a few dashes of each. But it is entirely possible to create the same tastes without these products. By using fresh or even prepared tomato puree, fresh or prepared horseradish, some homemade veggie juice, and spices, you can create a Bloody mix that doesn't miss the mark. Actually, you'll be able to taste the individual ingredients, the pucker and the spice, better than in the drinks made with those salted mixes.

And while using a juicer makes prep much easier, it isn't necessary to go out and buy one. You can get silky-smooth juice by blending your vegetables and running them through a strainer or cheesecloth.

Also, don't be afraid to be creative with your presentation. The preparation below is classic. But if you have salt-free pickled grapes, cherry tomatoes, or green beans lying around, throw them in, for heaven's sake. And instead of rimming the glasses with salt, spackle the tops with a blend of freshly ground black pepper, paprika, and lemon zest for color and extra spice.

**Makes 10 cups Bloody Mary**

- 4 large celery stalks, with extra stems for garnish
- 2 small red beets, trimmed and peeled
- 1½ red bell pepper, stemmed and seeded
- 4 cups no-salt-added tomato puree 1 (24-ounce jar has a little more than 3 cups, so you can always fill the jar with 1 cup water and shake to loosen the leftover tomato puree to make 4 cups)
- 1 to 2 teaspoons prepared low-sodium horseradish
- 1 to 2 teaspoons freshly ground black pepper
- 2 teaspoons smoked paprika
- ½ to 1 teaspoon cayenne pepper
- 2 lemons
- 1 tablespoon white wine vinegar
- Ice, for garnish

+ If you are using a juicer, juice the celery, beets, and bell pepper. Place the liquid into a pitcher or large mixing bowl and add the tomato puree.
+ If you are using a blender, put the celery, beets, bell pepper, and tomato puree into a blender. Pulse until you have a vegetable smoothie. Then make a sturdy pouch out of some folded cheesecloth and, over a pitcher or a large bowl, carefully pour the blended veggies into it. Gather the cheesecloth at the top to close and then squeeze. Really squeeze, many times, until all the juice runs out of the cheesecloth and all you have left inside is dry veggie pulp. If you don't have cheesecloth, you can also pour the veggie smoothie into a fine-mesh sieve and use a wooden spoon or the bottom of a ladle to press down on the puree, squeezing the juice through until you have strained every bit into the pitcher or bowl. Set all your vegetable scraps aside.
+ Now that you have your vegetable juice, add 1 teaspoon of the horseradish, 1 teaspoon of black pepper, the smoked paprika, cayenne, juice of 1 lemon, and vinegar to the pitcher or bowl. Whisk together and taste, adjusting the spices (oh hello, horseradish and pepper) according to your cocktail preferences. I like mine spicy!
+ Place the Bloody Mary mixture in the refrigerator to chill, 15 minutes minimum or 2 hours maximum.
+ When you're ready to serve, fill glasses with ice. Pour in Bloody Mary mixture and add a celery stalk for garnish. Cut the remaining lemon into wedges and offer them to guests as well for extra citrus punch. Finally, stir, sip, and savor.

+ **sodium count:**

Celery: 51mg per 1 large stalk; Beets: 64mg per 1 beet; Canned tomato puree: 15mg per ½ cup depending on brand; Prepared horseradish: 20mg per 1 teaspoon depending on brand

## BLOODY MARY SCRAPS ARE DELICIOUS

So you've made a stellar Bloody. Cheers! Clink! Drink!

But you've also made a pile of veggie scraps. Do not throw them away! You could make an entire brunch from them by giving the pile of fiber a quick chop and mixing it with avocado (a Bloody Guacamole); cooking them in a skillet with some oil and then throwing in a few eggs (a Bloody Scramble or a Bloody Frittata); using them in place of grated carrots in the Carrot Cupcakes recipe (page 246); or throwing them in a bread pan to make Bloody Mary Scrap Bread (recipe at right), which you can toast up for a nutrient-rich breakfast sandwich. Two dishes from one set of ingredients with no salt—that's some clever low-sodium cooking.

# BLOODY MARY SCRAP BREAD

**Makes one 9 by 5-inch loaf**

3cups all-purpose or bread flour plus extra if dough feels too sticky
2 tablespoons granulated white sugar
2 teaspoons sodium-free baking powder
2 teaspoons freshly ground black pepper
1 teaspoon chili powder or red chili pepper flakes
1½ cup veggie pulp
1 (12-ounce) can beer
1 tablespoon olive oil

+ Preheat the oven to 400°F.
+ In a mixing bowl, combine the flour, sugar, baking powder, black pepper, and chili powder with a wooden spoon. Make a well in the center and add the dry veggie pulp. Mix until distributed, breaking up any clumps with your spoon. Make a well in the center again and slowly add the beer, mixing as you pour. When all the beer is added, there may be some dry flour left in the bowl. So roll up your sleeves and get in there, and use your hands to give the dough a final mix and knead, incorporating any extra dry ingredients. Of course, if your dough is too sticky, add a little more flour (about ¼ of a cup should do the trick). And if it seems too dry, add a little extra water. Trust your instincts. You want the dough to be a slightly wet, but not can't-get-it-off-my-hands goopy.
+ Dump the batter into a greased 9 x 5-inch bread pan, spreading the dough with your hands or a spatula until it fills the pan evenly. Place the bread in the oven and bake for 30 minutes. When the time is up, drizzle the olive oil over the bread and put it back into the oven for 15 more minutes. To test if the bread is done, stick a knife in the middle of the loaf. If it comes out clean, it is ready to be devoured.
+ Take the Bloody bread out of the oven and allow it to cool before slicing, 15 minutes minimum. Eat as is or toast in a hot, oil-free skillet to make breakfast sandwiches.

# Bits + Bites

# CHAPTER 2

When's the last time you enjoyed a salt-free appetizer?

I'm guessing it's safe to say never, except for maybe the fruit that decorates the cheese plate, or the slim pickings from a bowl of salt-free nuts or that spread of crudités (fancy language for cut vegetables)—although those may have been salted too. You never really know. Either way, these nibbles don't count as real appetizers.

A truly good appetizer has all the makings of a full meal. It is just shrunk down to a mini bite, losing its size but keeping its big taste. Appetizers are composed, they are layered, and in my opinion, if you have enough of them, they can make a complete meal. I have great respect for appetizers; low-sodium ones just happen to be hard to find.

Something happened to me recently, though. As I started to blog about small low-sodium treats of my creation, people started to notice. When I joined friends at their homes for a dinner party, suddenly salt-free hummus showed up next to those plain sticks of carrots and celery. When I attended potlucks, friends offered jars of low-sodium pickles and bean dips that I could dig into. And when I got married, my wonderful caterers made sure I could stuff my white dress full of salt-free guacamole chips, dim sum, and mini tamales.

Try these recipes and start treating yourself to some itty-bitty bites. Because if big meals can be satisfyingly salt-free, then the small ones can be too.

*A truly good appetizer has all the makings of a full meal.*

# ORANGE PICKLED FENNEL

Surprise! Celery is kind of high in sodium—for a vegetable, that is. At 81mg per cup, I sometimes skip the stalk and use fennel in its place, which only has 45mg per cup. But this is no second hand substitute. Fennel not only has a similar crunch to celery; it also imparts a unique licorice flavor to classic recipes. Tuna fish and chicken salads suddenly get a whole lot sexier. And by pickling fennel in a mixture of citrus, vinegar, turmeric, and peppercorns, you can really make this bulb taste bright. As an added bonus, fennel and all of its various parts (including the seeds) are believed to act as a natural diuretic, which means it may help you shed off extra water weight, help lower blood pressure, and reduce edema. All welcome benefits if you are on a low-sodium diet.

**Makes 1 quart pickled fennel**
**Effort Level: Plan Ahead**

- 2 medium fennel bulbs, well washed
- 3 garlic cloves, peeled
- 1 (½-inch) piece of ginger, peeled and roughly diced
- 3 dried chile de arbol peppers or 1 teaspoon red chili pepper flakes
- 1 medium orange, grated zest or peel and juice of
- 1½ cups distilled white vinegar
- ½ cup apple cider vinegar
- ¼ cup granulated white sugar
- 1 teaspoon whole black peppercorns
- 1 teaspoon whole yellow mustard seed
- ¼ teaspoon ground turmeric

+ Cut off the stems and the bottom nub from the fennel bulbs and remove the outer layer if it looks old or bruised. Then cut both bulbs vertically in half, placing the flat side of each on a cutting board. To make your pickles, you can cut the fennel halves lengthwise into ½-inch spears, horizontally into crescents, or in whatever other shape and size you want. These are your treats and they'll pickle all the same. Once sliced, stuff the fennel, some of the soft fennel fronds from the stem, the garlic, ginger, chili peppers, and orange zest into your container. Set aside.
+ In a saucepan or small pot, mix 1 cup water with the distilled white vinegar, apple cider vinegar, sugar, juice from the orange, peppercorns, mustard seed, and turmeric. Bring the pickling liquid to a boil over medium-high heat, 6 to 8 minutes. Remove the pot from the heat and allow the liquid to cool, at least 20 minutes, or longer if you are using plastic containers.
+ When the liquid is lukewarm, carefully pour it into your containers, covering the fennel spears. If there is not enough liquid to completely cover the spears, add a bit more distilled white vinegar to the containers. The spears will shrink a bit in the hot liquid, so if you have any extra spears that did not initially fit in, go ahead and add them to the container. Finally, place the lid on the container and close it tightly. Give it 5 or 6 good shakes to mix and stick it in the fridge to cool.
+ In 48 hours, the fennel will be ready for munching. Resist the urge to taste before then, because the longer you wait, the more "pickly" they will be. But do try to finish them off within 2 weeks. It won't be hard.

## + note

You can use this same recipe for any kind of pickle—thinly sliced ginger, peppers, grapes, okra, cabbage, and even apples. Let the leftovers in your fridge speak to you. Then pickle them.

### + sodium count:

Fennel: 45mg per 1 cup chopped fennel, 122mg per bulb

# YES YOU CAN: A TALE OF TWO SALT-FREE PICKLES

As my meals began to transform from merely edible to totally enjoyable (even for salt-eaters), I started dedicating more time to my low-sodium experiments. I was quickly turning into a culinary fanatic, happy to spend hours in the kitchen. And as my obsession grew, I began to notice that I wasn't alone. I was surrounded by many other risk takers, bakers, and homemade bacon makers, all equally content to stand at a burner until late in the night.

There was the guy down the street who turned his garage into a home brewery, opening his tap to neighbors and ale connoisseurs alike. There was a group of young gentlemen who led foraging tours around the Bay, teaching locals how to pluck greens, mushrooms, and even fish from public spaces. And I discovered that the bookstore around the corner regularly sold urban-laid eggs at the counter. Which isn't so out of the ordinary, as the store is dedicated to books on cooking and food. But still, it's pretty extraordinary to buy a book on cakes as well as the eggs you'll use to make them.

Clearly, I was not the only one exploring new food grounds. And the creativity and exuberance for homespun food made me even more determined to take on new cooking projects and to continue pushing the low-sodium boundaries. That's when I met Karen Solomon, a fiery cook, author, and DIY goddess who hosts "Jam It Salons," events where self-taught cooks share their domestic fare with other interested palates. It wasn't a contest, simply a support group for adventurous food novices. And cheese, jam, tomato sauces, cured meats, and of course, cured vegetables were all welcome.

I figured this was the perfect place to test my latest low-sodium invention: salt-free pickles. They were a culinary oxymoron, but something I thought actually tasted pretty close to the real thing. Sometimes I'm skeptical, though, of my own judgment and my unsalted palate. And if the other jammers and picklers liked the taste, and if Karen approved, then I would know for certain that I was onto something.

A few days prior to the event, I sunk fennel spears in a mixture of orange juice, turmeric, mustard seed, peppercorn, and vinegar. I let them sit, shrink, and marinate. And the night of the "Jam It Salon" I opened my cans and waited. I told no one about the salt situation. And suddenly, from across the room, I heard a voice. It was Karen, asking, "Who made these? They're great!" My hand shot up in the air, and before saying anything else—like, "thank you," perhaps?—I blurted out, "There's no salt!" I was excited.

Having Karen's approval was proof that no-salt cooking could be full of flavor and that even in a snack known for its salty pucker, salt-free pickles could stand up to (even stand out from) the salty versions. I felt like David defeating a big, salty Goliath. And knowing that an expert pickle maker didn't notice the lack of salt gave me huge confidence, both in my pickles and in my other salt-free meals. This recipe was a winner. Even though, like I said, this wasn't a contest.

Forget the "cannots" and grab some cans to make these two tasty salt-free pickles—my diet-changing orange pickled fennel recipe and Karen's cumin-scented carrot recipe that she made over just for you. You may have thought these salty treats were off the safe list forever, but with some adjustments and aggressive spices (and advice from an expert) you can have this snack back.

# CUMIN-SCENTED PICKLED CARROTS

*Low-Sodium Guest: Karen Solomon, Author of Jam It, Pickle It, Cure It & Can It, Bottle It, Smoke It*

"Pickles with big, bold flavors—garlic, vinegar, dill seed—are naturally tangy and crisp. I love salt and I am a big fan of the kosher stuff for pickles. But trust me, this recipe is strong on bite and acidity, and you won't even miss the salt. These are the quintessential pickles to eat straight from the jar and, by all means, get experimental with other flavors by adding fresh ginger slices, jalapeños, or cinnamon sticks."

**Makes 1 pint pickled carrots**
**Effort Level: Plan Ahead**

- 1 garlic clove, lightly crushed
- 1 tablespoon dill seed
- 1 tablespoon whole black peppercorns
- 1 teaspoon fennel seed
- 1 teaspoon cumin seed
- About 12 ounces (roughly 6) fresh carrots, peeled, trimmed, and cut into large sticks
- Distilled white vinegar
- Water

+ In the bottom of a clean pint-size jar with a clean lid and tight-fitting band, place the garlic, dill seed, peppercorns, fennel seed, and cumin seed. Lay the jar on its side, and place as many carrots as possible into the jar, nestling them very snugly.
+ Turn the jar upright again and fill it halfway with vinegar and then top off the remainder with cold, fresh tap water, ensuring the vegetables are completely covered in liquid. Cover tightly and shake gently to distribute the spices.
+ Refrigerate for at least 3 to 5 days to let the vegetables pickle, then eat. Pickles will remain delicious for at least a month.

**+ sodium count:**
Carrot: 42mg per medium carrot

# BEET CARPACCIO TOWERS

Don't bother calling my editor—I didn't forget anything in the ingredient list below. This dish really is made from only three ingredients: beets, avocados, and a lime. And while it looks simple on paper, it manages to create complex flavors once it hits your palate—a feat that is outdone only by its deceptively easy, but stunning presentation. This dish has sweetness, a hint of natural salt (thank you, beets), richness from the avocados, and pucker from the squeeze of citrus. It is the perfect balance of flavors. And speaking of balance, the carpaccio towers can be expertly stacked using a clean, empty can (or plastic bottle) with the bottom and top removed. Or, if you don't have any cans or bottles, you can also use the funnel part of your food processor top to make the towers. No special spices or tools required. Serve with salt-free chips, a lightly oiled arugula salad, or simply a fork.

**Makes 4 to 6 carpaccio towers**

2 red or yellow beets, ends cut off
2 avocados
1 Zest and juice of 1 lime, divided
Aluminum Foil

+ Preheat the oven to 375°F.
+ Wrap each beet in a sheet of aluminum foil. Place the wrapped beets on a baking sheet and bake in the oven until the beets are soft to the touch, 30 to 40 minutes. Remove the pan from the oven and let the beets cool until you can comfortably touch the foil, 10 minutes. With the beets still wrapped, use the foil to rub off the outer layer of skin and place the peeled beets aside to continue cooling.
+ Cut each avocado in half and remove the seed. Use a spoon to carefully scoop the avocado flesh from the skin, attempting to keep it intact. Then dice the avocado halves into ¼-inch cubes. Sprinkle most of the lime juice over avocado to prevent browning. Divide the cubes into 4 to 6 even piles, depending on the number of servings. Divide each pile in half again, so you have enough avocado pieces to create a bottom and top layer for each tower.
+ When the beets have cooled, dice them into ¼-inch cubes and organize the cubes into 4 to 6 piles, depending on your number of servings.
+ To construct the towers, place a topless and bottomless can, a tall round cookie cutter, or a food processor funnel directly on your serving plate. Use a spoon to carefully fill your tower-making tool with one pile of avocado cubes. Press down lightly with the bottom of the spoon. Then, add a pile of beets on top of the avocado, pressing down lightly again. Finally, add the last pile of avocado on top of the beets, pressing down with the spoon as you gently remove your carpaccio tower from the tower-making tool. Repeat until you have made all the towers.
+ Grate some lime zest over the towers and sprinkle a bit of the juice on top for added brightness.

**+ sodium count:**
Beets: 64mg per beet;
Avocado: 14mg per avocado

# DELICATA COCKTAIL

My love for shrimp cocktail is how I know I'm my father's daughter. Just like him, I adore the taste of chilled shrimp against the smack of tangy cocktail sauce. But due to the sodium in shrimp and store-bought cocktail sauce, this dish needed a serious low-sodium makeover if I wanted to keep enjoying it.

The sauce was easy to create without salt. I simply mixed tomato puree with horseradish. As for the shrimp, though, I needed something that was slightly chewy, sweet, and hopefully similar in color. The answer was delicata squash, whose pink-orange color and scalloped shape makes a whimsical stand-in for the original. Plus, the name had a nice ring to it. And if delicata is not in season, go ahead and use a plump acorn squash. Consider it the jumbo prawn version.

**Serves 4**

- 2 delicata (or 1 acorn) squash
- 1 tablespoon olive oil or vegetable oil
- ¼ teaspoon garlic powder
- ¼ teaspoon paprika
- Freshly ground black pepper, to taste
- ¼ cup no-salt-added canned tomato puree or Salt-Free Tomato Puree (page 102)
- 3 teaspoons prepared low-sodium horseradish

+ Preheat the oven to 400°F.
+ Cut each delicata squash (or the acorn squash) into 1½-inch-thick rounds, discarding the ends. Then cut each round in half, making crescents, and remove the seeds and stringy parts by scraping the inside with a spoon. Feel free to save the seeds to toast later for an extra appetizer.
+ Place the squash crescents in a mixing bowl and drizzle them with the oil. Then add the garlic powder, paprika, and pepper to taste to the bowl and use your hands to rub the spices and oil all over the squash. Place the crescents on a greased or parchment paper–lined baking sheet and bake until the squash crescents are just soft enough to pierce with a fork, 5 to 8 minutes.
+ In a small dipping bowl, mix the tomato puree and the horseradish until well combined.
+ To serve, dangle the squash from the dipping bowl or lay the crescents out on a larger tray. Dip and enjoy.

**+ sodium count:**
Canned tomato puree: 15mg per ¼ cup depending on brand; Prepared horseradish: 20mg per 1 teaspoon depending on brand

**There are a few things we just inherently trust. Parents (excluding years 13 to 22); the Pythagorean theorem; weather predictions made by groundhogs; and when it comes to low-sodium cooking, nutrition labels.**

To live a successful and almost effortless low-sodium lifestyle, one has to be educated and diligent. In order to make smart choices, you have to know your stuff. You should be able to approximate the sodium content in the zucchini, fish dish, or plate of pasta you plan on eating. And, almost more importantly, you have to keep up to date on the information that is being provided. Because it often changes.

While writing a post for my blog, I proudly offered a recipe for shrimpless shrimp curry, because I thought shrimp was loaded with sodium. The data from USDA's National Nutrient Database for Standard Reference said that shrimp contains 480mg of sodium for 3 ounces. So far, everything adds up.

But here's where the issue arose. In my other trustworthy sodium reference book, the *Pocket Guide to Low Sodium Foods*, shrimp is listed as containing only 144mg of sodium for 3 ounces—a number that many of my blog readers adhere to, meaning that they continue to eat and enjoy shrimp. The inconsistency of information was surely disconcerting, for me and my readers, and it deserved further investigation.

Instead of panicking, though, I decided to go straight to the source. I wrote the good fellows and ladies of the USDA and asked for help. And only a few hours later, the airwaves boomeranged right back, and a little note from Dr. Jacob Exler arrived, explaining the following:

"We recently conducted a nationwide sampling and analysis of about 20 species of finfish and shellfish, including shrimp. The samples were all obtained from retail supermarkets and they represent what consumers would likely purchase.

The new sodium value is based on this sampling. The National Fisheries Institute tells us that seafood may come in contact with sodium solutions during their processing. It is likely that this is the reason for the higher sodium values. Our older data was mainly from the scientific literature and would not necessarily represent what is in the marketplace. I hope this answers your question."

Well, Jacob, it did. And here are the lessons I learned: First, when buying shrimp from your grocery store fish counter, it is hard to know the exact sodium content. Much like poultry, which can be plumped with salted brine in order to make the meat juicier, the sodium content in your shellfish will depend on the source. And the only thing you can do to avoid the "salted" versions is to know where your food comes from and how it was processed. Or buy it frozen, in a box, with a label.

As for the second lesson, this little shrimp adventure reminded me that whenever you reach a sodium impasse, there is always a way around it. At the start, I thought my go-to resource had been proven ineffectual. But quickly, my spirits rose and my confidence returned when I found out that not only was my resource still valuable, but I actually had a direct line to a real person. With answers.

It seems that yes, shrimp can be as low as 140mg of sodium per 3-ounce serving as long as it is not treated with salted solutions before it reaches the store. Just keep your eyes open, your brain alert, and your mouth talking to pick the right shellfish for your diet. And if you have any other questions, now you know you can just ask.

# PÂTÉ CAKE, PÂTÉ CAKE

I love chicken. Especially the thighs, which are juicy and flavorful. But it wasn't until I read *Good Meat*, by Deborah Krasner, that I realized I had been ignoring some of the chicken's best parts. Mainly its liver, which is cheap and even richer in taste than those leg muscles that I adore. As I've started buying whole, defeathered chickens and butchering the pieces myself at home (no big deal), I'm enjoying finding ways of using all the extra goodies in my cooking. This is how I found myself with a pound of chicken livers and my first attempt at pâté. The word used to make me quiver, but now it makes me shimmy with joy.

The caramelized shallots and butter in this dish add delicate earthy notes. The bourbon (or sherry) helps cut the fattiness of the protein and adds a husky taste that smolders in your throat long after that pâté is gone. The figs provide an appealing sweet note, not to mention a decorative touch. Creamy and decadent, this pâté is a pleasant surprise for you and your guests. And I'm not sure what's more impressive—the taste, or saying you made it from scratch. Serve with small toast points made from no-salt-added bread or salt-free crackers.

**Makes 2 to 3 small ramekins**
**Effort Level: Plan Ahead**

- 2 tablespoons (¼ stick) unsalted butter
- 2 shallots, finely chopped (about ⅓ cup)
- 2 large garlic cloves, minced
- 1 teaspoon minced fresh thyme or ¼ teaspoon dried
- 1 teaspoon minced fresh marjoram or ¼ teaspoon dried
- 1 teaspoon minced fresh sage or ¼ teaspoon dried
- ¼ teaspoon freshly ground black pepper
- ⅛ teaspoon ground allspice
- ½ pound chicken livers (see note left)
- 5 dried figs, stem removed and roughly chopped, plus a few thin slices reserved for garnish
- 2 tablespoons bourbon or sherry

+ Melt the butter in a medium, nonstick skillet over medium heat until it begins to brown and gives off a nutty flavor, about 3 minutes. Add the shallots and garlic and cook, stirring constantly until softened, 2 to 3 minutes. Lower the heat and add the herbs, pepper, allspice, livers, and figs. Continue cooking until the livers turn from pink to a light brown color on the outside, about 8 minutes. Pour in the bourbon or sherry and remove from the heat. Let the mixture sit for 5 minutes.
+ Put the mixture in a food processor and pulse until a puree is formed. If you find that the pâté is sticking to the sides of the processor bowl, use a spatula to push it back toward the blades. Continue processing until the mixture is smooth and then transfer it into small ramekins or a mini tart pan. Cover with plastic wrap, pressing it flat onto the top of pâté. Place in the refrigerator to chill for a minimum of 2 hours and up to 2 days before serving. Allow the pâté to come to room temperature before serving.
+ Garnish with the reserved sliced figs and serve.

## + note

One step that is essential to this dish is prepping the chicken livers. If you buy them from a butcher, you can ask him or her to do the dirty work for you. But if you want major kitchen credibility, then use a sharp paring knife to remove the white, sinewy parts and any of the darker, black-green pieces on the skin: these can create a bitter taste. I've done this many times myself and it is not difficult, just a little smelly. Offal smells awful. So be sure to get rid of your trash or compost ASAP.

### + sodium count:

Chicken livers: 80mg per ¼ pound

# TEMPURA

Tempura requires dirty hands and a bit of oil splatter. But if you're craving crunchy vegetables, you can make this salt-free treat quickly at home. For my version, I added cornstarch to the equation to help the batter stick to the vegetables and give the coating a puffier texture. Cornstarch actually gets clumpier than plain flour when fried and helps create the traditional lumpiness you want in tempura. I've also seen recipes that add an egg to the mixture, making a thicker batter. So feel free to experiment with your coating, the vegetables you use, and even how you cut them. Leave them whole, make them into nests of sliced matchsticks, or cut them into rounds. Turn your kitchen into a personal tempura lab and get sizzling. Serve warm with Umami Sauce (page 109) or wasabi Salt-Free Tofunnaise (page 103).

**Serves 4 to 6**

Vegetable oil
1 cup Pacific nori, shredded (scissors work best)
1 large zucchini, washed and sliced into 1-inch discs
1 Japanese eggplant, washed and sliced into 1-inch discs
1 medium daikon, washed, peeled and sliced into 1-inch discs
½ cup all-purpose flour
6 tablespoons cornstarch
1 cup pale ale or Japanese beer

+ Fill a wok or high-sided heavy-bottomed saucepan with about 2 inches of oil (this may use up your entire bottle of oil but you can reuse it once it cools for other frying adventures). Heat the oil over medium heat and as temperature rises, prep your workstation by laying out the shredded nori and vegetables on a plate and covering a cooling rack with paper towels to drain excess oil from the tempura.
+ In a medium bowl, mix the flour and 3 tablespoons of the cornstarch. Slowly drizzle the beer into the flour and cornstarch mixture, whisking as you pour. Continue to whisk the tempura batter until it is smooth and foamy. Pour the remaining 3 tablespoons cornstarch into a separate bowl.
+ When the oil has reached about 330°F, or it sizzles when you drop in a bit of batter, it's time to make the tempura. Working with one small group of vegetables at a time, dredge a few pieces in the cornstarch. Then immerse them in the batter, pulling apart any pieces that have stuck together. Place the battered vegetables on a slotted spoon and slide them into the hot oil. Fry until the coating starts to turn golden brown, 1 to 2 minutes. Flip and fry the opposite sides for 1 to 2 minutes, then immediately transfer to the paper towel–covered cooling rack. Repeat with the remaining vegetables.
+ For the nori, take a small handful of the shredded pieces and dredge them in the cornstarch. Then, as you did before, immerse it into the batter, forming a clump of batter-covered nori. Repeat the same frying steps as you did with the vegetable tempura and when the nori nest is crispy, remove it from the oil and transfer to the cooling rack or drain.
+ Place all the tempura on a plate and serve with your dipping sauces.

### + sodium count:

Zucchini: 26mg per large zucchini; Eggplant: 11mg per large eggplant; Daikon: 71mg per large daikon

# SEVEN-LAYER DIP

Traditionally, seven-layer dip is a rainbow of refried beans, sour cream, guacamole, pico de gallo, black olives, green onions, cheese, and lots of taco seasoning. But if you were to dip into this classic Super Bowl dish—often made with prepared and canned ingredients—you'd be dipping deep into your sodium allotment for the day.

Seven layers of low-sodium flavor, however, are not impossible to create at home. It takes some time and prep, but think of that extra effort as a secret eighth component. Serve with unsalted chips.

**Serves 4 to 6**

**Effort Level: Got Time to Spare**

- 3 cups cherry tomatoes (about two 8-ounce cartons), halved
- 6 garlic cloves, roughly diced
- 2 cups fresh or frozen corn (about 3 ears of corn)
- 1 red bell pepper, stemmed, seeded and diced
- 1 poblano pepper, stemmed, seeded and diced
- 1 (15-ounce) can no-salt-added black beans, drained and rinsed
- 1 cup beer (pale ale is best)
- 1 tablespoon honey
- 2 teaspoons ground cumin
- 1 teaspoon light or dark brown sugar
- ½ red onion, diced
- 2 ripe avocados
- 1 (6-ounce) container low-sodium plain Greek yogurt
- ¼ cup chopped fresh cilantro
- ½ jalapeño pepper, stemmed, seeded and finely diced
- 1 cup finely chopped red cabbage
- 3 green onions, thinly sliced (everything but the bulb)
- Salt-free corn chips or toasted tortillas

+ Preheat the oven to 375°F.
+ Place the tomatoes and garlic on a piece of aluminum foil and fold the sides over to make a little package. Make second one with the corn and a third package with the bell pepper and the poblano pepper. Place all 3 packages on a baking sheet and put them in the oven to cook for 35 minutes.
+ While the vegetables are roasting, mix the black beans, beer, honey, cumin, and brown sugar in a medium pot. Bring the mixture to a boil over medium-high heat and cook for 5 minutes. Then reduce the heat to medium and cook, uncovered, for 25 more minutes, stirring every 5 to 10 minutes to make sure no beans stick to the bottom of the pot. When the beans are soft and the mixture has thickened, remove the pot from the heat and allow the beans to cool for 15 minutes.
+ At this point, your roasted vegetables should be finished. Remove them from the oven and when the foil is cool enough to touch, transfer the ingredients from each foil package to separate prep bowls. Add the red onion to the tomato and garlic mixture. Scoop the avocados into the bowl with the corn and, using a fork, smash until it has a smooth, guacamole-like texture. Finally, put the Greek yogurt, cilantro, and jalapeño in another bowl, and mix until well combined. No need to do anything with the bell pepper and the poblano. Just tell them how delicious they look.
+ It is now time to make your layers. In a 2- to 3-quart glass bowl or high-sided dish, place the beans on the very bottom. Next, layer the cabbage over the beans, then add the roasted bell pepper and poblano, and spread the avocado mixture over that. Add in the tomato salsa, then the creamy yogurt sauce, and finally, a hearty sprinkle of green onions. Count to seven and dig in.

### + sodium count:

Cherry tomatoes: 7mg per 1 cup; Fresh Corn: 11mg per ½ cup; Frozen corn: 0mg depending on brand; No-salt-added black beans:10mg per ½ cup, depending on brand; Avocado: 14mg per avocado; Red cabbage: 19mg per 1 cup, chopped; Plain Greek yogurt: 60mg per 6-ounce container depending on brand

# SPICY SAUSAGE PEPPER POPPERS

Sausage Pepper Poppers. Try saying that ten times fast. It's hard. If you're looking for something easier to do, then make these bite-sized, low-sodium snacks instead.

With 0mg of sodium, trusty matzo meal makes the perfect substitution for herbed breadcrumbs, which can have more than 500mg of sodium per ¼ cup. And although they can taste bland on their own, by mixing them with savory meat and herbs, the final combination will burst with flavor. Just mix, fill, bake, and eat. And for the next tailgate or BBQ, swap these bites for saltier favorites like microwaveable mozzarella jalapeño poppers. The sausage filling and sweet peppers in this dish will more than make up for the fried cheesiness of the original game-day snack. Serve with low-sodium Ranch Dressing (page 100), Roasted Pepper and Tomato Salsa (page 99) or a yogurt-dill sauce.

**Serves 6 to 8**

- 1½ pounds ground pork
- 1½ teaspoons dried parsley
- ⅓ cup salt-free matzo meal
- 1 teaspoon freshly ground black pepper
- 1 tablespoon chopped fresh, dill or 1 teaspoon dried dill
- 1 teaspoon dried rosemary, broken up with your fingers
- 1 teaspoon smoked paprika
- 1 teaspoon garlic powder
- 1 teaspoon red chili pepper flakes
- ¼ teaspoon dried orange peel or freshly grated orange peel
- ⅛ teaspoon ground nutmeg
- 1 large egg, beaten
- 3 packages baby bell peppers (about a dozen per package)

+ Preheat the oven to 350°F.
+ In a medium bowl, mix together all of the ingredients, except the bell peppers. Be sure the herbs, spices, and egg are well distributed throughout the pork and don't be afraid to use your hands to combine. Then cut the tops off of the bell peppers and remove the core and seeds with your fingers.
+ To create a homemade piping bag, spoon the pork mixture into a plastic bag. Press out the air, twist the top closed, and use scissors to snip a ¼-inch opening at one of the bottom corners. Put the cut end into the open end of the pepper. Gently squeeze the pork mixture inside, pausing every so often to make sure the pork mixture is reaching the bottom. You can use the round bottom of a knife or your fingers to push the pork inside.
+ Place the stuffed peppers flat in rows on a lightly greased or parchment paper–lined baking sheet and bake in the oven for 1 hour. The peppers will soften and darken a bit in color and the pork will turn brown and crispy at the exposed end. Serve warm and pair with a low-sodium ranch dressing, roasted tomato salsa, or yogurt-dill sauce.

**+ sodium count:**

Pork: 63mg per ¼ pound; Egg: 71mg per large egg

# TAMARIND "TERIYAKI" CHICKEN SKEWERS

Long before I discovered my love of sashimi, I fell in love with the viscous, sweet taste of teriyaki. With anywhere from 300 to 700mg of sodium per tablespoon, however, teriyaki chicken from the local takeout is now out of the question. So, to meet my cravings, I let go of the original dish and focused on finding a substitute with a similar color, thick coating, and unique flavor. The low-sodium answer lay in tamarind paste—a sweet and tart concentrate made from tamarind seed pods. It is popular in Indian, Middle Eastern, and East Asian cuisines, and can even be found in Worcestershire sauce. Its acidic properties help tenderize meat, and in Ayurvedic medicine it is said to have heart-protecting properties. Or in Western medicine speak, it may help lower bad cholesterol.

While it is no teriyaki, this tamarind sauce sure makes a convincing look-alike. The savory sweetness of the tamarind will delight your palate. If you have any leftover herbs in your kitchen, like mint, cilantro, or even some green onion, dice and sprinkle them over the chicken at the end for some extra color and cool flavor. And to make a traditional bento presentation, serve with a slice of orange and crisp lettuce salad.

**Serves 6**

- 1 tablespoon tamarind paste (or substitute with pomegranate molasses)
- 1 tablespoon dark brown sugar
- 2 teaspoons unseasoned rice vinegar
- 2 teaspoons molasses
- ¼ teaspoon garlic powder
- 3 garlic cloves, diced
- ¾ cup water plus 2 tablespoons
- 1 tablespoon cornstarch
- 2 teaspoons sesame oil
- 8 boneless, skinless chicken thighs, cut into ½-inch-wide strips
- Bamboo skewers
- White toasted sesame seeds, for garnish
- 2 green onions, thinly sliced (everything but the bulb), for garnish

+ In a small pot or saucepan, mix together the first 7 ingredients (tamarind paste to ¾ cup water). Bring the mixture to a boil over medium heat, then reduce to low and cook for 10 minutes.
+ In a separate bowl, mix the cornstarch with the 2 tablespoons of water until it is dissolved and smooth. Add the cornstarch mixture to the pot and stir until it is well combined and the sauce begins to thicken like a glaze. Continue to cook and reduce by one third, 2 to 3 minutes. Then turn the heat to the lowest possible setting and cover the pot with a lid to keep the sauce warm.
+ In a large skillet, heat the sesame oil over medium-high heat. Add your chicken pieces and about a quarter of the sauce and cook for 5 minutes without stirring. Then toss the chicken pieces, doing your best to flip them over, adding another quarter of the sauce. Cook until the inside of the meat is white, 6 to 8 minutes more.
+ Remove the chicken from the heat and allow it to rest until the pieces are cool enough to handle. Weave the chicken onto the bamboo skewers, about 4 per skewer, and lay them flat on a serving dish or a large plate. Drizzle the remaining sauce over the skewers and sprinkle with white toasted sesame seeds and the sliced green onions. Serve and eat immediately.

### + sodium count:

Tamarind paste: 20mg per ounce depending on brand; Molasses: 10mg per 1 tablespoon; Chicken thigh (with skin): 87mg per ¼ pound

**+ sodium count:**

Chicken wing: 82mg per ¼ pound ; Canned tomato puree: 15mg per ½ cup depending on the brand; Celery: 32mg per medium stalk; Fennel: 45mg per 1 cup

# BUFFALO WINGS

Buttery, sweet, tangy, and tasty. I don't mean to brag, but I nailed this one.

Traditional Buffalo wings are usually made with prepared hot sauce, butter (lots and lots of butter), and salt. The hot sauce alone can cost you around 450mg of sodium—at least for one of the most popular brands. But with a little research and by reading the back of hot sauce labels, I came up with a spicy, buttery, and low-sodium concoction of my own. It has the same electric red color and taste of the original, and instead of frying the wings, I decided to go for a healthier version and baked the chicken instead. The result was equally tender bites with less oil splatter to clean.

Again, I don't mean to brag, but in terms of taste, look, and enjoyment, this gets pretty close to the original. Pair the wings with low-sodium ranch dressing and some celery sticks (or fennel fronds) to truly complete the low-sodium makeover.

**Serves 6 to 8**

- 1 red bell pepper, stemmed and seeded
- 1 Serrano pepper, stemmed
- 1 Fresno red pepper (or a jalapeño pepper), stemmed
- 2 tablespoons unsalted butter
- 2 tablespoons light or dark brown sugar
- 6 tablespoons no-salt-added tomato puree
- ¼ teaspoon garlic powder
- ¼ teaspoon onion powder
- ¼ teaspoon ground white pepper
- ¼ cup red wine vinegar
- ¼ cup beer
- 2 pounds chicken wings and drumettes, separated
- 6 medium celery (or fennel) stalks, halved or quartered
- Napkins or a bib, for serving (optional)

+ Turn the broiler to high.
+ Place the bell pepper, serrano pepper, and Fresno pepper in a baking pan and put it on the middle rack of the oven. Allow the peppers to roast until the skins chars and turn black, flipping and turning them a quarter-turn every 6 to 8 minutes. Remove the peppers from the oven, put them in a paper bag, close the top, and let them steam for 10 to 15 minutes. When you can comfortably touch the peppers, peel off the charred skin with your fingers and put the peppers into a blender, with their seeds and any roasting juices. Puree until smooth.
+ Turn off the broiler and preheat the oven to 425°F.
+ In a small pot or saucepan, melt the butter over medium heat until it begins to brown. Add the sugar, tomato puree, garlic powder, onion powder, white pepper, red wine vinegar, beer, and the pureed peppers. Cook the ingredients for 10 minutes and then remove the pan from the heat.
+ In a large bowl, mix the wings and drumettes with the hot sauce. Use a wooden spoon or tongs to mix (be careful—the sauce is hot) to ensure that all the wings are covered with the spicy stuff. Then remove the chicken from the bowl and place the wings and drumettes in a single layer on a large greased baking sheet. If you need to use 2 pans, that is okay. Just be sure that all of the chicken pieces touch the bottom of the pan. Place them into the oven and bake for 20 minutes.
+ Meanwhile, pour the hot sauce back into the pot or saucepan and, over very low heat, continue to let it reduce and thicken into a glaze.
+ After 20 minutes, flip the chicken pieces over to the other side and slather the remaining hot sauce glaze all over them. Cook for 20 minutes more then remove the wings from the oven. Place them on a large plate or platter and serve immediately with chopped celery (or fennel) and low-sodium Ranch Dressing (page 100).

# QUICK QUINOA MEATBALLS

The biggest salt-free challenge of meatballs is the breadcrumbs, which are essential to achieving the desired texture and are often soaked in milk, adding a good amount of sodium to these meaty bites.

To make a tasty meatball, with the right bite and no salt, I endured several failed attempts. I felt like a meatball Goldilocks. In my first version, I used plain matzo meal soaked in half-and-half. But they were just too mushy. In the next batch, I toasted no-salt bread to make breadcrumbs and soaked them in half-and-half again. This time, the texture was better, but they were just too much work. Finally, I had a new idea: meatballs made with quinoa, that nutty, funky grain that softens as it cooks but keeps a slightly toothy texture. They weren't your traditional meatballs, but they were airy and interesting. They were absurdly easy to make. They didn't need to be fried, toasted, or soaked in dairy. And they were just right. Sometimes you have to take a serious detour from the original recipe in order to find a satisfying, low-sodium replacement.

Beyond the pork and quinoa, this dish is flavored with a mix of warm cinnamon, spicy pepper, and other traditional Italian herbs. The meatballs work well as a toothpicked appetizer, served with either Salt-Free Ketchup (page 106) or mustard for dipping. Of course, you can make them into a full meal with some Chunky Red Tomato Sauce (page 108) and pasta noodles. Better yet, if you want to get supercreative, turn them into a deconstructed meatball sub sandwich and serve them over shredded basil and arugula, with pickled fennel on top. I did this recently and it was awesome.

**Makes 24 to 26 meatballs**

- ½ cup washed white quinoa
- 1 pound ground pork
- ½ cup diced shallot (about 2 medium shallots)
- 4 garlic cloves, smashed in a garlic press
- 2 large eggs
- ½ teaspoon freshly ground black pepper
- ½ teaspoon cayenne pepper
- ½ teaspoon paprika
- ½ teaspoon dried oregano
- ½ teaspoon dried parsley
- ¼ teaspoon ground cinnamon

+ Preheat the oven to 450°F. Line a baking sheet with parchment paper.
+ Put the quinoa and 1 cup water into a saucepan and bring to a boil. Once you have strong bubble action, reduce the heat to low, cover, and cook until the water is absorbed, 12 to 15 minutes. Check occasionally and stir to make sure no quinoa is burning at the bottom of the pan. Take the saucepan off the heat, transfer the quinoa to a medium mixing bowl, and allow it to cool for 10 minutes.
+ While the quinoa is cooling, add all of the remaining ingredients to the bowl. Using your hands or a spoon, mix until all the ingredients are evenly distributed and well combined.
+ Shape the meat mixture into balls that are a little smaller than a golf ball. Place them in even rows on the lined baking sheets. Place the sheet in the oven and cook the meatballs until they're slightly browned and crispy on top, 12 to 15 minutes. If you have a meat thermometer, the safe internal temperature for pork is 165°F.
+ Serve as suggested or find your own way to enjoy these little meat bites.

### + sodium count:

Quinoa: 0 to 10mg per 1 cup per serving depending on brand; Ground pork: 63mg per ¼ pound; Eggs: 71mg per large egg

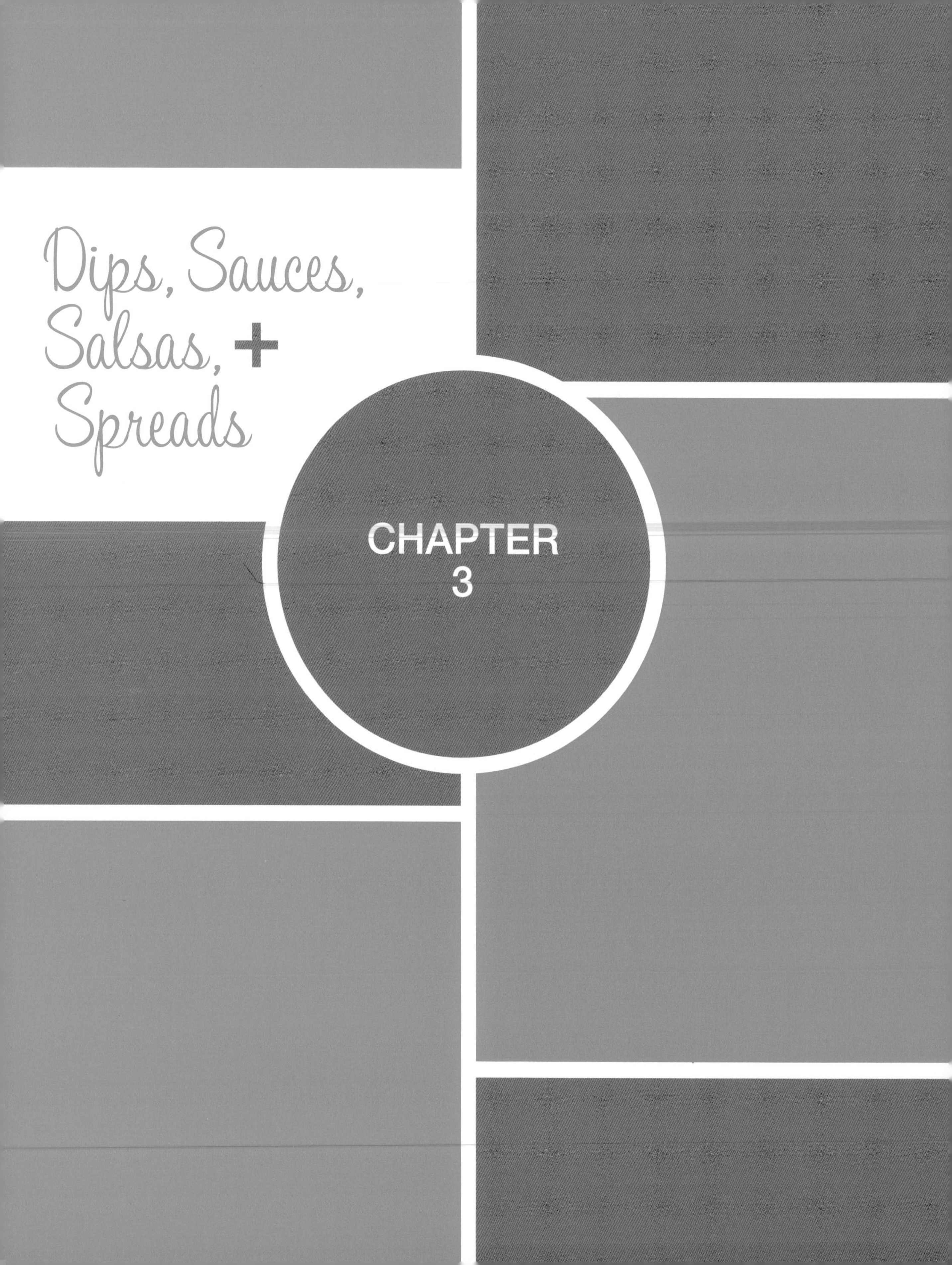

# Dips, Sauces, Salsas, + Spreads

## CHAPTER 3

One of my favorite local restaurants is a Belgian spot called Frjtz. They serve crepes, heaping bowls of mussels, and my favorite food of all, French fries—an item that they graciously make salt-free for me.

My love for Frjtz, however, goes beyond their perfectly crispy fries. I also adore their large menu of condiments. They have almost 30 choices, and while they are all loaded with salt, they are hugely inspiring. Thai Chili Ketchup. Pesto Mayo. Strawberry Mustard. Smoky Honey Mustard. Spicy Yogurt Peanut. Ginger Orange Mayo. BBQ. The list goes on and on, capturing any combination of flavors one could dream up. I'm waiting for chipotle chocolate butter. It's just a matter of time.

Even though I can't dip into Frjtz's endless list of condiments, it is a good reminder that classics are meant to be rewritten. And since it is still difficult to find low-sodium, salt-free condiments on restaurant menus and grocery store shelves, it's also a perfect excuse to get creative on your own. Chocolate chipotle butter, here we come.

With just a few minutes and a few ingredients, you can make creamy dips to dress up your food. Learning to make your own condiments will not only give you confidence in your kitchen, but will give you practice in fearless experimentation as well. Diced mangos, cayenne, and yogurt may spell dipping genius. It may also spell disaster. But until you try, you'll never know. Here are just a few ideas, tested and approved, to get you started.

*With just a few minutes and a few ingredients, you can make creamy dips to dress up your food.*

# ROASTED PEPPER + TOMATO SALSA

Gosh, I'm glad we're making this today. Popular brands of store-bought salsas can contain upwards of 200mg of sodium per 2 tablespoons, which, in my world, is a single dip in the salsa bowl. Meaning a few dunks into this sauce will add up to high sodium numbers quickly. And when you consider how easy it is to whip up a low-sodium version at home, buying prepared salsas no longer seems worth the salt or the money.

So can the canned stuff and start making your own. This version is spicy, tangy, and fresh, and by roasting your peppers and tomatoes first, you give it a standout smoky flavor that goes beyond simple diced tomatoes. It's an extra step that won't go unnoticed by salt-eaters. Serve with chips and be sure to experiment with other flavor combinations as well, adding grilled peaches, mango, avocado, jicama, and cucumber next time around. Put your stamp on salsa.

**Makes 3 cups salsa**

- 1 poblano pepper, stemmed and seeded
- 3 cups cherry tomatoes (about two 8-ounce cartons), halved
- 5 to 10 garlic cloves (depending on who you plan on kissing), chopped
- 1 cup fresh or frozen corn kernels
- 1 tablespoon olive oil
- 2 medium tomatoes, diced
- 1 jalapeño pepper, stemmed, seeded and finely diced
- 1 tablespoon chopped fresh cilantro
- 3 green onions, thinly sliced (everything but the bulb)
- ½ teaspoon freshly ground black pepper
- ½ teaspoon ground cumin
- Zest and Juice of 1 lime

+ Preheat the oven to 375°F.
+ Cut the poblano pepper in half and then slice it vertically into ¼-inch-wide strips. Dice the strips into little cubes and place them in a baking pan with the cherry tomatoes, garlic, and corn. Cover the vegetables with the olive oil and mix everything together. Bake until the pepper and tomatoes have shriveled and softened and the garlic and corn have turned a light brown, about 35 minutes.
+ Place the roasted pepper, tomato, garlic, and corn into a medium serving bowl, making sure to include all the roasting juices from the pan. Add the remaining ingredients (tomatoes through lime) and mix until well combined.

### + sodium count:

Poblano pepper: 7mg per pepper; Cherry tomatoes: 7mg per 1 cup; Fresh corn: 11mg per ½ cup; Frozen corn: 0mg per serving depending on the brand; Poblano pepper: 7mg per pepper; Cherry tomatoes: 7mg per 1 cup; Fresh corn: 11mg per ½ cup; Frozen corn: 0mg per serving depending on the brand

# RANCH DRESSING

Legend says that the original ranch dressing was developed in the 1950s by a real rancher. Visitors loved the tart taste of buttermilk mixed with green onion, garlic powder, and other herbs so much that the homemade condiment was soon bottled and commercially sold, taking over Italian dressing as America's favorite dip, and landing on everything from salad to crudités to pizza.

For low-sodium eaters, though, a few things stand in the way of enjoying ranch dressing. The combination of buttermilk, sour cream, and mayonnaise, as well as the salt in the herb and spice mix, all add up to sodium counts as high as 500mg per serving for some products (usually for only 2 tablespoons). But by looking at the packaging and breaking down the ingredient lists, it's easy to get back to basics and make a low-sodium version with all the farm flavors of the original.

To mimic the buttermilk, I used low-sodium Greek yogurt that has a similar sour bite, and I added some citrus juice for extra acid. Fresh herbs and a mix of garlic, onion, and mustard powder provide the familiar garden smells and tastes. And finally, a quick mix will blend everything together for a sauce confettied with herbs. Spoon this dressing over a salad or into a small serving bowl for dipping pleasure. It pairs well with chips, simple vegetables, Buffalo Wings (page 93) and Spicy Sausage Pepper Poppers (page 89).

**Makes 1½ cups**

- 1½ cups (two 6-ounce containers) low-sodium plain Greek yogurt
- Juice from ¼ lime (about 1½ teaspoons), taste to make sure it's ripe
- 3 to 4 teaspoons chopped fresh dill
- 3 to 4 teaspoons chopped fresh chives
- ⅛ teaspoon garlic powder
- ⅛ teaspoon onion powder
- ¼ teaspoon mustard powder

+ Mix all of the ingredients in a bowl until well blended. Snap. That was easy.

### + sodium count:

Plain Greek yogurt: 60mg per 6-ounce container, depending on brand

# HOMEMADE HORSERADISH

This gruff-looking root is low-sodium gold. Just a little bit of it will have your mouth on high alert, and it can add a lightning bolt of flavor to more muted dishes. I have been known to throw generous amounts of prepared horseradish into my cooked vegetables, mashed potatoes (the best!), and even toasted bread. That last example is a little ridiculous, but true. I have also seen horseradish used raw, thinly sliced in salads. And don't forget about red horseradish, which is just the root mixed with beets, giving it a bit of sweetness, natural sodium, and a cool color.

You can buy low-sodium horseradish in stores and it won't cost you too many sodium points. But you can also easily make your own horseradish at home. If you're ready to take on this root, grab your peeler, a food processor, and maybe some goggles, because the fumes are even stronger than a really stinky onion.

**Makes ½ to 1 cup prepared low-sodium horseradish**

1 horseradish root, 8 to 10 inches long
4 to 6 tablespoons water
1 tablespoon distilled white vinegar

+ Begin by peeling the rough, brown skin from the horseradish root until the white flesh is exposed. Rinse the peeled root so no dirt or grit remains, then roughly dice the root into small cubes and place them in a food processor with 2 tablespoons of the water and the white vinegar. Pulse the mixture, stopping from time to time to push the horseradish bits closer to the blades. Add a little more water and continue to pulse until the mixture transforms from grainy to creamy.
+ Before storing, drain the horseradish of any excess liquid. Place the puree in an airtight container and keep it in your refrigerator for up to 1 week.

**+ sodium count:**

Horseradish root: 2mg per 1 tablespoon

# SALT-FREE TOMATO PUREE

My neighborhood is dotted with small mom-and-pop Italian corner stores. Think: handmade pastas, sausages, cannolis, and plenty of neighborhood gossip. The people who run these establishments are some of the most accommodating folk I have ever met (they make ready-to-eat vegetable side dishes without salt), their shelves are equally obliging, and have introduced me to a world of low-sodium tomato products.

Whether it comes in a jar, a can, or even a box, there are now a host of salt-free tomato sauces and purees on the market that land in the 5 to 15mg of sodium per serving range. There are even options with roasted tomatoes and herbaceous basil, giving low-sodium eaters a much-deserved break from making everything from scratch.

But if you want to really tap into those Italian roots and avoid buying anything processed, then you can make tomato puree at home. The most difficult step is boiling and peeling the tomatoes. But the benefit of this added effort is a smoother final product and some delicate leftover tomato water that you can use for a cool summer cocktail.

**Makes 2 to 3 cups puree**

6 large tomatoes, stemmed

+ Fill a medium pot three-quarters way with water and bring to a boil over high heat. Fill a large bowl with water and ice and place it in the refrigerator. Using a paring knife, make small "x" marks on the bottom of each tomato and use the knife to core the tops. As soon as the water is fiercely bubbling, put the tomatoes in the water, cover with a lid, turn off the heat, and let them rest for 5 minutes.
+ Remove the cold water bath from the refrigerator and carefully transfer your hot tomatoes to the bowl with a slotted spoon. Let them sit until the skin near each "x" mark starts to peel back, about 5 minutes more. Peel the skin off each tomato with your hands and then cut the tomatoes in half and spoon out the seeds. Working in two batches, place the skinned and seeded tomatoes in a blender or food processor and puree.
+ Put the pureed tomatoes in a small pot or saucepan and cook over medium to medium-low heat until the puree has reduced to a consistency of your liking, 10 to 15 minutes. Allow the puree to cool for 10 minutes, and place it in an airtight container. Store the puree in the refrigerator for 1 week or freeze for up to 3 months.

## + sodium count:

Tomatoes: 9mg per large tomato

## + note

Another great trick is to freeze your sauce in an ice cube tray so you have small portions available without having to unfreeze and refreeze the entire batch. These cubes also make a fun addition to a Bloody Mary (page 72) or to that leftover tomato water that you got from peeling your tomatoes.

# SALT-FREE TOFUNNAISE

Only two years ago you still had to order salt-free chips, beans, and other condiments online, but today more and more low-sodium products are hitting the market—including a brand of mayonnaise made from hempseed oil, which has only 5mg of sodium per 1 tablespoon serving. It is a bit oily tasting, but it has the perfect mayo texture and flavor. And as most store-bought mayo can land between 70 and 100mg of sodium per tablespoon, this is a welcome addition to my cooking arsenal.

Since we are on a homemade cooking roll, though, I thought I'd give you an option for making this creamy spread at home. And that's what gets me, finally, to the recipe. Thank you for being so patient.

I learned the trick from several wise vegan cooks, who replace the egg with silken tofu. I was a bit skeptical at first, but a good blend in the food processor, with some garlic and a hint of vinegar, convinced me that this sodium-free mayonnaise is going to change my life. Or at least the frequency with which I make deviled eggs. As usual, play around with the flavors. Add curry powder, dill, dried onions, horseradish, pickled fennel, or even salt-free wasabi powder to make unique spreads and dips.

**Makes 1½ cups tofunnaise**

1 package silken tofu (about 1½ cups)

¼ teaspoon garlic powder

2 teaspoons apple cider or white vinegar

+ Place all of the ingredients into a food processor and blend until combined and smooth. Add more vinegar for extra tang.
+ Use. Enjoy. Keep for 1 week in the refrigerator.

### + sodium count:

Silken tofu: 0mg depending on brand

# ROASTED BUTTERNUT RICOTTA DIP

This dip started out as a filling for a simple galette that I made for a tart contest. Yes, I enter tart contests from time to time. The tart turned out well, but the filling was extraordinary. So good, in fact, that my sous-chef for the day (my mom) and I finished off an entire bowl of leftovers while the galette baked. It was proof that this filling, now a dip, had to be a recipe of its own. And because of the orange coloring, it not only tastes great but it also looks like a sharp cheddar spread, making it a perfect addition to a low-sodium "cheese" plate. Serve with salt-free crackers, chips, or even toasted tortilla triangles for dipping pleasure.

**Makes 2 cups dips**

½ small butternut squash
1 tablespoon olive oil, plus 2 teaspoons for drizzling
4 garlic cloves, chopped
½ cup low-sodium ricotta
⅓ cup mascarpone
2 tablespoons chopped fresh thyme leaves
½ teaspoon freshly ground black pepper

+ Preheat the oven to 375°F.
+ Using a knife, cut the squash into 2 halves. Pick one half to use, reserve the rest to boil and blend for soup on another night. Then peel or cut off the hard outer rind of the squash until you get to the bright orange flesh. Cut the squash vertically in half and remove any seeds and fiber. Finally, give it a good chop, cutting the squash into cubes.
+ Place the squash cubes on a greased or parchment paper–lined baking sheet and drizzle 1 tablespoon of olive oil over them. Spread the squash out in a single layer and place the sheet in the oven. Bake until softened, about 30 minutes. Remove the baking sheet from the oven and set the squash aside to cool.
+ As the squash cools, heat the remaining 2 teaspoons of olive oil in a small skillet. Add the garlic and cook over medium heat until softened, about 3 minutes.
+ Place the cooked garlic in a food processor and add the baked squash, ricotta, mascarpone, thyme, and pepper. Pulse until the mixture is combined and smooth. Spoon the spread into a serving dish and chill until you're ready to serve.

**+ sodium count:**

Butternut squash: 6mg per 1 cup cubed; Low-sodium ricotta: 24mg per ¼ cup depending on brand; Mascarpone: 15mg per 2 tablespoons depending on brand

# SALT-FREE KETCHUP

If you could only have one condiment, what would it be?

These days I would say honey mustard, mainly because there are a few delicious salt-free versions available in stores. But if you had asked me before my kidneys failed, I would have unequivocally answered ketchup.

It is good on almost anything—eggs, French fries, burgers. I'd even put it on pancakes if I had to prove my point. But ketchup in all its gloppy goodness can reach up to 165mg of sodium per tablespoon. And while salt-free versions do exist, many contain sodium substitutes that are high in potassium, which can be an issue for some kidney patients. As I dearly missed my sloppy joes and ketchuped potatoes, I knew I needed to come up with an easy-to-make version of my own.

With some quick research online, I realized the essential ingredients were tomatoes, vinegar, sugar, and some black or white pepper. And with that simple groundwork, you can let your imagination run wild. Spice this ketchup however you like, whether you give it an Asian twist with ginger and curry, a Tex-Mex spin with cumin, or a fruity essence with some peach. Who needs a one-note condiment when you can have many?

**Makes about 3 cups ketchup**

- 3 cups no-salt-added tomato puree
- ¾ cup apple cider vinegar
- ¼ cup packed dark brown sugar
- 1 teaspoon freshly ground black pepper

+ In a small pot or saucepan, bring all of the ingredients to a brisk simmer over medium heat. Cover with a lid and cook until reduced by one-third, about 15 minutes. If using the ketchup right away, keep it warm in the pot over low heat covered with the lid. Or, if it is being saved for later use, place the ketchup in an airtight container and refrigerate it for up to 1 week, if you can wait that long to use it.

**+ sodium count:**

Canned tomato puree: 15mg per ½ cup depending on the brand

# TOMATO-LESS KETCHUP

While I had conquered salt-free homemade ketchup, it turned out that I still had another challenge. Many kidney patients cannot eat tomatoes due to their high potassium level, and while I was speaking at a kidney patient support group, one darling woman (whom we'll call Margaret, because I never got her name) said she dearly missed eating the red condiment. My heart melted and I knew I had to come up with a substitute for her and everyone else who must ditch the savory fruit and all the wonderful sauces that come with it.

I started throwing out ideas for a thick, easily puree-able substitute. Pumpkin? No, too much potassium. Squash? Potassium. Bell peppers? Finally, a winner. And if you ask me, the perfect swap.

So for Margaret and everyone who loves ketchup and red sauce as much as I do, here is a salt-free, tomato-less ketchup that I made just for you.

**Makes 2 cups ketchup**

- 3 red bell peppers, stemned and seeded
- ¼ cup apple cider vinegar
- ½ cup packed dark brown sugar
- ½ teaspoon balsamic vinegar
- 1 teaspoon freshly ground black pepper
- ¼ teaspoon no-salt garlic powder
- ¼ teaspoon smoked paprika

+ Roughly chop the bell peppers into large chunks and then place them in a food processor or blender. Add the apple cider vinegar and blend until you have a pepper and vinegar smoothie. Yum.
+ Pour your blended bell pepper and vinegar mixture into a small pot or saucepan, add the brown sugar, balsamic vinegar, black pepper, garlic powder, and paprika and bring to a brisk simmer over medium heat. Cover with a lid and cook over low heat until the mixture has reduced by one-third, about 15 minutes. If using the ketchup right away, keep warm in the pot on low heat covered with the lid. Or, if it is being saved for later use, place it in an airtight container and refrigerate. Ketchup will stay good for 1 week.

### + sodium count:

Red bell peppers: 5mg sodium per medium pepper

# CHUNKY RED TOMATO SAUCE

Bottled tomato sauces, flavored with herbs, roasted tomatoes, and other spices, can add up to 1,280mg of sodium per cup—almost the recommended daily limit in a single bowl of spaghetti oh-nos. But cans of salt-free tomatoes (crushed, roasted, and pureed) do exist. And by using these or fresh tomatoes, it is easy to whip up a pasta-worthy sauce in no time. The recipe below is just my personal favorite blend of vegetables and other aromatics. I love the crunch of fennel seed and the meaty quality of the mushrooms, and I think it tastes splendid with some browned ground pork served over a pile of noodles. As usual, use this as a starter recipe and then feel free to adjust according to your tastes and needs.

**Makes 3 to 4 cups sauce**

- 3 fresh tomatoes or 4 cups no-salt-added tomato puree
- 2 medium carrots (see note left)
- 1 teaspoon olive oil
- 5 garlic cloves, finely chopped
- ¼ red onion, finely diced
- 1 portabella mushroom, diced, brown gills and stem removed (see note below)
- ¼ teaspoon freshly ground black pepper
- ¼ teaspoon fennel seed
- ¼ teaspoon ground nutmeg
- 1 teaspoon dried oregano
- 1 teaspoon dried basil
- 2 teaspoons red wine vinegar
- ¼ teaspoon red chili pepper flakes

+ Place the tomatoes and carrots in a blender or food processor and puree until smooth.
+ In a medium pot or saucepan, heat the olive oil over medium heat. Add the garlic and onion and cook, stirring, until softened, 2 to 3 minutes. Add the mushroom and cook, without stirring, for 5 minutes.
+ Pour the tomato mixture into the pot or saucepan and add the remaining ingredients. Bring to a boil and cook for 5 minutes. Reduce the heat to low, cover the pot with a lid, and simmer for 15 to 20 minutes. Finally, remove the lid and cook until the sauce has reduced by one-third, about 10 minutes.

## + note

If you are short on time or energy, dice the carrots and skip the blending process. It won't really affect the taste, just the texture, and the sauce will be even chunkier.

## + note

Cremini, button, or any other kind of mushroom would be equally delicious in this recipe. Add them to the pot or skip the portabella all together. Use what you have!

### + sodium count:

Tomatoes: 6mg per medium tomato; Canned tomato puree: 15mg per ½ cup depending on brand; Carrots: 42mg per medium carrot; Portabella mushroom: 8mg per 1 cup diced

# UMAMI SAUCE

I remember the day that my low-sodium diet truly turned around. I had just bought Donald A. Gazzaniga's book *The No-Salt, Lowest-Sodium Cookbook*, and as I flipped through the recipes, I landed on "Soy Sauce Replacement." I had never considered the idea of replacements before. Or that I could mimic something as salty as soy sauce, which contains over 1,000mg of sodium per tablespoon.

I made Mr. Gazzaniga's Soy Sauce Replacement, and while it didn't taste exactly like the original—there is just no way you can replicate the taste of all that salt—it did have a similar Asian essence. And when mixed with other components for marinades or BBQ sauces, it provided the right amount of savory sweetness.

Taking my cue from the king of substitutes, I created my own version that I use whenever a recipe calls for soy or teriyaki or fish sauce. And I'm calling it umami sauce, as I want your palate to seek out the savory quality, not the salt.

**Makes about 1 cup sauce**

- 1 cup water
- 1 tablespoon unseasoned rice vinegar
- 1 teaspoon molasses
- ½ teaspoon dark brown sugar
- ½ teaspoon garlic powder

+ Mix all of the ingredients together and refrigerate until ready to use. The sauce will keep in the refrigerator for 1 month.

### + sodium count:

Red Wine: 10mg per 1 tablespoon, depending on brand

# BALSAMIC BLUEBERRY STEAK SAUCE

As I mentioned earlier, I was lucky enough to travel abroad to Italy just months before getting sick. While I was there, I was also lucky enough to eat at a restaurant called Acqua al Due, where I experienced a dish that has stuck with me ever since: Blueberry Balsamic Steak.

I had never tasted such a deeply rich reduction sauce before, and I dreamt about it for months after I returned home. I also didn't know that good, aged balsamic tastes like dark bitter chocolate. And when I removed the salt from my life, I realized that this rich concoction could be a perfect replacement for salty steak sauces, which can have over 500mg of sodium per 2 tablespoons.

So reader, meet Balsamic Blueberry Steak Sauce. It is rich, a bit bitter, and subtly sweet: a perfect complement to the fatty and naturally salty quality of the meat. And don't let this be the only fruit sauce you try on top of your proteins. Be bold with your combinations and experiment with what is in season. If you get "cooking block," just follow the wise adage that "what grows together goes together." And if you're craving some extra heat, add half a roasted poblano pepper to the sauce for more of a spicy, BBQ-style sauce.

**Makes 1½ cups sauce**

- 1 teaspoon olive oil
- 2 garlic cloves, finely minced
- ¼ Vidalia onion, finely diced
- 6 tablespoons balsamic vinegar
- 2 tablespoons dark brown sugar
- 4 teaspoons honey
- 2 teaspoons molasses
- 2 cups (1 pint) blueberries

+ In a small saucepan, warm the olive oil over medium heat. Add the garlic and the onion and cook, stirring, until softened, about 5 minutes.
+ Add the remaining ingredients to the pot and stir until combined. Increase the heat and bring the mixture to a low boil, cooking for another 5 minutes. Reduce heat to low, cover the pot with a lid, and simmer for 25 minutes. Make sure to keep an eye on the sauce and if it is reducing too quickly, turn the heat down or off.
+ Take the lid off the pot and, with the back of a wooden spoon, pop the blueberries against the side of the pot, releasing their juices. Increase the heat to medium and reduce the sauce until it reaches your preferred thickness, 6 to 8 minutes more. And if you want the sauce to be free of blueberry skins, strain it through a fine-mesh sieve before serving.
+ Spoon the sauce on a juicy piece of steak and enjoy. Refrigerate any leftover sauce in an airtight container for up to 1 week.

### + sodium count:

Molasses: 10mg per 1 tablespoon depending on brand

Just follow the wise adage: "What grows together, goes together."

# ROASTED EGGPLANT HUMMUS

I love hummus. The combination of chickpeas, lemons, and tahini is pretty spectacular on its own. And when paired with salt-free rice cakes, it makes a quick snack for breakfast, lunch, or any time you need to munch on something.

But for this version, I wanted to add something special to the mix. Taking a cue from hummus's cousin—babaganoush—I threw roasted eggplant and garlic in the oven, and in a little under an hour, it became soft, smoky, and sweet. To play up these flavors, I added smoked paprika, cumin, and cayenne to the mix as well, and after a quick spin in the food processor or blender, the spread is ready to devour. Serve with salt-free chips, crackers, or sliced, seedless cucumber.

**Makes 2 to 3 cups hummus**

- 2 large globe eggplants, stemmed and peeled
- 3 tablespoons plus 2 teaspoons olive oil
- 2 heads garlic
- 2 tablespoons tahini
- Juice of 1 lemon (about ¼ cup)
- 1 teaspoon prepared low-sodium horseradish
- ½ teaspoon freshly ground black pepper
- 1 teaspoon smoked paprika
- 1 teaspoon ground cumin
- ½ teaspoon cayenne pepper
- ½ teaspoon garlic powder
- 1 (15-ounce) can no-salt-added chickpeas (garbanzo beans), drained and rinsed
- 1 tablespoon chopped fresh flat-leaf parsley, for garnish (optional)

+ Preheat the oven to 375°F.
+ Slice the eggplant lengthwise into 3 pieces and then cut each crosswise in half. Place the eggplant on a greased or parchment paper–lined baking sheet and drizzle with 2 tablespoons of the olive oil, spreading it all over with your hands.
+ Slice just the top off the heads of garlic so that the garlic flesh is exposed. Put both heads into a piece of aluminum foil and drizzle each with 1 teaspoon of the olive oil. Wrap up the foil so no garlic is exposed and place it on the baking sheet alongside the eggplant. Bake until the eggplant is soft and has turned a deep purple-brown color, 1 hour and the garlic is soft. Your kitchen will smell delicious.
+ While the eggplant and garlic are roasting, mix the tahini with 1 tablespoon of water and blend until it is smooth. Add the lemon juice, horseradish, pepper, paprika, cumin, cayenne, and garlic powder to the tahini mixture.
+ Remove the eggplant and garlic from the oven, separate the cloves from the head. Place them on a cutting board, and smacking your palm on the flat side of a knife, smash them to squeeze out the softened flesh. It's a great stress reliever. Discard the flaky outer skin, scrape the roasted garlic flesh pulp and transfer it to a blender or food processor.
+ Add the eggplant and tahini mixture to the garlic in the blender or food processor and puree. Add the chickpeas and remaining 1 tablespoon of olive oil and continue to blend until the mixture is smooth and spreadable, about 2 minutes.
+ Spoon the hummus into a serving bowl, garnish with roughly chopped parsley, and serve.

### + sodium count:

Eggplant: 11mg per eggplant; Prepared horseradish: 20mg per 1 teaspoon depending on brand; No-salt-added chickpeas: 10mg per ½ cup depending on brand

CHAPTER
4

# Salads

I officially broke up with salads in 2004. I had been eating gluten-free for almost four years and I was sick and tired of dining out and only eating leafy greens, with no dressing, few toppings, and not much flavor. Salad was the symbol of my limitations—boring, bland, and mediocre—and I swore off them as part of my defiance that salt-free food was a culinary afterthought. It was a clean break and we didn't see each other for some time.

Then a few years later, I was hungry and dining out and was left with one option: a salad. Reluctantly, I agreed, and thirty minutes later I received the stallion of salads—a mature dish that had class and personality and loads of fresh flavors. This was a meal that was not high-maintenance or demanding in its preparation, but ambitious in its composition and taste.

Forget about a simple bed of romaine (no offense, romaine) or butter lettuce. This salad didn't have a single salad leaf on the plate. It was made from diced squash, zucchini, asparagus, tomatoes, and slices of orange, all fresh from the garden in back of the restaurant and covered in finely chopped thyme, dill, parsley, and lemon zest. There were no spices, no dressings, no grilled chicken pieces, tortilla chips, or salt. Just a spring mix that married in their natural nectars.

After that passionate evening, salads and I got back together and began to have quite a torrid affair. I experimented with adding grains, like quinoa and rice, to the vegetable mix of flavors and using citrus juice or even fried eggs to replace typical dressings. I even revisited leafy greens, attracted to the mischievous bitterness of chicories and the frisky spice of arugula.

I have since changed my opinions about salads. And I know now that, when done right, they don't have to be an unsatisfying holdover until you can find something else to eat. They can actually be the star of the meal.

*I have since changed my opinions about salads. And I know now that, when done right, they don't have to be an unsatisfying holdover until you can find something else to eat.*

# RICOTTA WITH PUMPKIN CRUMBS

I try not to be a jealous person. But a salad topped with fried goat cheese definitely makes me seethe with envy. I just love the idea of it—raw greens paired with toasted cheese. Clean yet creamy.

While goat cheese is out of the question (around 90 to 150mg of sodium per ounce, depending on brand and firmness), I thought ricotta might work. The texture is similar: soft and curdy. And by mixing it with some herbs and pepper, you can add flavor to its generally plain taste. To mimic the crunch of the breadcrumb crust, I skipped the typical coating and decided to make a toasted pumpkin seed crumble instead, which adds color as well as an element of surprise. I also kept the cheese fry-free, as I like the crisp flavor of the cool ricotta. And to complete the makeover, I switched the typical salad greens with peppery arugula and sliced pear, which I mixed with some salt-free vinaigrette.

Voilà. Cheese salad. Low in sodium.

**Makes 4 small salads**

- ½ cup salt-free pumpkin seeds
- 1 cup low-sodium ricotta
- Freshly ground black pepper
- ½ teaspoon dried dill
- ½ teaspoon dried thyme, crushed with fingers
- ¼ teaspoon garlic powder
- 1 tablespoon honey
- 2 pears, halved, cored and thinly sliced
- 4 cups arugula, coarsely chopped
- ¼ cup olive oil
- 2 teaspoons champagne or balsamic vinegar

+ Warm a small skillet over medium-high heat and add the pumpkin seeds. Occasionally shake the pan to keep the seeds from sticking to the bottom and burning, and cook until toasted, about 3 minutes.
+ Add the toasted seeds to a food processor and pulse to make toasted pumpkin seed crumbs. Pour them into a bowl and set aside.
+ In another small bowl, mix the ricotta with freshly ground pepper (about 8 good twists), the dried dill, dried thyme, garlic powder, and honey. With your hands, form 4 patties out of the seasoned ricotta cheese, put them on a plate, and set them in the freezer for 2 to 3 minutes to firm up. Then roll each patty in the pumpkin crumbs until completely covered.
+ To finish the salad, toss the pears, arugula, olive oil, and vinegar in a large mixing bowl and put equal portions on 4 individual plates. Place the ricotta patties on top of the salad and serve.

**+ sodium count:**

Pumpkin seeds: 5mg per ¼ cup; Low-sodium ricotta: 24mg per ¼ cup depending on brand

# DAIKON + CUCUMBER SALAD

Daikon and cucumber make a perfect pair. They have similar round shapes, which work well for presentation. And while the cuke provides a cool crispness, the daikon adds its own snappy pepper flavor. A simple mix of rice vinegar and sesame oil coats the veggies, and a sprinkle of black sesame seeds and basil finish the look.

If you have a mandoline to cut the vegetables, it will not only cut prep time in half, but the uniform slices help make this super simple salad look super elegant. Just be sure not to cut your finger in half. Mandolines can be dangerous, and if you don't have one, a sharp knife works just as well. Also, if watermelon radishes are available, prepare them like the daikon and add them to the bowl. The fuchsia pink lends an extra splash of unexpected color.

**Serves 6 to 8**

- ½ cup unseasoned rice vinegar
- 1 tablespoon granulated white sugar
- 2 teaspoons sesame oil
- ½ pound daikon radish, peeled and sliced into thin rounds
- ½ English or seedless cucumber, sliced into thin rounds
- 1 teaspoon red chili pepper flakes
- Handful of fresh basil leaves
- Black sesame seeds

+ In a medium bowl, whisk together the vinegar, sugar, and oil. Add the daikon, cucumber, and chilli pepper flakes and toss to combine. Cover and chill in the refrigerator.
+ Right before serving, tear the basil into pieces and add the basil and the sesame seeds to the salad. Gently toss to mix and serve.

**+ sodium count:**
Daikon: 71mg per large daikon

# PICKLED BEET + QUINOA SALAD

The next time you want to stand out at a picnic or BBQ, bring this salad. The tangy beets, creamy avocado, and nutty red quinoa blend together for superstar taste and gorgeous color. It's full of nutrients, spice, bright herbs, and crunchy texture—the red quinoa pearls adding bite and protein to the dish. Other than needing to make the pickled beets ahead of time, this dish is a snap to put together. And it will be eaten just as quickly.

**Serves 2 as a main; 4 as a side**

**Effort Level: Plan Ahead**

Pickled Beets

- Grated zest and juice of 1 medium orange
- 1 cup distilled white vinegar
- ½ cup apple cider vinegar
- ¼ cup granulated white sugar
- 1 teaspoon whole black peppercorns
- 1 teaspoon yellow mustard seed
- 2 large red or yellow beets
- 3 garlic cloves
- 3 dried chile de árbol peppers or 1 teaspoon red chili flakes

Quinoa Salad

- ¾ cup washed red quinoa
- 1 pound radishes (2 bunches)
- 2 avocados
- 2 small tomatoes or 1 red bell pepper
- ¼ cup chopped fresh chives
- Splash of red wine vinegar

+ This recipe involves a multi-day process and before you do anything else, you have to pickle your beets. First, zest the orange and set the zest aside. In a small pot or saucepan, mix 1 cup water with the distilled white vinegar, apple cider vinegar, sugar, orange juice, peppercorns, and mustard seed. Bring the liquid to a boil over medium-high heat and once it really starts bubbling, remove it from the stove. Allow the liquid to cool for at least 20 minutes, or longer if you are using a plastic container.
+ While the liquid cools, peel the beets with a vegetable peeler and discard the peels. Cut the bottom nub and top root from the beets and then cut the beet vertically in half. Place the flat side of one beet half on your cutting board, like you are slicing an onion. Cut the beet vertically into ½-inch sticks and then cut the slices horizontally into cube-like shapes (the ends will be more rounded). Repeat with the other beet half and when finished, stuff the beet cubes, garlic, chile peppers, and orange zest into a container. Set aside.
+ When the liquid is lukewarm, carefully pour it into your container. The beets should be covered in the pickling liquid; if not, add a bit more distilled white vinegar. Put on the lid and close the container tightly. Give it 5 or 6 good shakes and stick it in the fridge to cool. In 48 hours, the beets will be ready and they will stay fresh in the fridge for a week.
+ Once your beets have pickled, it's time to make a salad. Put the quinoa and 1½ cups water into a small pot over medium-high heat and bring to a boil. Lower the heat to medium, cover the pot with a lid, and continue to cook until all the water is absorbed, about 15 minutes. Check occasionally and stir to make sure no quinoa is burning at the bottom. You'll know that the quinoa is ready when its white tendrils appear and it is soft enough to chew. Take the pot off of the heat and let the quinoa cool for 10 minutes.
+ Meanwhile, wash and cut the radishes into quarters. Dice the avocados and the tomatoes into ¼-inch cubes. I leave the seeds in the tomatoes and use their juices as a light dressing for the salad, but feel free to remove the seeds if you prefer. Strain the beets from their pickling liquid and spices, and put them in the salad bowl with the diced vegetables. Add the cooled quinoa, sprinkle the chives on top, splash in the vinegar to taste, then mix, and serve.

### + sodium count:

Beet: 64mg per beet; Quinoa: 0 to 10mg per serving depending on brand; Radish: 45mg per 1 cup; Avocado: 14mg per avocado; Tomatoes: 5mg per small tomato

## GIMME A BEET

We're going to talk about a topic that often makes people uncomfortable.

Beets.

There. I said it.

These oddly shaped little buggers give many eaters—healthy, adventurous, curious, and beyond—major pause. They look strange. They seem like they're difficult to peel, if that is even how you are to prepare them. And when it comes to actually cutting into the tubers, well, you better prepare for a bloodbath. Those suckers will happily dye everything around you a deep shade of red.

When it comes to choosing a vegetable to cook, beets were rarely at the top of my list. I'd much rather leave them underground where they won't stain my white pants, not to mention my hands and cutting board and cupboard and dishtowels. I'd rather cut up a well-behaved radish instead.

But when it comes to successful low-sodium cooking, one must be adventurous, constantly braving new ingredients, whether it is a spice, an herb, a cooking technique, or a vegetable. It is about surprising your palate. Or even more importantly, it is about surprising yourself. So let's give those beets a second look.

Their juice is used in a lot of commercial products, including red velvet cake and even ketchup. They can be pickled, made into chips, or simply sliced and eaten. And it is even said that they are a natural aphrodisiac. So upon further investigation, beets are clearly meant to be loved. And eaten. And eaten with love.

A perfect way to showcase beets is in a salad. You and your guests won't know what hit you. Shaved, cubed, cooked, or raw, beets add a tinge of natural salt, gorgeous color, and either a crunchy or slightly supple texture (depending on how you cook them) to your mix of greens. And if you are ready to rock out with some fresh beets, then follow these tips to make it the most pleasant experience possible. Discover the new world of color and taste at your low-sodium, and now red, fingertips.

1. If you are wearing something you love, put on an apron. Or throw on some old T-shirt that is already covered in dog slobber or paint. That way, you can prepare your beets without worry.
2. To easily peel the beet skin, hold the beet in your nondominant hand while scraping the peeler toward you with the other hand. This method makes peeling any odd-shaped vegetable a lot easier.
3. If you are cooking the beets, wash, trim and wrap them unpeeled in aluminum foil. Throw them in a 350°F oven to roast. After they have cooked, allow them to cool and then use the foil to rub off the skin. This keeps the juicy mess to a major minimum.
4. A single beet can contain upward of 64mg of sodium, which doesn't mean you shouldn't eat them. Just be aware that they naturally contain sodium and use this to your advantage for dishes that you want to taste saltier. It's a great way to enhance flavor without picking up the shaker.

# GREEK SALAD WITH PICKLED BEET "OLIVES"

While olives come in a diverse range of colors, shapes, and flavors, they all have a common denominator: a salty, tangy brine, that perks up milder ingredients like fish, chicken, and greens.

So I challenged myself to find a low-sodium olive substitute for an olive-heavy dish. And I found the answer in pickled beets. Get ready to pucker up.

**Serves 4 to 6**

**Effort Level: Plan Ahead**

Pickled Beet "Olives"

- 1 cup distilled white vinegar or white wine vinegar
- ½ cup water
- 2 tablespoons granulated white sugar
- ½ cup orange juice
- 1 teaspoon whole brown mustard seed
- 1 teaspoon whole black peppercorns
- 1 medium yellow beet, peeled
- 3 garlic cloves, roughly diced

Greek Salad

- 1 red bell pepper, stemmed and seeded
- 1 green bell pepper, stemmed and seeded
- 1 large fennel bulb
- 6 cups (one 8-ounce package) romaine heart leaves, washed and dried
- 2 tablespoons red wine vinegar
- 2 tablespoons olive oil
- ½ cup low-sodium ricotta
- 2 tablespoons chopped low-sodium sun-dried tomatoes
- 1 tablespoon fennel seed
- 1½ cup cherry tomatoes, halved
- ¼ cup diced seeded cucumber
- Freshly ground black pepper

+ To make your pickled beet "olives," start at least a day ahead.
+ In a small pot or saucepan, mix the vinegar, water, and the sugar. Add the orange juice, mustard seed, and the peppercorns. Bring the pickling liquid to a boil over medium-high heat, then reduce to a simmer and cook, 6 to 8 minutes. Remove from the heat and allow it to cool for at least 20 minutes or longer.
+ While the liquid is cooling, cut the beet into olive-size cubes and place them with the garlic in a clean container.
+ When the liquid is lukewarm, pour it into your container, covering the beets. Close the container tightly, give it 5 or 6 good shakes, and stick the beets in the fridge to cool. In 24 to 48 hours, they will be ready to eat and will stay fresh in the fridge for 1 week.
+ Once your beets have pickled, it's time to roast your bell peppers. Put them in a baking pan and place under the broiler. Turn the broiler to high and check every 5 minutes or so to see if the skin has blistered and charred. Then, using tongs, rotate the peppers to blister and char the other sides.
+ Remove the bell peppers from the oven and put them in a paper bag. Close the top and allow them to steam for 15 minutes. When cool to the touch, slide the skin off the peppers and discard. Slice the flesh horizontally into thin strips and then chop in half. Set aside.
+ To prepare the fennel, cut the stems and the bottom nub from the fennel bulbs and remove the outer layer if bruised. Cut the bulbs vertically in half. Place the flat side of each half on a cutting board and slice the fennel into thin, crescent-shaped spears. Discard the hard core and set the fennel spears aside.
+ Chop the romaine leaves into bite-size pieces and put them in a large mixing bowl, gently tossing with the red wine vinegar and olive oil. Next, place the ricotta, sun-dried tomatoes, and fennel seed in another bowl and mix.
+ To assemble the salad, spread the romaine on a serving dish or platter. Cover with rows of green peppers, fennel, tomatoes, beet, cucumbers, and red peppers. Sprinkle with ricotta and freshly ground black pepper.

**+ sodium count:**
Beet: 64mg per beet; Fennel: 45mg per 1 cup, 122mg per bulb; Low-sodium ricotta: 24mg per ¼ cup depending on brand; Sundried tomato: 5mg per serving depending on brand; Cherry tomatoes: 7mg per 1 cup

# SALAD OF GRAPEFRUIT + AVOCADO WITH TOASTED PUMPKIN SEEDS

*Low-sodium guest: Chef Traci Des Jardins, Jardinière and Mijita Cocina Mexicana*

This salad is like a beautiful waltz—a spicy, Mexican waltz—where the ingredients are perfectly in step with one another. On the first bite, the crunch of the pumpkin seeds dances with the snap of the jicama, and the lemony essence of the coriander keeps up with the citrus.

Upon a second taste, however, the ingredients suddenly switch partners and move on to a new pairing. The nutty oils of the pumpkin seeds now melt with the smooth avocado, and the bright pop of the coriander ignites the hot jalapeño.

Hot, cool, slick, and sweet, this salad hits all the right notes. It is dizzyingly delicious and a perfect example of why Chef Des Jardins is a master of her craft. It is also proof that, with the right technique, carefully chosen elements, and combination of spices, a simple list of ingredients can transform into something quite elegant.

**Serves 6**

- ⅓ cup salt-free pumpkin seeds
- 1 tablespoon coriander seed
- 1 jalapeño pepper, thinly sliced into rounds
- ⅓ cup plus 1 tablespoon olive oil
- 1 medium jicama, peeled
- 2 ruby red grapefruits
- Juice of 1 lime
- ¼ cup fresh cilantro leaves
- 2 avocados, pitted, peeled, and sliced

+ Toast the pumpkin seeds, coriander seeds, and sliced jalapeño in a skillet with 1 tablespoon of olive oil until fragrant. Set aside to cool. (You can also make extra pumpkin seeds and set out as a snack.)
+ Cut the jicama into small *batonnets* about 3 inches long. Slice off the ends of both grapefruits and set them flat on a cutting board. Using a sharp knife, remove the peel and all of the bitter white membrane from the grapefruit. Then hold the grapefruit over a large bowl (to collect the run-off juices) and use a paring knife to carefully slice between each membrane, removing the sections. Place the sections into the bowl with all that wonderful grapefruit juice. Add the jicama, the remaining ⅓ cup olive oil, the lime juice, and cilantro leaves. At the last possible moment, add the sliced avocado and blend gently. Place onto individual plates or in a salad bowl and garnish with the pumpkin seeds, coriander seeds, and sliced jalapeños.

**+ sodium count:**

Avocado: 14mg per avocado;
Pumpkin seeds: 5mg per ¼ cup

# CHINESE FIVE-SPICE PLUS ONE CHICKEN SALAD

*Low-sodium guest: Steven Foung, father-in-law and low-sodium innovator*

> "This usually calls for salty soy sauce. But I learned from Jess that a little extra garlic works as a wonderful alternative. I mixed the Chinese five-spice mix with garlic powder and used that as the rub for the chicken. For broiling just about any meat, I use olive oil to add flavor. The real secret: using chicken thighs rather than breasts, which tend to be much more tender. The rest is straightforward and sodium-free."

**Serves 2 to 4**

**Effort Level: Plan Ahead**

- 4 boneless, skinless chicken thighs
- 2 tablespoons plus 1 teaspoon sesame oil
- 2 to 3 tablespoons salt-free Chinese five-spice
- 1 tablespoon garlic powder
- 3 tablespoons unseasoned rice vinegar
- 2 tablespoons granulated sugar
- ⅛ teaspoon olive oil
- ½ cup vegetable oil
- ½ package mai-fun noodles
- ½ head iceberg lettuce, cut into ¼-inch strips
- ½ head Savoy cabbage, cut into ¼-inch strips
- 1 lemon
- 1 cup unsalted, roasted almonds or cashews, coarsely chopped

+ Get ready to get your hands dirty. Place the chicken pieces in a bowl and rub them with 2 tablespoons of the sesame oil. Then mix the Chinese five-spice with half of the garlic powder and rub it all over the chicken. Cover the bowl with plastic wrap and place it in the fridge to marinate for 2 to 12 hours.
+ When you're ready to get cooking, preheat the oven to 350°F.
+ Place the thighs in a greased or nonstick pan and bake for 15 minutes. Remove the pan, flip the thighs over, and bake for another 10 minutes. Test one piece by cutting into the center. If it is white, remove the chicken from the oven.
+ Meanwhile, prepare the dressing. Whisk the vinegar and sugar until dissolved, 2 minutes. Continue to whisk as you drizzle in the remaining sesame oil, the olive oil, and the remaining garlic powder.
+ Now it's time to make your crispy mai-fun. These noodles puff up immediately, so make sure you have tongs and a paper towel–lined plate ready. Heat the vegetable oil in a wok or high-sided pan over medium-high heat. When the oil is spitting hot, add the mai-fun noodles, use tongs to remove them once they puff, 30 seconds. Transfer them to the paper towel-lined plate to drain and cool.
+ Slice the cooled chicken into ¼-inch strips and toss them with the lettuce and cabbage. Add the dressing, using your hands to mix. Squeeze some lemon juice over the salad, sprinkle on the nuts, and top with the crispy noodles.

### + sodium count:

Chicken thigh (with skin): 87mg per ¼ pound; Lettuce: 10mg per cup shredded; Savoy cabbage: 20mg per cup shredded

# CURRY CHICKEN SALAD

*Low-sodium guest: Magdalena Cabrera, mother-in-law and low-sodium innovator*

"I found a salty version of this recipe in a magazine and decided to take a stab at "unsalting it". I was pretty new to cooking for my lovely daughter-in-law, so I felt a bit out of my league. But she had already taught me some key substitutions, so I hit the ground running.

As I prefer a tart apple, I chose a Pink Lady or a Granny Smith in lieu of the sweeter Fuji. I also knew that celery has some naturally occurring sodium, so the logical and fun replacement was fennel bulb. When it came to raisins, well, I like them in oatmeal, raisin cookies, and couscous, but that's about it. So I grabbed an equal amount of dried cranberries for some extra zing and tartness to add to the dish. I totally omitted the almonds, but a nut eater could add them. The next time I make it, I might throw in some pumpkin seeds. As for that delicious dressing, I chose to use crème fraîche. And tah-dah! A salt-free curry chicken salad."

**Serves 4 to 6**

- 3 boneless, skinless chicken breast halves
- 2 tablespoons olive oil
- ¼ teaspoon onion powder
- ¼ teaspoon garlic powder
- 1 Pink Lady or Granny Smith apple, cored and diced
- 3 green onions, thinly sliced (everything but the bulb)
- ½ cup diced fennel bulb, outer layer and core removed
- ⅓ cup golden raisins (or cranberries)
- ½ cup crème fraîche, low-sodium plain soy yogurt, or no-sodium mayo (see note)
- 2 teaspoons curry powder
- 1 teaspoon honey
- ½ teaspoon peeled and grated fresh ginger
- Pinch of cayenne pepper

+ Coat the chicken with 1 tablespoon of olive oil and then rub it with the onion powder and garlic powder. Set aside.
+ Put the remaining tablespoon of olive oil in a medium skillet and warm over medium heat. Add the chicken and cook until the skin inside is no longer pink, 8 to 10 minutes on each side. Take the chicken out of the pan and set aside to rest, 10 minutes. When ready, chop the chicken into ¼-inch cubes and put them into a salad bowl with the apple, green onion, fennel, and raisins.
+ In another small bowl, combine the crème fraîche, curry, honey, grated ginger, and cayenne pepper. This is your dressing. Spoon it over the salad and toss to coat. Cover the salad bowl with foil or plastic wrap and then place it into the refrigerator to chill for at least 1 hour before serving.

## + note

Add a pinch of cayenne if you like extra kick and use Salt-Free Tofunnaise (page 103) or soy yogurt in place of the crème fraîche to lower the sodium count even further.

### + sodium count:

Chicken breast (with skin): 71mg per ¼ pound; Fennel: 45mg per cup, 122 per bulb; Raisins: 16mg per cup; Crème fraîche: 10mg per 2 tablespoons; Plain soy yogurt: 15mg per 6-ounce container, depending on brand

# THE BRUTUS: WARM CHICORY + BREAD SALAD WITH SARDINE LEMON DRESSING

Sometimes one cannot merely replicate a recipe without sodium, especially when it has only a few ingredients, and those happen to be very salty. Take Caesar salad, for example. In its most classic form, it includes lettuce, Parmesan cheese, croutons, and dressing made from anchovy paste, which alone can account for 363mg of sodium per 2 tablespoons. So I did what any ambitious Roman would do; I did away with Caesar and decided to use its most basic elements to create a low-sodium salad filled with creamy sardine dressing, peppery chicories, and warm bread. Fractions that come together for a recipe that truly rules.

**Serves 4 as a main; 6 as a side**

- 2 cups no-salt-added sliced bread, cut into 1-inch cubes
- ½ teaspoon finely diced or pressed garlic (2 to 3 cloves)
- Olive oil
- ½ teaspoon red wine vinegar
- 4 to 5 no-salt-added canned sardines
- 2 tablespoons fresh lemon juice
- Freshly cracked black pepper
- 1 small head radicchio (½ pound), cleaned and roughly chopped
- 1 small head frisée (½ pound), cleaned and roughly chopped
- 1 pound spring lettuce mix, cleaned and roughly chopped
- ⅛ teaspoon garlic powder

+ Preheat the oven to 350°F.
+ Put the cubed bread in a 9 x 11-inch baking pan and bake until crisp, 20 to 25 minutes, turning the bread chunks every 5 to 8 minutes to make sure they toast evenly and don't burn.
+ While the bread is toasting, mix the garlic with ¼ cup of olive oil in a mixing bowl and allow it to marinate for 20 minutes. It will really bump up the garlic flavor in the dressing, if you like that sort of thing.
+ Remove the bread from the oven and set aside to cool. Make the dressing. Using a whisk, slowly add the red wine vinegar to the garlic and oil mixture, whisking while you pour. Set aside.
+ Mince the sardines and put them into a mortar and pestle. Add ½ teaspoon of olive oil and grind into a paste-like consistency. (Note: if you don't have a mortar and pestle, you can do this in a bowl with the back of a fork.)
+ Add 2 teaspoons of the sardine paste, the lemon juice, and cracked pepper to taste to the oil and vinegar mixture. Give it a brisk whisk until all of the ingredients are well combined. Taste the dressing and add more sardine paste and pepper as needed.
+ In a large skillet, warm 1 tablespoon of olive oil over medium-high heat. In batches, add the radicchio, frisée, and spring lettuce, and cook until slightly warm and softened, using tongs to toss it in the pan, 1 to 2 minutes. Remove the lettuces from the pan and put them immediately into a serving bowl. Add a little more oil to the skillet and repeat until all the lettuces are warmed. Add the dressing to the serving bowl and gently toss.
+ Add a little more olive oil to the skillet if it is dry and cook the toasted bread cubes over high heat until they have an oily sheen and get a bit crispier, 2 to 3 minutes. Sprinkle them with the garlic powder and then add them to the salad bowl. Toss and serve immediately.

### + sodium count:

No-salt-added bread: 10mg per slice depending on brand; No-salt-added canned sardines: 70mg per can depending on brand; Radicchio: 9mg per 1 cup shredded; Frisée: 13mg per 1 cup chopped; Lettuce: 10mg per 1 cup shredded

# KALE-NORI SALAD

Just a quick warning: all your other salads are going to be jealous of this one. This salad doesn't have to do much to look or taste good. The kale only requires a quick cook in a skillet and some shredded nori (whose dark green hue makes the kale's coloring look even more radiant) to look fresh and alive. After throwing on some cooked noodles, sesame seeds, and a light dressing, it's ready to go.

This salad is impressive at a potluck. It's simple enough to make for a weeknight meal. It even tastes good cold for lunch the next day. It's so easy and flavorful that you'll be shocked you've never made this before. Just be sure to visit your other salads once in a while, too.

**Serves 2 to 4**

- 1 tablespoon sesame oil, plus more for garnish
- 1 tablespoon peeled and diced fresh ginger
- 4 garlic cloves, diced
- 6 cups chopped lacinato kale leaves, cut into ½-inch-wide ribbons (stems removed)
- 3 tablespoons unseasoned rice vinegar
- 1 to 2 tablespoons toasted sesame seeds
- ¼ teaspoon ground white pepper
- 2 green onions, thinly sliced (everything but the bulb)
- Quarter-size bundle of no-salt-added soba noodles
- ½ sheet Pacific nori
- Red chili pepper flakes

+ In a large skillet or wok, warm the sesame oil over medium-high heat. Add the ginger and garlic and cook, stirring, for 2 to 3 minutes. Reduce the heat to medium and add the kale in several batches, cooking until it is bright green and wilted, about 3 minutes per batch.
+ With all the cooked kale in the wok, add in the rice vinegar, toasted sesame seeds, and white pepper. Stir the ingredients and cook for 2 minutes more. Transfer the kale mixture to a bowl. Add the green onions, reserving a small handful for garnish. Give it one final mix and place the salad in the fridge until you're ready to eat.
+ Meanwhile, fill a pot with water and bring it to a boil. Add the soba noodles and cook for 4 minutes (or according to the package directions). Immediately drain the noodles and rinse with cold water. Set them in a bowl, drizzle in a bit of sesame oil so the noodles don't stick, and allow them to cool for at least 15 minutes. While the noodles cool, using scissors shred the nori into very thin 2-inch strips. Cut until you have about ¼ cup of shredded nori pieces and save any extras for a weeknight rice bowl.
+ Is it time to eat? Perfect.
+ You can serve this dish family style on a large platter or in separate bowls. Either way, place the soba noodles at the bottom of your chosen serving dish and then pile the kale-kelp salad on top. Sprinkle with the reserved green onions, the shredded nori, and some chili pepper flakes to taste, and finish with a drizzle of sesame oil.

## + sodium count:

Kale: 29mg per 1 cup chopped

## + note

This recipe can be made up to 24 hours ahead of time. Just put the undressed salad and soba noodles into separate bowls, cover, and refrigerate. When the dinner or lunch bell rings, simply assemble the dish as directed.

CHAPTER 5

# Stocks, Soups, + Stews

There is no greater convenience food salt offender than canned soup. Many brands clock in at over 1,000mg sodium for a single can. And even the low-sodium versions are merely a lower-percentage version of the original saltier ones, meaning they can still land you somewhere in the 400 to 800mg range per serving, which may only be one cup. And who actually eats just one cup of soup?

Making low-sodium soup at home, however, is actually very easy. With fresh vegetables, an oven, homemade stocks, and a trusty blender, you can avoid the salt and still get the soup on the table in minutes, without much effort, cleanup, or time.

But (BUT!) here's the thing. The flavors you're accustomed to tasting—the chicken noodle, the cream of tomato, the mushroom barley—aren't so much the braised meat, the blended vegetables, or the earthy bits of wheat. When you crack that can and bring that steaming spoon to your lips, your palate is lusting for, wanting, and expecting the taste of salt. And there's no real way to mimic that.

So before you dig in, you will have to redefine flavor. Give yourself time to adjust to soup without all that sodium, and in time you'll begin to taste not just salted chicken noodles, but you'll notice individual notes of green parsley, roasted corn, and caramelized garlic that stew and simmer in the pot.

Give yourself time to adjust to soup without all that sodium.

Of course, adding a little extra zing or spice to your soup never hurts. And you can increase the complexity of a simple soup, without spending extra time, money, or sodium points, with these five simple tricks:

1. Roast or caramelize your vegetables first—this will bring out the natural smoky and sweet notes of tomatoes, cauliflower, onions, corn, fennel . . . well, you get the point.
2. Top it off with fresh herbs. Not only does a little mint or dill perk up your taste buds, but it can also turn a monotone bowl of pureed cauliflower into something that looks refined.
3. Add a dollop of heavy cream or crème fraîche to give richness and silky texture.
4. Citrus notes or a dash of vinegar can lend a surprising brightness to both creamy and brothy soups.
5. A pinch of spice is always nice. Stir in some curry powder or sprinkle in some red chili pepper flakes before serving.

# LEFTOVER CHICKEN OR MEAT BONE STOCK

Save the bones! Pork chops, ribs, chicken legs, wings, and backs—after the meat is long gone, store these picked over bits in a plastic bag. Label them with the date and put them in the freezer. And when you want to make a recipe that calls for chicken, beef, or any other kind of meaty stock, you'll be ready to go, without having to run to the store. And don't worry about cleaning them off. The spice and sauce residue from the first time they were cooked will only add to the flavor of the stock. This is recycling at its tastiest.

**Makes 10 cups stock**

- Leftover meat bones
- 2 medium carrots, scrubbed and cut into chunks
- 1 celery stalk, cut into chunks
- 1 onion, peeled and cut into quarters
- 5 garlic cloves
- 12 cups water (3 quarts)
- 10 sprigs fresh flat-leaf parsley
- ½ teaspoon whole black peppercorns

+ Preheat oven to 450°F.
+ Place the bones in a baking pan and roast in the oven for 20 minutes until the tops brown. Remove the pan from the oven, turn the bones over and add the carrots, celery, onion, and garlic to the pan. Place the pan back in the oven and roast for the bones and vegetables 20 minutes more.
+ Remove the pan from the oven and transfer the contents to a large stockpot (4-quart or larger). Pour some of the water into the baking pan and using a spoon, scrape up all the brown bits on the bottom. Pour this pan liquid with all those meat juices, into the stockpot.
+ Add the remaining water, the parsley, and peppercorns to the stockpot. Bring to a boil. Reduce the heat to low and simmer for 1½ hours, occasionally skimming the surface to remove the foam that forms on the top.
+ Strain the stock through a fine-mesh sieve or cheesecloth and discard all of the solids. Allow the stock to cool to room temperature, 45 minutes to an hour, and refrigerate for another 45 minutes to an hour. When the stock has cooled, a layer of fat will form at the surface. Remove the fat solids with a spoon and discard.
+ Use the stock within the next 3 days or freeze in an airtight (and labeled!) container for up to 2 months.

**+ sodium count:**

Carrot: 42mg per medium carrot; Celery: 51mg per large stalk

# ONE-POT VEGETABLE STOCK

Grab those wilting veggies and herbs; it is time to make some vegetable stock. Depending on what you have in your refrigerator, feel free to sub and swap with the ingredients listed below. Play with other additions, like dried chili peppers, ginger, corncobs, celery root, and other spices and herbs to switch up the flavor profile of your seasoned stock. And if you adjust the amount of water, just keep in mind that with less liquid, you can achieve a more concentrated flavor. But you'll have fewer cups of stock to use, now and for later meals.

**Makes 6 cups stock**

- 2 medium carrots, peeled and chopped into 2-inch chunks
- 1 fennel bulb, trimmed and chopped into 2-inch chunks (but feel free to add trimmings to pot)
- 1 daikon radish, peeled and chopped into 2-inch chunks
- 1 onion, peeled quartered
- 5 garlic cloves
- 2 tablespoons white wine vinegar
- 8 cups water (2 quarts)
- 10 sprigs fresh flat-leaf parsley
- 5 sprigs fresh oregano
- 5 fresh or dried shiitake mushrooms
- ½ teaspoon whole black peppercorns

+ Place a 3-quart (or larger) stockpot over medium heat. Some people like adding a little olive oil here to brown the vegetables, but I like to just throw them in a dry pot and let them sear. I think it makes the stock taste cleaner at the end. Either way, with or without olive oil, add the carrots, fennel, daikon, onion, and garlic and brown them, about 3 minutes. Stir occasionally to loosen the vegetables from the bottom of the pot and to keep them from burning.
+ Add the white wine vinegar and deglaze any brown bits that have formed on the bottom of the pot. Add the water, parsley, oregano, shiitake mushrooms, and peppercorns. Using a spoon scrape the bottom of the pot to release any additional brown bits and stir a few more times. Raise the heat and bring the liquid to a boil. Reduce to a simmer and cook for 45 minutes to an hour, stemming any foam that rises to the surface.
+ Strain the vegetable stock through a fine-mesh or cheesecloth and discard the solids. Allow the stock to cool to room temperature before placing in the refrigerator. Use the stock within 3 days or freeze in an airtight container for up to 2 months.

## + note

If you want fish-flavored stock, simply add leftover fish bones (strong fish flavor) to the pot.

### + sodium count:

Carrot: 42mg per medium carrot; Celery: 32mg per medium stalk; Fennel: 45mg per 1 cup, 122mg per bulb; Daikon: 71mg per large daikon

# CHEF AMARYLL'S THOUGHTS ON SALT-FREE COOKING

*Low-sodium guest: Chef Amaryll Schwertner, Boulette's Larder*

I met Chef Amaryll Schwertner a few years ago at my favorite place on earth, the Ferry Plaza Farmer's Market in San Francisco. At the time, I was working at the Center for Urban Education about Sustainable Agriculture (CUESA), writing descriptions of fruits and vegetables for their website. Can you see why this place was a dream? And while the Ferry Building was full of farm-fresh food stands, it was still difficult to find a truly satisfying, low-sodium lunch option.

After a few months of eating ripe avocados with a spoon, I finally decided to walk into Boulette's Larder, Chef Amaryll's restaurant. I asked the kind woman at the counter if, perhaps, there was anything on the menu that was not made with salt. And to my surprise, I was greeted with the following answer: first, if I told them in the morning that I was coming in for lunch, they could make me a salt-free meal, and second, none of their broths are made with added salt and did I want some that afternoon?

As the bay was clouded over with fog, my answer was undoubtedly yes, and Chef Amaryll herself quickly boiled some fresh kale in a quart of salt-free poultry broth, which I slurped, oohed, and sloshed over for the rest of the day and well into the evening.

# RICH POULTRY BROTH

*Low-sodium guest: Chef Amaryll Schwertner, Boulette's Larder*

"When many cooks talk about seasoning, they are talking about salt. When I talk about seasoning, I am talking about something different. In my stocks, I use spices, vegetables, and proteins for flavor, and if I want more, I'll reduce it. It is rich without salt and you can taste the purity of the protein and the mirepoix. Salt belongs on the table, but it shouldn't be the only flavor people are familiar with. Because it is limiting to the palate if salt is all you can taste in food. You'll lose the world of flavor in food itself. "

**Makes 10 cups broth**
**Effort Level: Got Time to Spare**

- 2 whole chickens (backbone, head, and feet can also be included) For additional texture and poultry flavor, also add 2 guinea hen legs or 2 turkey wings (all brine-free)
- 1 large carrot, scrubbed and chopped
- 1 parsnip, scrubbed and chopped
- 1 large leek, cleaned and cut in halved
- ½ white or yellow onion studded with a whole clove
- 2 spring garlic shoots or 2 whole heads garlic
- 12 cups water (3 quarts)
- Fresh herb bouquet (parsley, chervil, coriander, lemongrass, bay, thyme, and celery are all appropriate)

+ Preheat the oven to 425°F.
+ Wash and cut up the chicken into 8 pieces—head, backbone, and feet included if possible—or have your butcher do this for you. Set the chicken pieces and bones into a large (16-quart) soup or stockpot on the stove.
+ Next, place the guinea hen or turkey wings and the vegetables (carrot, parsnip, leek, onion, garlic) in a roasting pan and cook them in the oven until they are caramelized, 30 to 40 minutes. Discard any fat and place the roasted guinea hen and turkey wings into the stockpot. Reserve the vegetables, as they are considered aromatics and are to be added midway through the process or after the stock has come to a boil. Add 2 cups of the water to the roasting pan and scrape up all of the browned and caramelized bits. Add this liquid to the stockpot and pour in the remaining 10 cups water.
+ Bring the pot to a rolling boil and then reduce to a simmer. For the first hour of cooking, continually check on the stock and skim the foam from the surface. Then add the roasted vegetables and the bouquet of herbs as separate ingredients or tied together in cheesecloth.
+ Allow the stock to simmer, uncovered, for 5 or more hours. When ready, gently pour the stock through a mesh sieve or cheesecloth into another container, and cool completely before refrigerating.
+ Use as a soup broth; reduce for a sauce or vinaigrette; use to braise meats or vegetables; or as the liquid for a risotto.
+ At this point the chicken is mostly spent, but I do have a suggestion for how to use the chicken meat. We make dog food with the thoroughly picked chicken and mashed vegetables mixed with our multigrain cereal and formed into a nutritious patty. This is only possible because we use no salt in our stock-making process.

### + sodium count:

Carrot: 42mg per medium carrot; Celery: 32mg per medium stalk; Fennel: 45mg per 1 cup, 122mg per bulb; Daikon: 71mg per large daikon

# ROASTED GARLIC, FENNEL, + CORN CHOWDER

Garlic has crazy chameleon-like properties. The strength of its taste can completely change depending on how it is cooked and even how it is sliced. If you want it spicy and tart, leave it raw and cut into a fine dice. If you want it sweeter and more delicate, roast it or cut it into larger slivers and cook until softened.

In this recipe, the garlic goes the sweeter route and gets roasted, becoming quite velvety in texture. Once it hits the soup, it melts like butter, infusing its flavor throughout the liquid base. And when mixed with the sugary corn and fennel, this soup transforms into something slick, savory, and sweet.

**Serves 2 as a main; 4 as a side**

1 whole head garlic
3 teaspoons olive oil
1 fennel bulb, roughly chopped
1½ cups fresh or frozen corn kernels
¼ teaspoon ground white pepper
2 cups water
1 tablespoon heavy cream
1 tablespoon chopped fresh chives

+ Preheat the oven to 375°F.
+ To roast the garlic, slice off the top of the bulb so that the garlic flesh is exposed. Put the whole bulb into a piece of alumunum foil and drizzle with 1 teaspoon of the olive oil. Place the foil packet in a baking pan and place it in the oven. Roast until the garlic is soft, about 40 minutes. Remove the garlic from the oven and, when cool to the touch, separate the cloves from the head. Place them on a cutting board and, smacking your palm on the flat side of a knife, smash them to squeeze out the softened pulp. Discard the flaky outer skin and set the roasted garlic paste aside.
+ Add the remaining 2 teaspoons olive oil to a large stockpot and warm over medium heat. Add the fennel and cook, stirring, until softened, about 5 minutes. Add the corn and cook, stirring, until it begins to soften as well, about 5 minutes. Add the white pepper, roasted garlic paste, and water. Reduce the heat to a gentle simmer and cook for 15 to 20 minutes.
+ Take the pot off the heat and allow the soup to cool for 15 minutes. Using your immersion blender or a standing blender, puree until the consistency is smooth and creamy. At this point, you can add an extra step of running the soup through a sieve if you want it to be supremely silky. Otherwise, pour the pureed liquid directly back into the pot. Heat the soup until it is gently simmering and then cook to the desired thickness, 10 to 12 minutes more.
+ Just before serving, mix in the heavy cream. Remove the pot from the heat and ladle the steaming soup into bowls or mugs, and top with chives.

### + sodium count:

Fennel: 45mg per 1 cup, 122mg per head; Fresh corn: 11mg per ½ cup; Frozen corn: 0mg depending on brand; Heavy cream: 5mg per 1 tablespoon

# UMAMI BROTH

Umami. The elusive fifth taste. Described as "savory," most people associate umami with soy sauce, fish sauce, and other high-sodium, highly delicious Asian products. And for a very long time, I thought umami was out of the question for a low-sodium diet. Then I did some reading.

According to the Umami Information Center—yes, there is apparently a center for everything—the desired umami taste comes from a group of amino acids called glutamates that—gasp—occur naturally in food, not just in bottles of soy sauce. The more glutamate compounds an ingredient has, the higher its umami level. And things like mushrooms and tomatoes are brimming with them.

It isn't just the glutamate that can lead to umami, either. Other scientific-sounding ingredients, like inosinate (found in bonito fish flakes, which can have 0mg of sodium depending on the brand) and guanylate (found in shiitake mushrooms, which also contain little to no sodium) can create umami flavor as well.

So salt-free umami isn't so difficult to find after all. And when a recipe calls for a product that has high umami flavor, but is also high in salt—like fish sauce, miso paste, or soy sauce—use this low-sodium umami mushroom broth instead.

**Makes 4 cups broth**

6 fresh or dried shiitake mushrooms
1 teaspoon peeled and diced fresh ginger
2 whole star anise
6 whole cloves
6 cups water

+ Put the mushrooms and spices into a medium stockpot (at least 4-quart) and fill with the water. Bring to a boil and cook for 10 minutes. Reduce the heat to low and cover the pot. Cook for another hour.
+ When the broth is ready, strain it through a fine-mesh sieve and discard all of the solids. Allow the broth to cool and then pour it into an airtight container. Store in the refrigerator for up to 3 days and or in the freezer for a month.

**+ sodium count:**

Shiitake mushroom: 2mg per mushroom

# EGG DROP SOUP

Let me begin by saying this: get yourself to a cooking class. It doesn't matter what the theme is or even if you will be able to eat the food. Taking cooking classes will improve your low-sodium skills by teaching you about different techniques and cuisines you never dared to try.

I learned how to make egg drop soup in one such cooking class. And while I did not taste a spoonful of the dish we made that evening, I was guided through every step of the process, from making a slurry to swirling in threads of yolk. And by following along that evening, I gained the guts and know-how needed to make my own low-sodium version at home.

Obviously, the biggest challenge in this dish is creating a low-sodium broth. But in class, I talked to the instructor about what salt-free flavors I could use, like garlic, ginger, and even chicken bones, to make my own base for the soup. I eventually came up with my umami broth, which has Asian flair while remaining mild enough to let the shiitake mushrooms, green onion, and silky egg threads in the recipe shine. But you could definitely use salt-free chicken broth or vegetable stock if you have some on hand. My father-in-law also informs me that many people add corn and shredded chicken leftovers to the soup for extra flavor and texture. So now that you have the basics, give this egg drop soup your own twist.

**Serves 4**

- 2 large eggs
- 4 cups Umami Broth (page 140)
- 1 tablespoon cornstarch
- ¾ cup sliced shiitake mushrooms
- ½ cup Umami Sauce (page 109)
- 3 green onions, thinly sliced (everything but the bulb)
- ½ teaspoon peeled and finely minced fresh ginger
- ¼ teaspoon ground white pepper
- Salt-free chili oil or red chili pepper flakes, for garnish

+ Crack the eggs into a small bowl and lightly beat with a fork. Unlike scrambling eggs, you want most of the yolk and whites to remain unmixed. So just give it a few whisks and then let it be.
+ In a covered pot, bring the umami broth to a gentle simmer over medium-low heat. When warm, remove ½ cup of the stock and, in a small bowl, mix this with the cornstarch until dissolved. This is your slurry, or thickening agent. Set aside.
+ Add the mushrooms, umami sauce, three-quarters of the sliced green onions, the ginger, and white pepper to the umami broth. Bring to a boil. Add the cornstarch mixture, stir, and cook for 2 minutes. Reduce the heat to a very gentle simmer and cook for 15 minutes more.
+ Now for the impressive stuff: to make the luscious egg ribbons, gently stir the pot clockwise with a spoon while slowly pouring in the eggs in a thin stream from the bowl with the other hand. Continue stirring and pouring until all the egg is used in the soup. Increase the heat to medium, until you see some small bubbles, and then cook for 5 minutes more.
+ Ladle the soup into individual bowls and garnish with the remaining green onions. Offer salt-free chili oil and chili pepper flakes at the table for guests who want more heat.

**+ sodium count:**

Egg: 71mg per large egg

# MINESTRONE SOUP

I like to refer to minestrone as the casserole of soups. A loose interpretation of the dish is a blend of vegetables that melt together in a light broth, slowly soaking in the flavors of herbs, vinegar, and maybe even beans, all made more robust by the addition of noodles.

The recipe below is just one variation of what is possible. I like the colors, flavors, and textures of these ingredients. I also love the way cabbage tastes and feels when boiled. But if you have green beans or kale wilting in the refrigerator or slow-roasted tomato sauce from the evening before, throw it in. Experiment until you find a minestrone that fits your personal flavor profile.

**Serves 4 to 6**

- ½ cup dried split peas
- 1 (15-ounce) can no-salt-added cannellini beans, rinsed and drained
- 1 cup water
- 2 teaspoons olive oil, plus an extra drizzle
- 2 shallots, chopped
- 4 garlic cloves, finely chopped
- 2 medium carrots, peeled and cut into ¼-inch cubes
- 1 large tomato, diced
- 1 quart (4 cups) One-Pot Vegetable Stock (page 135)
- 1 tablespoon red wine vinegar
- ¼ teaspoon freshly ground black pepper
- Freshly grated nutmeg (about 6 to 8 rubs on a microplane grater)
- ½ cup pasta (farfalle, fusilli, and conchiglie work well)
- 2 cups shredded Savoy cabbage (core removed)
- 1½ cups chopped cremini mushrooms
- ¼ cup chopped fresh flat-leaf parsley

+ Bring a small pot of water to a boil. When it is bubbling, remove it from the heat. Add the split peas, cover the pot, and set them aside to soften while you start the soup.
+ In a blender, puree half of the cannellini beans with the water. Set aside. This will be used later as the thickening agent in the soup. Reserve the remaining beans.
+ Heat 2 teaspoons of olive oil in a large stockpot over medium-high heat. Add the shallots and garlic and cook, stirring, until softened, 2 to 3 minutes. Add the carrots and let them soften and brown, about 5 minutes. Move the vegetables to one side of the pot, making a well in the center, and pour in the diced tomatoes. Cook, without stirring, allowing them to sear on the bottom, about 2 minutes. Add the vegetable broth, vinegar, pureed bean mixture, and the drained split peas. Bring the entire mixture to a boil and cook for 5 minutes more. Then lower the heat so that the liquid gently simmers. Season with the black pepper and nutmeg, and stir until combined. Cover the pot and cook for 35 to 40 minutes, stirring every 15 minutes to ensure that none of the ingredients stick to the bottom of the pot.
+ When the soup is almost ready, bring a separate medium pot of water to a boil. Add the pasta and cook until al dente, 6 minutes or a few minutes less than the instructions on the package. Drain the pasta and rinse with cold water.
+ When the split peas have softened, add the cabbage, mushrooms, and the reserved whole beans to the pot. Cook for 10 minutes more.
+ Add the pasta, parsley, and a drizzle of olive oil. Cook for 5 more minutes and then remove the soup from the heat. Ladle into bowls and serve warm.

### + sodium count:

No-salt-added cannellini beans: 40mg per ½ cup depending on brand; Carrot: 42mg per medium carrot; Tomatoes: 9mg per large tomato; Celery: 32mg for 1 medium stalk; Fennel: 45mg per cup, 122mg per bulb; Daikon: 71mg per large daikon; Noodles: 0 to 10mg depending on brand; Savoy cabbage: 20mg per cup shredded

# MUSHROOM BROTH BARLEY SOUP

Hearty doesn't even begin to describe this soup.

If this soup starred in a romance novel, it would be the rugged, outdoorsy Prince Charming. This soup would wear flannel and it would know how to survive on a deserted island and with only a comb. And it would also be able to nurse a hummingbird back to life while reciting Shakespearean sonnets. Because this soup is deep, manly, and yet surprisingly delicate.

Mushrooms are clearly the stars of this dish—their name is in the title—and I've used three different kinds to bring out as much of their woodsy flavor as possible. But don't forget about the barley. You'll be equally satisfied by the plump bites, which soak up all the yummy umami (yumami?) mushroom flavor and then burst when they hit your mouth.

**Serves 4 to 6**

¼ cup dried mushrooms (any kind will do, but I like medley mixes as they tend to be the cheapest)
1 tablespoon plus 2 teaspoons olive oil
1 medium leek, sliced, washed, and thinly sliced into half-moon shapes (use the whole thing except the bulb)
¼ cup sliced shallot
5 garlic cloves, diced
2 carrots, peeled and diced
1 large daikon radish, peeled and diced
6 fresh shiitake mushrooms, stemmed into ¼-inch slices
8 cups water
1 pound cremini mushrooms, cut into ¼-inch slices
1 teaspoon whole yellow or brown mustard seeds
2 teaspoons whole black peppercorns
½ teaspoon freshly ground black pepper
Pinch of red chili pepper flakes
2 teaspoons no-salt-added tomato paste
10 sprigs fresh thyme leaves or 1 teaspoon dried thyme
2 teaspoons sherry
½ cup red wine
¾ cup pearl barley
1½ cups chopped kale, leaves and stems

+ Using a food processor, pulse the dried mushrooms into a fine powder and set aside.
+ In a 5-quart stockpot, warm 1 tablespoon of the olive oil over medium heat. Add the leek, shallot, and garlic and cook, stirring, until softened, 3 to 5 minutes. Add the carrots and daikon and allow them to soften, about 5 minutes. Add the shiitake mushrooms, half of the cremini mushrooms, the crushed dried mushrooms, and the water. Bring to a boil, reduce to a simmer, and cook, uncovered for 15 minutes.
+ Add the mustard seeds, peppercorns, black pepper, chili pepper flakes to taste, tomato paste, thyme, sherry, red wine, and barley. Cover the pot, and simmer over medium heat for 45 minutes. Take a bite of the barley and if it is still too hard, cook for 10 to 15 more minutes.
+ When there are 10 minutes left on the clock, remove the lid and add the kale to the pot. Then, in a large pan, heat the remaining 2 teaspoons olive oil. Add the remaining cremini mushrooms and brown them, without stirring, for 5 minutes. Give the mushrooms a stir so that you turn most of them to their other side and cook, undisturbed, for 3 to 5 minutes more.
+ Ladle the soup into bowls and top each with some of the browned mushrooms.

### + sodium count:

Leek: 18mg per leek; Carrot: 42mg per medium carrot; Daikon: 71mg per large daikon; Tomato paste: 10mg per 2 tablespoons depending on brand; Kale: 29mg per 1 cup chopped

# SWEET FRENCH ONION SOUP + RICOTTA CRACKERS

Rich beef broth, slow-cooked onion, and pungent cheese are melted over crusty croutons. This is a French onion soup, a comfort food to be enjoyed slowly, with a napkin and accordion music in the background. And this soup is entirely possible to make without salt.

Upon first look at that description, you might think that a truly satisfying, low-sodium French onion soup is just an oxymoron. But because reduced beef broth has its own natural saltiness, you can actually get very close to the real deal, "*sans sel*." And you will still achieve that kiss of beefy, salty broth that lingers on your lips long after you've finished the bowl.

If you want a truly low-sodium version, though, I've made this soup before without the beef broth and used both pork bones and mushrooms to make stock instead. It's less beefy, obviously, but just as good. And if you feel it can no longer be considered French onion soup, then by all means, call it something different. Like Semi-French Onion Soup. Or Italian Onion Soup. Or (insert your name here)'s Onion Soup.

**Serves 4 to 6**

**Effort Level: Got Time to Spare**

Soup

- 4 beef back ribs (if you can only find ribs with the meat on the bone, roast them in the oven at 400°F until the meat is cooked and can be cut off of the bone, about 40 minutes)
- 8 cups water
- 2 tablespoons unsalted butter
- 3 large yellow onions, thinly sliced
- 2 large red onions, thinly sliced
- ¼ teaspoon granulated white sugar
- 1 teaspoon dried thyme
- ¼ teaspoon garlic powder
- ¼ teaspoon onion powder
- Pinch of black pepper
- 2 bay leaves
- ¼ cup red wine
- ¼ cup sherry

+ To make the beef broth, place the beef bones and water in a large stockpot and bring to a boil. Cook for 10 minutes and then reduce to a simmer. Cover with a lid and cook for 1 to 2 hours. (Note: This can also be done in a slow cooker to save time.)
+ When the broth has cooked, discard the bones and allow it to completely cool. Then, to reduce the fattiness, use 1 to 2 paper towels to skim the surface of the broth. Chill the broth in the refrigerator for at least an hour. This will cause the fat to harden at the top so you can skim it off before adding it to your soup. You should have about 6 cups of broth.
+ When you're ready to make the soup, place 2 tablespoons of butter in a 5-quart stockpot and melt over medium heat until browned, 2 to 3 minutes. Add the yellow and red onions and cook for 40 minutes, adding the sugar 10 minutes into the cooking to help them caramelize, stirring occasionally to make sure they are not burning. The onions will start to shrink down and the red ones will begin to lose their color.
+ While the onions caramelize, prepare the ricotta crackers.

- Place the 4 tablespoons of chilled butter and the flour in a food processor and pulse until the mixture has a crumbly texture. Add the remaining cracker ingredients and pulse again until it forms a dough ball. Roll out a large piece of plastic wrap or wax paper on your work surface and place the dough ball on top. Using your hands, roll the dough out into a 12-inch-long, snake-like log and wrap it in plastic wrap or wax paper. Gently press down along the top to give it a rectangular shape and then place it in the freezer for 20 minutes to harden. This will make it easier to cut the cracker squares.
- Meanwhile. Add 2 cups of the beef broth to the onions. Give it an aggressive stir, scraping the bottom and sides of the pot to loosen all the brown flavor bits at the bottom of the pot. Bring the soup to a boil, and cook covered for 10 minutes. Then add 3 more cups of beef broth, the thyme, garlic powder, onion powder, black pepper, bay leaves, wine, and sherry. Lower the heat so that the broth is barely simmering and move the lid off center so that there is a slight opening. Cook for 30 minutes or until the soup has reduced by one-third. Remove and discard the bay leaves.
- Preheat the oven to 375°F.
- Take the ricotta dough out of the freezer and discard the plastic wrap or wax paper. Using a serrated knife, cut rectangular biscuits (like slices from a mini baguette) that are about 1 inch wide and ½ inch thick. Place the crackers on a greased or parchment paper–lined baking sheet and put them in the oven. Bake until they get crisp and golden, 20 to 25 minutes. Remove the baking sheet from the oven and set the crackers aside.
- When the soup is ready, ladle into small bowls and place the crackers on top or along the side of the soup just before serving. Bon appetit.

Ricotta Crackers

4 tablespoons (½ stick) unsalted butter, chilled and cubed
1¼ cups all-purpose flour
¾ cup low-sodium ricotta
2 tablespoons salt-free herb spice blend, like Herbes de Provence
½ teaspoon freshly ground black pepper
½ teaspoon dry mustard powder
½ teaspoon garlic powder
Grated zest of 1 orange

**+ sodium count:**
Low-sodium ricotta: 24mg per ¼ cup depending on product

This is comfort food to be enjoyed slowly, with a napkin and accordion music in the background.

CHAPTER 6

# Vegetables

I used to hate everything green. Even avocados, which I didn't eat until I was fourteen, and guacamole literally got shoved into my mouth. Thank goodness for that. But until then, avocados were green, so I was determined that they wouldn't taste good, like broccoli and beans and everything else of that color.

When my diet became limited, however, vegetables had to become a part of my daily intake. It was time to grow up, in many ways, and whether they were red, white, yellow, purple, or even green, I was going to have to learn to like vegetables. And much to my surprise, I didn't merely cope with them; I fell in love with them.

I couldn't believe I had denied myself the natural flavors in Brussels sprouts, cabbage, chard, and asparagus. And don't even get me started on kale. When it's fresh and in season, kale is pure craziness. It is a health powerhouse, and whether it is cooked in a bit of olive oil or served raw with a spritz of citrus, it doesn't need much else to taste good.

*When it's fresh and in season, kale is pure craziness.*

That leads me to this last point about greens. These days, I rarely eat a dinner without a side of vegetables. But they don't have to be as fancy or as time-consuming as Green Bean Casserole or Gratin-Tatouille. You can keep your vegetables quick and simple by:

1. Washing your greens, throwing a tablespoon of olive oil in a skillet, and cooking them for 5 minutes over medium heat until they are shiny and softened.
2. Preheating the oven to 400°F, dicing up some root vegetables, mixing them with herbs and olive oil, and roasting for 45 minutes until they turn soft and golden brown.
3. Filling a pot with a little water, putting in a steaming basket, filling it with vegetables, covering, and cooking until they reach your desired doneness.

# MINTED RADISHES + PEAS

As a side dish, peas and carrots never really appealed to me. Overcooked vegetables without much else on them seem to be the perfect symbol of bland food, which is exactly what I'm trying to avoid. But my opinion greatly changed after a month-long eating adventure in New Zealand (also known as my honeymoon), where night after night, I was surprised to find peas on the menu. And I was even more surprised to love the taste.

The trick? Mint and a bright squeeze of citrus, turning this TV dinner side into an elegant accompaniment for a gamy entrée or simple pasta. I took this extraordinary combination back home as a souvenir and to give the dish a bit of extra bite and color, I nixed the traditional carrots and added radishes, which get juicy (not mushy) with a quick braise. Their sweetness also helps accentuate the natural sugar flavor of the peas, which will convince even the biggest vegetable-avoiders to give peas a chance.

**Serves 6 as a side**

- 3 cups fresh or frozen peas
- 2 teaspoons olive oil
- ½ large white onion, finely diced (about 1 cup)
- 3 garlic cloves, finely diced
- 1 pound radishes (about 2 bunches), trimmed and cut into thin slices
- Freshly ground black pepper
- 2 green onions, thinly sliced (everything but the bulb)
- Grated zest and juice of 1 lime
- ¼ cup loosely packed fresh mint leaves

+ Before you do anything, fill a medium bowl with ice and water and put it in the refrigerator. If you are using fresh peas, you will need to shell the peas from their pods first, so turn on some music, because it will take a bit of time.
+ Bring a small pot of water to boil and dunk the peas in it for 1 to 2 minutes. Immediately remove them from the hot water, drain, and place into your cold water bath until the peas are cool, about 5 minutes. Drain the peas again and set aside.
+ Warm the olive oil in a large skillet over medium heat. Add the white onion and garlic and cook, stirring, until softened, 2 to 3 minutes. Add the radish slices and cook, stirring occasionally, until they begin to turn translucent, 2 to 3 minutes. Add 5 twists of the pepper grinder and remove the pan from the heat.
+ Put the garlic, onion, and radish mixture into a salad bowl. Add the peas, green onions, lime zest, and half of the juice. Take a bite and add more lime juice or pepper to taste.
+ Layer the mint leaves, one on top of another. Roll them lengthwise until you make a little mint cigar and slice the roll crosswise, cutting the leaves into thin ribbons; this is called chiffonade. Gently mix in the mint and serve immediately.

### + sodium count:

Fresh peas: 7mg per 1 cup; Frozen peas: 35mg per ½ cup depending on brand; Radish: 45mg per 1 cup

# MEDITERRANEAN ROASTED CAULIFLOWER

In 2008, I teamed up with three other food bloggers whom I had never met before. It was like Internet dating for people who liked to cook. After an initial successful meal, we decided to meet up quarterly and cook beyond our culinary comfort zones. We each had our dietary constraints: *Food & A Frying Pan* uses only fresh, organic goods; I, of course, am salt-free; and *Tao of Pao* likes to explore the world through food. She also likes hamburgers. A lot.

Cooking with this team of adventurous eaters quickly expanded my spice rack. It also showed me how much loved ones and even new friends wanted to learn how to cook low-sodium to better support and feed me. And even more impressively, I realized just how quickly people caught on.

During a recent dinner trip to the Mediterranean, the food club gals wanted to take on a Caspian cauliflower dish that is usually made with roasted cauliflower, tomatoes, capers, Kalamata olives, and parsley. After a low-sodium brainstorm, they decided to replace saltier components (capers and olives) with other Mediterranean tastes, like vinegar, raisins soaked in wine, lemon juice, and pine nuts—additions that were aromatic and savory and complemented the sweetness of the tomatoes and the cauliflower. It is a comforting yet bright dish and is equally delicious on a muggy summer evening or a stormy night—however the Mediterranean winds blow.

**Serves 4 to 6**

- ½ cup raisins
- ½ cup red wine
- 2 medium cauliflower heads, cored, leaves removed
- 3 teaspoons olive oil
- 2 cups diced tomatoes
- ¼ teaspoon red chili pepper flakes
- ¼ teaspoon freshly ground black pepper
- ½ cup chopped fresh flat-leaf parsley
- Grated zest and juice of 1 lemon
- ½ cup salt-free pine nuts
- ½ teaspoon red or white wine vinegar

+ Preheat the oven to 350°F.
+ Mix the raisins with the wine in a small bowl and set aside.
+ With your hands, separate the cauliflower into individual florets and set aside.
+ In a large skillet, warm 1 teaspoon of the olive oil over medium heat. Add the cauliflower florets and stir occasionally until they start to soften and brown, about 10 minutes. Add the remaining 2 teaspoons olive oil and raise the heat to medium-high, continuing to cook and stir until the florets begin to brown, about 10 minutes.
+ Add the tomatoes, chili pepper flakes, black pepper, and ¼ cup of the parsley. Mix well and continue to cook for 5 minutes more. Remove from the heat.
+ Transfer the cauliflower and tomato mixture to a 9 x 12-inch baking pan or a similar-sized casserole dish. Drain the raisins from the wine and add them to the cauliflower along with the lemon grated zest, the pine nuts, and vinegar. Mix to combine and then place the baking pan into the oven for 30 minutes.
+ When you're ready to eat, remove the pan from the oven and add half of the lemon juice and the remaining parsley. Give it a few gentle mixes and taste the seasoning. Add additional lemon juice if needed. Serve warm.

### + sodium count:

Cauliflower: 16mg per ½ cup, 176mg per medium head; Tomato: 6mg per medium tomato

# ZUCCHINI, SQUASH, + EGGPLANT GRATIN-TATOUILLE

This dish is the culmination of three vegetables, two French cooking techniques, and a single notion that I desperately wanted to make ratatouille for this cookbook. Traditional ratatouille is made from tomato, eggplant, and zucchini, and depending on who's cooking it, the ingredients can be stewed, baked, or even stuffed into a crêpe.

That's when the idea of a gratin swept in. In this technique, vegetables are set in a shallow dish, mixed with an egg and butter sauce, and topped with bread crumbs and cheese. While the classic potato gratin is the best-known example, cauliflower, spinach, and, you guessed it—ratatouille ingredients can be used as well.

I made my gratin with thinly sliced rounds of green, yellow, and purple vegetables. And instead of soaking them in butter, egg, or cream, I used the third ingredient of the ratatouille trifecta, the tomato, as the base for the baking sauce. With a laundry list of spices, you won't miss the cheese. Bread crumbs can be spread over the top with olive oil for a classic gratin topping. Or simply turn the broiler on for the last five minutes to make it extra crispy.

**Serves 4 to 6 as a side**

- 3¼ teaspoons olive oil
- 1 white onion, diced
- 2 garlic cloves, minced
- 1 medium zucchini, trimmed
- 1 medium yellow crookneck squash, trimmed
- 1 medium Japanese or Chinese eggplant (the long skinny kind), trimmed and ends discarded
- 1½ teaspoon dried oregano
- ½ teaspoon freshly ground black pepper
- ¼ teaspoon smoked paprika
- Chunky Red Tomato Sauce (page 108)
- Freshly grated nutmeg

+ Preheat the oven to 350°F.
+ Heat 1 teaspoon of the olive oil in a skillet. Add the onion and garlic and cook, stirring, until softened, 2 to 3 minutes. Remove from the heat and set aside.
+ Slice the zucchini, squash, and eggplant into ¼-inch-thick rounds.
+ In a medium bowl, using your hands, mix the zucchini, squash, and eggplant with 2 teaspoons of the olive oil, the oregano, black pepper, and paprika until the vegetables are evenly coated. (Note: If you would like to keep the zucchini, squash, and eggplant separate for aesthetic reasons, mix the olive oil and spices in a separate bowl first. Then place the zucchini, squash, and eggplant into 3 separate bowls and divide the olive oil and spice mixture evenly between them.)
+ Lightly grease a 3½-quart casserole dish with the remaining ¼ teaspoon olive oil. Spread the cooked onion mixture evenly on the bottom of the dish.
+ Begin to layer the zucchini, squash, and eggplant on the bottom of the casserole dish. Once it is covered, pour half of the chunky tomato sauce on top, using a spoon or spatula spread it out evenly. Then make a second layer of vegetables as you did before and pour the remaining tomato sauce on top of the second layer, again using the spoon or spatula to spread it out evenly.
+ Grate nutmeg over the entire dish and bake in the oven for 40 minutes. Remove the gratin-tatouille and serve warm.

### + sodium count:

Zucchini: 16mg per medium zucchini; Eggplant: 11mg per large eggplant; Tomatoes: 6mg per medium tomato; Canned tomato puree: 15mg per ½ cup, depending on brand; Carrots: 42mg per medium carrot; Portabella mushroom: 8mg per cup diced

# PANEER IN SPINACH PEPPER SAUCE OR SAAG PANEER

Just when I thought cheese was no longer a diet option, I found paneer. I must have turned over the package ten times, as I couldn't believe what I saw: 5mg of sodium per ounce.

This delicious cheese is popular in South Asian and Persian cuisine. It is firm in texture and can be grilled or fried, and it stays sturdy when drowned in a variety of delicious sauces. Although it is sometimes referred to as Indian cottage cheese, I think it tastes more like a hard mozzarella and it can bring welcome contrast to otherwise silky dishes. Just like this one.

Serve over rice or with lentils for a full meal.

**Serves 4 to 6**

- 1 pound fresh spinach, well washed
- 1 tablespoon plus 2 teaspoons sesame oil
- 2 cups cubed low-sodium paneer (or firm low-sodium tofu, cut into ½-inch cubes)
- 4 garlic cloves, finely diced
- 1 teaspoon grated fresh ginger
- ½ yellow onion, finely diced
- 1 red bell pepper
- 1 large tomato, washed and diced
- 2 teaspoons curry powder
- ⅛ teaspoon ground white pepper
- Red chili pepper flakes
- ¼ cup plain soy yogurt

+ Bring a small pot of water to boil and blanch the spinach in it for 1 minute. Immediately remove it from the water and place it in a colander to drain. Rinse with cold water and when cool to the touch, use your hands to tightly squeeze the spinach and wring out the liquid. Do this 4 to 5 times until no more water comes out, then cut the spinach into thin ribbons. Set aside.
+ In a wok or saucepan, heat 1 tablespoon of the sesame oil over medium-high heat. Add a handful of cubes of paneer (or tofu) and fry until their skin bubbles and turns golden brown, 3 to 5 minutes. Flip them over and fry their opposite sides, 3 to 5 minutes more. Take out the paneer (or tofu) and set aside on some paper towels to drain off the oil. Repeat with the remaining paneer and cover to keep warm.
+ Add the remaining 2 teaspoons sesame oil to the pan and lower the heat to medium. Add the garlic, ginger, and onion and cook, stirring, until softened, 2 to 3 minutes. Then, remove from the heat and transfer the garlic, ginger, and onion to a blender or food processor. Add the bell pepper and diced tomato and puree until the sauce is smooth.
+ Reheat your wok or saucepan over medium heat and pour in the blended sauce. Bring it to a boil and cook for 2 minutes, then lower the heat to a simmer and stir in the spinach, curry powder, white pepper, chili pepper flakes, and yogurt, and continue to cook for 5 minutes more.
+ Remove the pan from the heat, stir the paneer, and serve warm.

### + sodium count:

Spinach: 24mg per 1 cup; Tomato: 9mg per large tomato; Paneer: 5mg per 1 ounce depending on brand; Plain soy yogurt: 15mg per 6-ounce depending on brand

# GREEN BEAN CASSEROLE WITH ORANGE CINNAMON SAUCE

Bright greens, a creamy sauce, and a crunchy topping—this is green bean casserole. But for my version, a turmeric and cinnamon roux replaces canned soup. Shallots and mushrooms replace fried onions. And the flavors remain comforting and bright, meaning that Thanksgiving Turkey will be taking a backseat next November.

**Serves 4 to 6**

- 1½ pound fresh green beans, trimmed
- 2 tablespoons plus ½ teaspoon olive oil
- ¼ white onion, finely diced
- 2 garlic cloves, chopped
- 2 tablespoons unsalted butter
- 2 tablespoons all-purpose flour
- ½ cup half-and-half mixed with 2 cups water
- 1 teaspoon dried thyme
- ¼ teaspoon paprika
- ¼ teaspoon freshly ground black pepper
- ¼ teaspoon ground turmeric
- ¼ teaspoon ground cinnamon
- Grated zest of 1 orange
- 2 large shallots, thinly sliced
- ½ pound white button mushrooms, thinly sliced

+ Preheat the oven to 350°F.
+ Fill a medium bowl with water and ice and place it in the refrigerator for 10 minutes. Next, fill a pot (at least 2 quarts or bigger) with water and bring to a boil. Cook the green beans in the boiling water for 3 to 4 minutes. Remove them from the pot with a slotted spoon, draining any excess water back into the pot, and dunk the beans in the bowl of ice water to set the color and stop the cooking. When they are cool to the touch, drain the beans again and set them aside in a dry bowl.
+ In the same pot you used to cook the beans, heat ½ teaspoon of the olive oil over medium heat. Add the onion and garlic and cook, stirring, until softened, 2 to 3 minutes. Remove to a small bowl and set aside.
+ In the same pot, melt the butter over medium heat for 1 to 2 minutes. Whisk in flour until it is combined, and cook for 2 minutes. Pour in the half-and-half mixture and continue to whisk until the sauce thickens, 6 to 8 minutes. Be patient—it really will thicken. Add the thyme, paprika, pepper, turmeric, cinnamon, and orange zest. Continue to stir until smooth, 2 to 3 minutes, then remove from the heat. This is a good time to taste a fingerfull of your work and adjust the seasoning to your liking. Add the cooked garlic and onion bits to the creamy sauce and mix to combine.
+ Cut the green beans in half and place them in a 3½-quart casserole dish. Pour the sauce on top, and gently toss so all of the beans are coated with the sauce. Place the casserole in the oven and cook for 45 minutes.
+ Meanwhile, place the shallots and mushrooms in a small bowl and mix with the remaining 2 tablespoons olive oil. When the green beans are cooked, remove the dish from the oven and turn the broiler to high. Spread the marinated shallots and mushrooms evenly on top of the beans, and return the dish to the bottom rack of the oven. Broil until the shallots and mushrooms are crispy and lightly browned, 3 to 5 minutes. Keep an eye on them so they don't burn.
+ Remove the casserole from the oven and serve while warm.

### + sodium count:

Green beans: 33mg per 1 cup; Half-and-half: 15mg per 2 tablespoons

# SUMMER SUCCOTASH

When I think of summer, I think of corn and squash. And when I think of corn and squash, I think of succotash. Now succotash is not traditionally made with squash, carrots or tomatillos or a handful of the ingredients that I decided to use. In its original form, it included hominy, (i.e. corn kernels treated in a salty, alkaline solution), lima beans, and a tomato-based broth for some background noise. But I changed things up a bit to boost flavor and lower the sodium.

**Serves 4 to 6**

- 2 ears husked corn (or 2 cups frozen corn)
- 1 tomatillo, husks removed and washed (warm water helps remove the goo)
- 1 poblano pepper, stemmed and seeded
- 2 tablespoons olive oil
- 2 medium yellow summer squash, diced
- 6 garlic cloves, diced
- 1 small shallot, diced
- 3 medium carrots, peeled and cut into half circles
- 2 large juicy tomatoes, diced
- ¼ cut water
- ⅛ teaspoon freshly ground black pepper
- ⅛ teaspoon dry mustard powder
- 1 or 2 pinches red chili pepper flakes
- Grated zest and juice of 1 lime

+ Turn the oven broiler to high.
+ Place the corn, tomatillo, and poblano pepper in a baking pan and then place the pan on the middle rack in the oven. Roast the vegetables until the corn kernels begin to brown and the skins on the tomatillos and peppers bubble and turn black, about 5 minutes. Using tongs, give the vegetables a quarter-turn and roast them for 5 minutes more. (If you're using frozen corn kernels, just toss them slightly so they roast evenly). Repeat turning the vegetables until every side of the corn, tomatillo, and pepper has been roasted and charred, about 20 minutes. Remove the pan from the oven and put the poblano pepper in a paper bag, close the top, and let it steam for 15 minutes. Set the corn, tomatillo, and their roasting juices aside.
+ While the poblano steams, heat 1 tablespoon of the olive oil over medium heat in a small skillet. Add the summer squash to the pan and brown, about 5 minutes on each side. Turn off the heat and set aside.
+ If you used fresh corn, remove the kernels by standing the cob on one end and cutting downward with a sharp knife. Continue to rotate the cob and cut until all the kernels are removed. Set aside.
+ When you can comfortably touch the poblano pepper, peel off the charred skin and roughly dice both the poblano and tomatillo into small cubes and set aside with any residual juices.
+ In a medium pot, warm the remaining 1 tablespoon olive oil over medium heat. Add the garlic and shallot and cook, stirring, until softened, 2 to 3 minutes. Add the carrots and cook for another 3 minutes. Finally, add the corn kernels, poblano pepper, tomatillos, tomatoes, water, black pepper, ground mustard, and chili pepper flakes to taste to the pot. Bring to a boil and cook for 3 to 5 minutes. Reduce the heat and bring the mixture to a gentle simmer. Add half of the reserved summer squash and juice from half of the lime to the pot. Cook until the succotash starts to thicken, about 15 minutes. Stir occasionally to make sure nothing is sticking to the bottom of the pot.
+ To serve, scoop heaping spoonfuls of the succotash into a bowl and top with leftover squash and lime zest. Cut the remaining half of the lime into wedges and offer to guests for an additional punch of flavor.

**+ sodium count:**

Fresh corn: 11mg per ½ cup; Frozen corn: 0mg depending on brand; Carrot: 42mg per medium carrot; Tomatoes: 9mg per large tomato

Besides being easy to make, the succotash is super versatile as well.

# ZUCCHINI LEMON GARLIC PASTA NOODLES

This is a fun and quick way to spice up your usual greens. Seven ingredients and ten minutes in the pan make a light side of vegetables that will pair well with any fish or meaty main dish. They make a great pack-and-go lunch as well.

+ To make your noodles, wash the zucchini. Peel the skin lengthwise, starting with the outer green layer, and be sure to rotate the zucchini a quarter turn after every peel, so that you keep each peel, or "noodle," about the same width. When you get down to the seeded part of the zucchini, put down the peeler, pick up a knife, and chop the innards into a fine dice. Put the zucchini noodles and diced bits aside.
+ Cut the garlic into thin, round slices. Heat the olive oil in a skillet over medium heat. Add the garlic slices and brown, 3 to 5 minutes. Then add the diced zucchini bits and the chili pepper flakes, and cook for another 2 to 3 minutes. Add the zucchini noodles cook until they soften, 2 to 3 minutes, and remove the pan from the heat. Place the zucchini noodles in a mixing bowl and add the grated lemon zest and half of the juice, the parsley, and black pepper. Give the noodles one final toss and serve immediately.

**Serves 2 to 4**

2 large zucchinis
2 large garlic cloves
1 teaspoon olive oil
Red chili pepper flakes
Grated zest and juice of 1 lemon
5 sprigs fresh flat-leaf parsley, leaves roughly torn
Freshly ground black pepper

## + sodium count:

Zucchini: 26mg per large zucchini

# POLANGSAK DAL

Trying new cuisines is a great way to discover new flavor combinations and new ingredients. That's why we're going to India. This particular recipe is all about letting ingredients transform with time and heat. The hard yellow onions melt into buttery strands. The firm red lentils, high in protein, turn into milky, beige porridge. And the snappy spinach turns into green threads that get woven throughout the dish. A handful of spices and a bit of low-sodium dairy completes the velvety dal. Serve it over rice and top with tofu or diced tomatoes for a complete meal.

**Serves 4**

- 1 cup dried red split lentils, rinsed
- 1 medium yellow onion, sliced into ¼-inch thick strips
- 3 garlic cloves, smashed in a garlic press
- 2½ cups water
- 1 pound fresh spinach
- 1 teaspoon peeled and grated fresh ginger
- ½ to 1 teaspoon chili powder
- ½ teaspoon ground cumin
- ¼ teaspoon ground white pepper
- 2 tablespoons plain soy yogurt
- 1 lemon or lime, sliced into 4 wedges

+ Add the lentils, onion, and garlic to a medium pot or saucepan with the water. Bring to a boil and cook for 5 minutes. Reduce the heat so that the liquid is barely simmering. Cover and cook until the lentils have a creamy texture and turn golden-yellow, 20 to 25 minutes.
+ Meanwhile, bring another small pot of water to a boil. When the bubbles are rolling, dunk in your spinach and cook for 1 minute. Immediately remove it from the water and place into a colander to drain. Rinse with cold water, and when cool to the touch, use your hands to tightly squeeze the spinach and wring out the liquid. Do this 4 to 5 times. You now have a tight bundle of spinach. Place this bundle of spinach on a cutting board and begin cutting it crosswise into ribbons. Then, cutting in the opposite direction, give the ribbons a couple of good chops. Set the spinach bits aside.
+ When the lentils are done, add the ginger, chili powder, cumin, and white pepper and mix until combined. Increase the heat to high and cook, uncovered, until the remaining liquid evaporates, 3 to 5 minutes.
+ Lower the heat and add the chopped spinach and yogurt, stirring it until incorporated throughout. Cook for a final 2 to 3 minutes.
+ Your dal is now ready to devour. Serve with the lemon or lime slices so guests can squeeze to their liking for added brightness and flavor.

**+ sodium count:**

Lentils: 12mg per 1 cup; Spinach: 24mg per 1 cup; Plain soy yogurt: 15mg per 6-ounce container depending on brand

# QUICK KIMCHI + CRISPY TOFU SALAD

Kimchi comes in jars. It's bright red. It's salty. It was once just a Korean side dish or topper for steamed rice. But now it can be found in pancakes, on pizzas, and in major grocery store aisles. And while you cannot make an exact replica without the salt—which is an essential part of the fermentation process—you can get close with similarly punchy ingredients like chili oil, nori, vinegar, sugar, garlic, and sesame oil. The cabbage takes at least a day to soak in all the good flavors, so prepare ahead for this salad. The rest is simple and easy to assemble. Oh, and before I forget, don't skip the crisped tofu. It adds welcome firm bite to the otherwise slick greens.

**Serves 2 to 4**

**Effort Level: Plan Ahead**

- 6 loosely packed cups chopped savoy or Napa cabbage
- ½ cup water
- 6 garlic cloves, smashed in a garlic press
- ½ sheet Pacific nori
- 5 tablespoons sesame oil
- ¼ cup unseasoned rice vinegar
- 2 green onions, thinly sliced (everything but the bulb)
- Juice of ½ lime
- 1 teaspoon diced ginger
- ½ teaspoon granulated white sugar
- ½ to 1 teaspoon salt-free chili oil
- 2 cups cubed firm tofu, ½ inch high and 1 inch wide
- ¼ teaspoon ground turmeric
- Toasted white sesame seeds
- Red chili pepper flakes

+ Put the cabbage, water, and the garlic into a pot and bring to a rolling boil over medium heat. Cook until the cabbage is soft and wilted, 8 to 10 minutes. Meanwhile, using scissors, shred the nori into very thin 2-inch strips. Cut until you have about ½ cup of shredded nori; save any extra.
+ In an airtight container, whisk together 2 tablespoons of the sesame oil, the rice vinegar, nori, three-quarters of the green onions, the lime juice, ginger, sugar, and chili oil.
+ When the cabbage and garlic mixture has cooked, remove the pot from of the heat and drain out any leftover liquid. Transfer the cabbage and garlic to the container with the rice vinegar marinade. Place the lid on top, shake vigorously to coat. Place the tofu, 2 tablespoons of the sesame oil, and the turmeric in another airtight container, and shake it gently to spread the oil and spice. Place the cabbage and tofu containers in the refrigerator and marinate for 24 hours.
+ When you're close to eating time, heat 1 tablespoon of the sesame oil in a skillet over high heat. Take the cubes of tofu out of their marinade and, working in batches, fry until their skin bubbles and turns golden brown, 3 to 5 minutes. Flip them over, sprinkle some sesame seeds on top, and fry the opposite sides, 3 to 5 minutes more. Repeat until all the tofu cubes are cooked. They are now yellow, crispy, and ready to be eaten.
+ To serve, place a serving of kimchi salad in bowls or on a plate and then layer the tofu on top. Sprinkle with leftover green onion slices, more sesame seeds, and chili pepper flakes, to taste if desired.

### + sodium count:

Savoy cabbage: 20mg per 1 cup shredded; Cabbage (general variety): 13mg per 1 cup shredded; Tofu: 0 to 10mg depending on brand

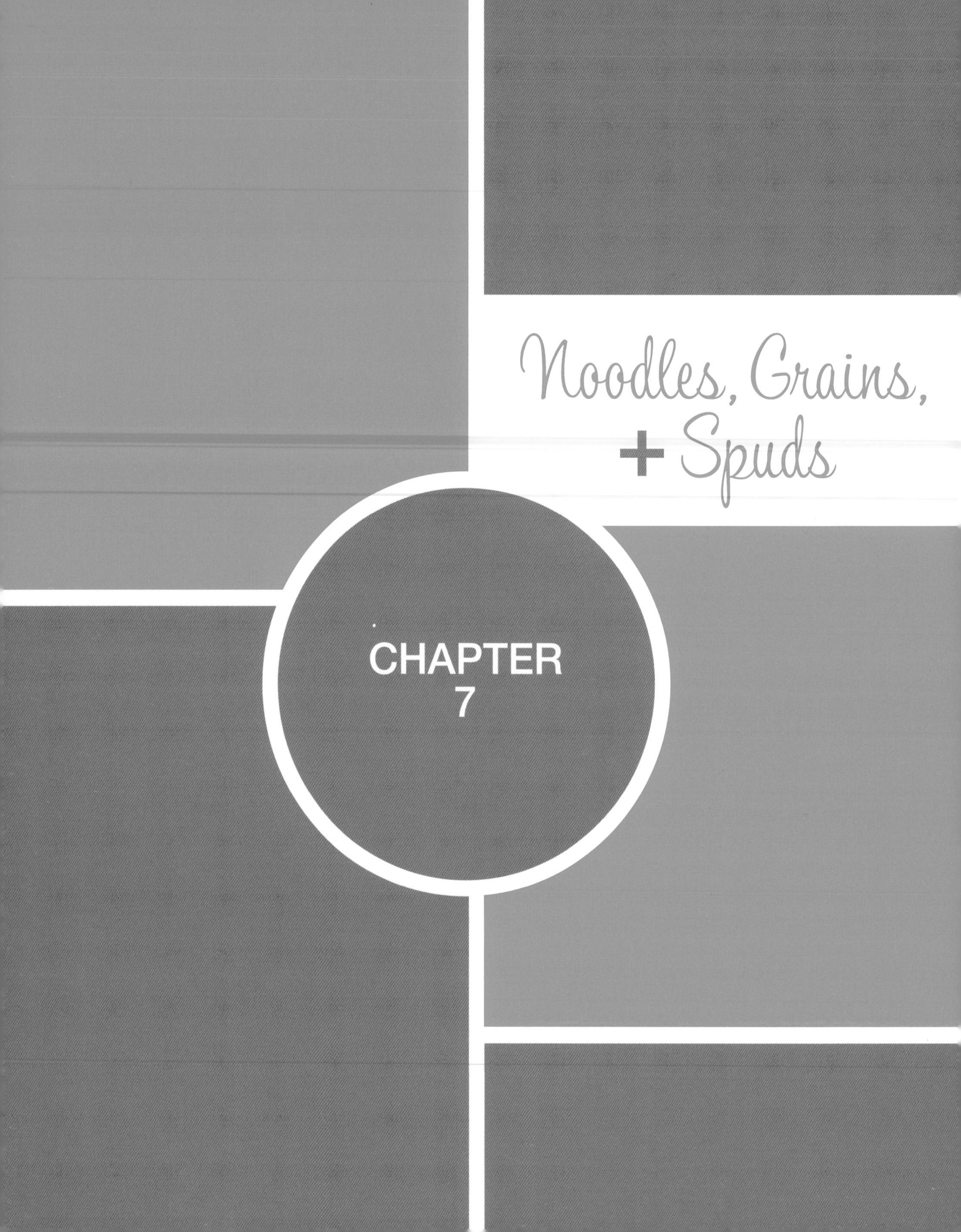

# Noodles, Grains, + Spuds

CHAPTER 7

Dearest potato, noodle, bean, and speck of rice,

I am a gal who likes feeling full; a task that at times seems impossible on a low-sodium diet. For years, I felt like I was eating on empty. Salads were good, chicken was scrumptious, and a quick stir-fry was delicious. But all these dishes lacked the weight of the awesome carbohydrate. That starchy, spongy addition that soaks up every ounce of flavor and juice in a meal, honoring the time and love that was poured into it.

I bided my time with salt-free crackers and tortilla chips sprinkled over my soup. A fine substitution; but I must admit, I always felt as if I was settling.

Then you arrived with your twisty, chunky, plump bites and my food was never the same. Stews suddenly had heftiness, simple vegetables were meatier, and even new friends, like quinoa, cannellini beans, and brown rice added unexpected nutty and buttery flavors. What a surprise.

Of course, sometimes we may spend meals apart. But, as they say, distance makes the heart grow fonder. So if I pass you up for a date with some simple greens, just know I'll see you sometime later this week for a dreamy pasta dinner.

Loyally yours.

*I'm a gal who likes feeling full; a task that at times seems impossible on a low-sodium diet.*

# BEET CARROT HASH CAKES

With bright colors, punchy herb flavor, and the natural sodium found in beets, these low-sodium patties easily compete with the classic potato pancake. They work well for breakfast and brunches, and make a dashing side for a meaty main course. I like serving them with low-sodium Greek yogurt, crème fraîche, or even salt-free Ranch Dressing (page 100). Squeezes of orange or lemon also work nicely, or you can dress it with a simple mixture of white wine vinegar, chopped garlic, and dill.

Although I typically like to use fresh herbs in recipes to add a bright, finishing touch, since the herbs are being cooked in hot oil, dried dill is a better choice here. But if you have fresh dill to sprinkle on top at the end, by all means use it. You can never overdo the dill.

**Makes 10 to 12 palm-size patties**

- 3 medium carrots, peeled
- 2 large red beets, peeled
- 1 large Yukon potato, peeled
- ¼ cup all-purpose flour
- 2 teaspoons dried dill
- 2 teaspoons freshly ground black pepper
- 2 large eggs
- Safflower or canola oil, for frying

+ To begin, grate the vegetables with either a hand grater or, for a faster solution, a food processor fitted with a grater attachment. You should end up with approximately 2 cups of grated carrots, ¾ cup of grated beets, and ¼ cup grated potato. But if you have more or less, don't fret. The recipe will still work.
+ Put the grated vegetables into some cheesecloth, or just into your hands, and squeeze them over the sink into a bowl, forcing out the liquid. You'll be surprised how much juice is in there and you want the vegetables to be as dry as possible for a solid patty and a crispy fry. And as a bonus, you can save or freeze the juice for salt-free Bloody Marys.
+ Place your grated (and liquid-free) vegetables in a mixing bowl and add the flour, dill, and pepper. With your hands, mix all the ingredients together until well combined. Next, crack both eggs into the bowl and mix again until everything is combined. Wash your hands and set the mixture aside.
+ Now for the fun part. Set up a cooling rack or a plate covered with a paper towel next to your stove. This is where your fried goodies will have a place to drain off their excess oil. Put 2 tablespoons of oil in a skillet and heat over medium-high heat. To see if the oil is ready, test it by putting a small bit of the hash batter into the pan. If it hisses at you, it is ready.
+ With your hands, form a few, loosely packed palm-size patties out of the carrot, beet, and potato batter. Using a spatula, carefully slide the patties into the pan. Cook the patties undisturbed until a brown crust forms on the bottom, about 5 minutes. Flip over the patties and cook the opposite sidesfor another 5 minutes, again pressing on the cakes with the spatula once or twice. Transfer the crispy patties to the cooling rack or the paper towel–plate and repeat with the remaining batter until it is gone. Raise and lower the heat as needed to keep the patties from burning, and add extra oil if needed, keeping a thin layer of slick stuff on the bottom of the pan at all times. And if your patties do fall apart, looking more like hash than cake, don't stress. They will taste just as good.
+ Serve warm with suggested garnishes (see head note) and enjoy.

**+ sodium count:**

Carrot: 42mg per medium carrot; Beet: 64mg per beet; Potato: 22mg per large potato; Eggs: 71mg per large egg

## HERBS: DRIED VERSUS FRESH

Throughout this book, you'll see both dried and fresh herbs being used. While I generally just use whatever I have lying around, for the purposes of your culinary education, I thought I'd give you some simple rules for choosing between fresh or dried herbs during your own cooking adventures.

Dried herbs or fresh sturdy herbs, like rosemary and thyme, work best when food is cooked, stewed, or baked for a long time. More delicate, leafy herbs, like cilantro, basil, and tarragon, often wilt and become muted with too much heat. They are most vibrant when added at the very end of prepping a dish.

Of course, you can always just use what you have on hand. In that case, a good ratio for conversion is 1:3, that is one part dried herbs is equal to 3 parts fresh herbs. And if you are stocking up on dried herbs, it is best to store them in a dark, cool space and to crush larger pieces in your fingers before you add them to your pot or pan. This will release the pungent aromas hidden inside. Replace dried herbs as soon as their color fades.

# RICH POTATO, SHALLOT, + FRESH HERB PIE

*Low-sodium guest: Chef Hubert Keller, Fleur de Lys*

"This recipe is based on a traditional Alsatian recipe, *tourte Alsacienne*, a classic potpie stuffed with meat and a creamy quiche-like custard, and cooked in a decorated terra-cotta mold. I have simplified it in my recipe by adding the custard before cooking the pie, and I have given it a low-sodium and vegetarian twist. Allow about 1½ hours to prepare. The pie is easier to serve if you let it rest after cooking and it reheats well. I recommend serving it with a spinach or frisée salad."

**Serves 8 to 10**

**Effort Level: Got Time to Spare**

Pie Crust

2 cups all-purpose flour, plus extra for rolling
6 tablespoons (¾ stick) cold unsalted butter, cut into ½-inch chunks
6 tablespoons cold solid shortening, cut into ½-inch chunks
4 to 6 tablespoons ice water

Filling

1 pound Yukon gold or other yellow potatoes (2 medium potatoes), peeled
½ tablespoon virgin olive oil
¾ cup minced shallots
3 garlic cloves, finely minced
Freshly ground black pepper

+ Preheat the oven to 375°F.
+ Place the flour in a food processor fitted with the steel blade. Add the butter and the shortening and pulse until the flour forms little pea-size clumps. Add the ice water 1 tablespoon at a time and continue to pulse until you can gently squeeze a handful of the dough and it holds together like clay. Gather the dough into a ball, flatten it into a 4-inch disk, and wrap it in plastic wrap. Chill the dough in the refrigerator for at least 1 hour or up to 2 days.
+ When you're ready to make your pie, generously flour your rolling pin and work surface. Roll out the chilled pastry dough into a very thin circle, about 1/16 inch thick. Carefully place it in a 9-inch pie dish, bringing the dough up the sides and trimming off any excess. If the dough breaks apart a bit, just press it back together. Then make a ball with the excess dough, wrap it in plastic wrap, and place it back in the refrigerator. You'll use this for the top of the pie later.
+ Prick the bottom of the pastry dough a few times with a fork and cover it with some parchment paper. Fill the pie crust with 1½ cups of dry beans or pastry weights and bake the crust in the preheated oven for 20 to 25 minutes. Remove the pie pan from the oven, and remove the beans or pastry weights and discard the parchment paper. Return the crust to in the oven and bake until it turns a light golden color, 3 to 5 minutes. Transfer the crust to a wire rack to cool for about 15 minutes.
+ While the crust is cooling, put the potatoes in a large pot, cover them with water, and bring to a boil. Reduce the heat and simmer until the potatoes are just soft

enough to poke with a fork, 10 to 15 minutes. Drain the potatoes in a colander, rinse with cold water, and let them cool.

+ Meanwhile, heat the olive oil in a small skillet and add the shallots and garlic. Cook over medium heat until softened, stirring frequently, 8 to 10 minutes. Add black pepper to taste and a tablespoon of water if the skillet becomes too dry. Remove the shallots and garlic from the heat and set aside.
+ Beat the eggs in a mixing bowl. Add the heavy cream or half-and-half, thyme, parsley, chives, and cooked garlic and shallots. Whisk well and set aside. Take out your extra pastry dough from the fridge.
+ Once the potatoes have cooled, slice them into very thin rounds (⅛ to ¼ inch thick). Line the bottom of the pastry shell with half of the sliced potatoes, overlapping each slice. Ladle half of the egg and cream mixture into the pie dish and then add another layer of potatoes, overlapping them again. Fill with the remaining egg and cream mixture. The potatoes and cream sauce filling will reach the top of the pie dish.
+ Flour your work surface and rolling pin, and roll out a thin layer of the leftover pastry dough into a circle large enough to cover the pie. Whisk the egg yolk and water together in a small bowl and brush it over the dough and along the rim. Carefully place the dough lid over the pie and press along the rim to seal. Cut off any excess dough with scissors or a knife and cut out a small hole in the center of the lid to allow the steam to escape.
+ Bake the pie in the middle of the oven for 30 to 40 minutes. Remove and let the pie rest for 10 minutes before serving.

3 large eggs
¾ cup heavy cream or half-and-half
2 tablespoons finely minced fresh thyme
3 tablespoons finely minced fresh flat-leaf parsley
3 tablespoons finely minced fresh chives

Egg Wash

1 large egg yolk
½ teaspoon water

**+ sodium count:**

Potatoes: 13mg per medium potato; Eggs: 71mg per large egg; Heavy cream: 5mg per 1 tablespoon; Half-and-half: 15mg per 2 tablespoons

# POTATOES POUTINE WITH MUSHROOM GRAVY

Originating in Quebec, poutine consists of French fries piled high with dark gravy and chewy cheese curds—great for late night snacking. But lately, chefs from all over are giving poutine a healthy new look, which means it is time for a low-sodium version, too. Mushroom gravy replaces the meat sauce and, if you crave the curd, roast some low-sodium paneer for a similar, cheesy texture. The result is no ordinary French fry salad. It's clean, salt-free poutine.

**Serves 4 to 6**

3 cups water
½ cup dried mushrooms (a mixed variety works best)
5 medium Yukon potatoes, scrubbed and cut into thick wedges like steak fries
2 tablespoons olive oil
½ teaspoon dried parsley
¼ teaspoon dried dill
1 teaspoon dried rosemary
¼ teaspoon onion powder
2 tablespoons unsalted butter
1 medium shallot, diced
2 tablespoons all-purpose flour
¼ teaspoon dried thyme or tarragon
1 teaspoon sherry
⅛ teaspoon freshly ground black pepper
¼ cup low-sodium paneer, cut into ½-inch cubes

+ Preheat the oven to 400°F.
+ Fill a small pot with the water and bring to a boil. Add the mushrooms, cover the pot with a lid, turn off the heat, and let them soak and soften for 30 minutes. Drain the mushrooms and reserve the liquid. You will be using it in the recipe.
+ Meanwhile, place your potato wedges in a bowl and add the olive oil, parsley, dill, rosemary, and onion powder. Use your hands to toss everything together until the potatoes are evenly coated in the oil and spices. Then arrange the potatoes in a single layer on a greased baking sheet and place in the oven. Bake until the skin starts to darken and bubble a bit, 25 minutes. Use a spatula or tongs to flip the wedges to their opposite sides and return the baking pan to the oven, and bake for 25 minutes more, for a total of 50. The potatoes are done when the wedges are golden brown and crispy.
+ While your spuds are crisping on their second sides, it's time to make the gravy. Melt the butter with the shallot in a small saucepan. Cook, stirring, until the butter browns and the shallot soften, 3 to 5 minutes. Then add the flour and whisk vigorously until the butter mixture begins to thicken, about 2 minutes. Slowly add in 1 cup of the mushroom soaking liquid, stirring constantly to keep the sauce creamy. Add another ½ cup of mushroom liquid and keep whisking to work out any flour lumps. Continue adding in the mushroom liquid until you have used 2 cups. Increase the heat to medium and begin to reduce the gravy.
+ Take a moment to quickly dice the soaked mushrooms and add them with the thyme (or tarragon), sherry, and pepper to the saucepan. Stir until all the ingredients are combined. Reduce the heat to very low and allow the sauce to reduce slowly until the fries are done, 10 to 15 minutes.
+ Just before serving, place the cubed paneer on an aluminum foil–lined baking sheet and place it in the oven until the top of the cheese browns, 6 to 8 minutes.
+ When all the components are ready, put the poutine together. Pile a handful of crispy potato fries on a plate, drizzle gravy over them, and sprinkle the top with the paneer cubes. Enjoy.

**+ sodium count:**
Potato: 13mg per medium potato; Paneer: 5mg per 1 ounce depending on brand

# ROASTED CAULIFLOWER–BROWN RICE RISOTTO WITH LEMON, WALNUT, + MASCARPONE

*Low-sodium guest: Food52.com and Gingerroot*

As I was ramping up my blog, I began posting recipes on a brand new site called *Food52.com*, headed by two genius *New York Times* food writers and cookbook authors, Amanda Hesser and Merrill Stubbs. Their weekly contests, themed by ingredient, supplied me with constant inspiration and it motivated me to take innovative approaches to classic dishes. Their prompts also led me to make many of these recipes you hold in your hands, and most importantly, their support and guidance gave me the confidence to write this book.

It seems fitting, then, that for their contribution they wished to honor their users and pick a recipe from the thousands in their growing database. This one comes from Gingerroot (real name, Jennifer), whose recipes continue to receive numerous editor nods and wins for their creativity and crafty cooking techniques, like steaming cauliflower in aluminum foil before roasting so that it does not dry out.

Merrill adds that this particular dish is a great example of how to create robust flavors without using salt. She says that roasting the cauliflower and garlic intensifies their sweetness, and that lemon juice is an ingredient one should always have in his or her back pocket when cooking with little to no sodium. "Like salt, it brightens and lifts the other flavors in a dish."

---

+ Preheat the oven to 425°F.
+ Tear off two 12-inch square pieces of aluminum foil and set aside on a baking pan. In a medium bowl, toss the cauliflower florets with a few glugs of olive oil and half of the chopped garlic.
+ Lay out the cauliflower mixture on one of your foil squares in a single layer. Top with a second piece of foil and fold up the edges on all sides to create a sealed packet. Roast in the oven for 15 minutes.
+ While the cauliflower is roasting, combine the chicken stock and 4 cups of water in a saucepan. Cover, bring to a boil, then reduce to a simmer.

+ Carefully pry off the top piece of foil to expose the cauliflower (watch out for the hot steam)! Shake the foil slightly to move the pieces around. Roast the cauliflower for 6 minutes more, until tender and browned but still moist. Remove the baking pan from the oven. When cooled, coarsely chop the cauliflower florets.
+ Transfer the chopped roasted cauliflower to the original medium bowl. Add the lemon zest and 2 tablespoons of the lemon juice. Set the bowl aside.
+ In a medium-sized pot or 5-quart Dutch oven, melt the butter over medium heat. Add the onion and remaining chopped garlic and cook, stirring, until fragrant, about 5 minutes. Add the cauliflower leaves and continue cooking and stirring until the onion softens and begins to become translucent. Stir in the rice and cook, stirring, for 1 minute. Add the vermouth and stir until absorbed, about 5 minutes.
+ Pour 1 cup of the simmering broth into the rice (I use my soup ladle). Cook, stirring constantly, until absorbed. You want the mixture to be simmering, not boiling, so adjust the heat if necessary. Continue cooking and adding broth, 1 cup at a time, stirring constantly and allowing each addition to be absorbed before adding the next, until the rice is just tender and creamy, about 45 minutes. Fold in the cauliflower-lemon mixture and stir to combine. Add the mascarpone and mix again. Turn off the heat.
+ Mix in the parsley and several grinds of black pepper to taste. If the risotto is too thick, thin it with a bit of the remaining broth (there will be a little left). Serve the risotto with a drizzle of walnut oil and sprinkle with the toasted walnuts and enjoy.

**Serves 4 as a main; 6 as a side**

3 cups cauliflower florets
Extra-virgin olive oil
2 garlic cloves, finely chopped
3½ cups salt-free chicken stock
Grated zest and juice of 1 Meyer lemon
2 tablespoons unsalted butter
⅓ cup sweet onion, finely chopped
½ cup finely chopped cauliflower florets (thick, fibrous stalks discarded)
1½ cup short-grain brown rice
⅓ cup vermouth
2 generous tablespoons mascarpone
1 tablespoon finely chopped fresh flat-leaf parsley
Freshly ground black pepper
Walnut oil or more olive oil, for drizzling
¼ cup salt-free walnuts, lightly toasted in a 350°F oven for 5 to 7 minutes, finely chopped

### + sodium count:

Cauliflower: 16mg per ½ cup; Mascarpone: 15mg per 2 tablespoons depending on brand

# VEGGIE BURGERS + PORTABELLA BUNS

Supposedly packed with vegetables, healthy grains, and less fat than the beef version, the store-bought vegetarian patty seems like a good choice for meatless Mondays or attempts at vegetarianism. It even tastes like a good choice, especially when piled high with condiments and pickles. But when you look beyond the delightful pictures of tomatoes and leafy greens on the package of frozen patties and catch sight of the nutritional information, you'll discover that many of these products replace the rich flavor of meat with loads of salt.

Many store-bought veggie burgers contain a whopping 400mg of sodium per patty or more, as well as other ingredients that don't grow in your garden. And we haven't even gotten to the bun yet, which can be another 400mg of sodium, totaling two-thirds of your daily intake.

But don't fear. A low-sodium veggie burger is here. Actually, right here after this intro. It is loaded with vegetables and nuts for nutrients and color, beans for bulk, and ricotta for that creamy taste. And while you can simply use bread crumbs to thicken the patty, I decided to use salt-free tortilla chips that were going stale in my cupboard. It was a random move, but I really like the corn flavor they add. Definitely give it a try if you have some lying around.

I also like serving these burgers by stacking them on a grilled portabella mushroom. You can't really pick it up to eat it and it is more of a knife-and-fork presentation, but what's more veggie burger than serving it on a sesame-sprinkled veggie bun? Top it with anything from Salt-Free Ketchup (page 106), to sliced fennel, or any of the other fun toppings described at the end of the recipe.

## + note

Got leftovers? Make the extra patty batter into falafel! Roll it into small balls and place them on a greased or parchment paper–lined baking sheet. Preheat oven to 400°F and cook until golden and crispy, 15 to 20 minutes. Serve with cucumber slaw or inside some butter lettuce with a simple tahini dressing made from tahini, lemon juice, and a drizzle of olive oil.

## + note

Use a spoon to easily remove the gills from the portabellas. Gently scoop out the brown part until the white mushroom flesh is exposed.

+ In a food processor fitted with the metal blade, pulse the tortilla chips until they turn into medium-size crumbs. Transfer the crumbs to a small bowl and set aside. Add the pine nuts and garlic to the food processor and pulse until they are coarsely chopped. Add the next 11 ingredients (chickpeas through cardamom) and pulse again until all of the ingredients are chopped and mixed together. Pour the mixture into the bowl with the tortilla chips and, with your hands, mix until everything is well combined. Form patties that are 3 to 4 inches in diameter and place them on a plate or baking sheet.
+ In a large skillet, heat a teaspoon of vegetable oil over medium-high heat. Add 3 patties to the pan and cook until the surface has a light brown sear, about 6 minutes. Flip the patties and cook on the opposite sides for another 6 minutes. Place the patties on a plate or baking sheet and cover with aluminum foil to keep warm. Wipe out the skillet, add another teaspoon of oil, and repeat until all the veggie burgers are cooked.
+ Preheat the broiler.
+ While the patties are browning, moisten the top half of the mushrooms with a few drops of olive oil and sprinkle them with the sesame seeds. Place the mushrooms on a greased baking sheet and place in the oven on the second to the highest rack. Broil until the mushrooms soften and start to let out their juices, 3 to 5 minutes. Then remove the mushrooms from the oven and cool until they can be handled, 1 to 2 minutes.
+ To assemble the burgers, layer from bottom to top with any or all of the following: mushroom bun, veggie patty, Salt-Free Ketchup (page 106), sliced avocado, Dilly Burger Pickles (page 176), cucumbers, and sliced fennel. Dig in.

**Serves 4 to 6**

20 salt-free tortilla chips, ground to make ½ cup tortilla crumbs
½ cup salt-free pine nuts (or pumpkin seeds or walnuts)
4 garlic cloves
1 (15-ounce) can no-salt-added chickpeas (garbanzo beans), rinsed and drained
1 medium carrot, peeled and chopped
1 large egg
¼ cup low-sodium ricotta
3 tablespoons diced sun-dried tomatoes (optional)
½ teaspoon freshly ground black pepper
½ teaspoon onion powder
½ teaspoon paprika
½ teaspoon ground cumin
½ teaspoon fennel seed
½ teaspoon ground cardamom
Vegetable oil, for frying
1 portabella mushroom per person, gills and stem removed (see note page 174)
Olive oil
1 tablespoon toasted white sesame seeds

### + sodium count:

No-salt-added chickpeas: 30mg per ½ cup depending on brand; Carrot: 42mg per medium carrot; Egg: 71mg per large egg; Low-sodium ricotta: 24mg per ¼ cup depending on brand; Sun-dried tomatoes: 0 to 15mg per serving depending on brand; Portabella mushroom: 8mg per 1 cup chopped or whole mushroom

# DILLY BURGER PICKLES

A perfect topping for those veggie burgers on the previous page.

**Makes 1 quart pickles**
**Effort Level: Plan Ahead**

- 3 pickling cucumbers, sliced into rounds or spears
- 3 garlic cloves, roughly chopped
- ¼ cup roughly torn fresh dill
- 2 dried chile peppers
- 1 cup water
- 1½ cups distilled white vinegar
- ½ cup apple cider vinegar
- ¼ cup granulated white sugar
- 1 teaspoon whole black peppercorns
- 1 teaspoon whole yellow mustard seed
- ¼ teaspoon anise seed
- ¼ teaspoon ground turmeric

+ Place the cucumbers, garlic, dill, and dried chile peppers into a 1-quart container. Set aside.
+ In a pot, mix the water with the distilled white vinegar, apple cider vinegar, sugar, black peppercorns, yellow mustard seed, anise seed, and turmeric. Bring to a boil over medium-high heat and as soon as the liquid is at a full boil, turn off the heat and remove the pot from the heat. Allow the liquid to cool for 20 minutes, or longer if you are using a plastic container.
+ When the liquid is lukewarm, carefully pour it into your container. Your vegetables should be covered in the pickling liquid; if not, add a bit more distilled white vinegar. The cucumbers will also shrink in the hot liquid, so if you have any extras, go ahead and stuff them in when there is room. Put on the lid and close the container tightly. Give it 5 or 6 good shakes and put it in the refrigerator to cool.
+ In 48 hours the pickles will be ready for munching. Resist the urge to taste, because the longer you wait to eat them, the more "pickly" they will be. But do try to finish them off within 2 weeks.

### + sodium count:

Cucumber: 1mg per ½ cup sliced and practically sodium-free

# YAKISOBA

For cooking inspiration, I started taking recipes from Mark Bittman's columns in the *New York Times* and giving them salt-free makeovers. Even though Mr. Bittman's recipes aim to be super straightforward and fuss-free, I was looking for challenges. So I skipped his soups and salads and purposefully searched for salt-dependent foods. I found yakisoba.

In Mark's own words, "There are thousands of ways to make yakisoba, many of them good. All contain noodles and vegetables, and usually some protein. The dish is always fried in a pan and finished with a somewhat sweet sauce that is put together quickly, from condiments. All of this provides plenty of leeway."

With that intro, I took Mr. Bittman's allowance for leeway, and I made my own low-sodium adjustments. First, I attacked the sauce: a mixture of ketchup, soy sauce, Worcestershire, mirin, and, oh my kidneys, Tabasco. To replace the ketchup, I used my no-salt-added tomato puree; for the mirin, sodium-free products do exist but you can always mix ½ cup sake with ⅙ cup granulated white sugar. I swapped molasses for Worcestershire; and a few shakes of chili oil for Tabasco. And I ended up with a sweet, spicy, no-salt sauce that sticks to every noodle. Thanks, Mark.

**Serves 2 to 4**

- 1 (9.5-ounce) package no-salt-added udon noodles
- 1½ teaspoons sesame oil
- 2 tablespoons no-salt-added tomato puree
- ¼ cup sodium-free mirin (or filtered sake)
- 1 teaspoon molasses
- ¼ cup Umami Sauce (page 109)
- ½ teaspoon salt-free chili oil
- 2 tablespoons peeled and chopped fresh ginger
- 4 garlic cloves, diced
- 2 cups sliced mushrooms (like shimeji, enoki, or shiitake)
- ¾ pound pork shoulder, chopped into 1-inch strips
- 2 cups shredded Napa cabbage
- 3 medium carrots, peeled and cut into thin matchsticks
- 3 green onions, thinly sliced (everything but the bulb)

+ Bring a pot of water to a boil. Add the udon noodles and cook according to the package directions. Drain the noodles. Place them in a bowl and sprinkle them with ½ teaspoon of the sesame oil so that they don't stick together. Set aside.
+ In a small bowl, make the yakisoba sauce by whisking together the tomato puree, mirin, molasses, umami sauce, and chili oil. Set aside.
+ In a wok or a large skillet, heat the remaining 1 teaspoon sesame oil over medium-high heat. Add the ginger, garlic, and mushrooms and cook, stirring, until they begin to brown, 3 to 5 minutes. Add the pork and cook for 10 minutes. Add the cabbage, carrots, and half of the green onions, and cook for 5 more minutes. Add the udon noodles and the yakisoba sauce, toss well, and cook for 3 to 5 minutes more.
+ Spoon heaping portions into bowls, sprinkle the remaining green onions on top, and slurp away.

## + sodium count:

Canned tomato puree: 15mg per ½ cup depending on brand; Molasses: 10mg per 1 tablespoon; Pork Shoulder: 55mg per 3 ounces, 74mg per ¼ pound; Cabbage (general variety): 13mg per 1 cup shredded; Carrot: 42mg per medium carrot

# BAKED MACARONI + PEAS

To recreate the richness of mac 'n' cheese, without the sodium, I made a milky coconut and cauliflower sauce, jazzed up with bright green peas and the surprise addition of mace, a spice that helps balance the savory and sweet flavors, and makes this mac 'n' peas taste like mac 'n' cheese.

**Serves 4 as a main, 6 as a side**

- 3 cups (about 12 ounces) pasta shells or macaroni noodles
- 1 cup fresh or frozen peas
- 1 medium head cauliflower, stem removed and broken into florets
- 3 tablespoons unsalted butter
- 3 tablespoons all-purpose flour
- 1 13.5-ounce can light coconut milk
- 2 teaspoons mace
- 2 teaspoon garlic powder
- 1 teaspoon ground white pepper
- Grated fresh nutmeg (about 6 good scrapes across a Microplane grater)
- Sprinkle of paprika and sprinkle of chili powder (if you like spice)

+ Preheat the oven to 375°F.
+ Fill a medium pot with water and bring to a boil. Add the pasta and cook until slightly al dente, about 6 minutes or according to the package directions.
+ Remove the pot from the heat. Using a slotted spoon, remove the noodles from the pot reserving the water in the pot, and run the noodles under cold water to stop the cooking process. Put the noodles in a bowl and then bring the same pot of water to a boil again. Dunk the peas in the pot for 1 to 2 minutes and immediately remove them, using the same method as for the noodles, and run them under cold water until they are cool to the touch. Add them to the noodles.
+ Pour out the water until you have just a few inches left in the pot. Place a metal steamer in the pot and make sure the water sits below the steamer. Place the cauliflower florets on the steamer. Cover with a lid and cook over medium heat until the cauliflower is soft enough to eat, 6 to 8 minutes. Remove the cauliflower from the heat and place half of it into a blender with ½ to ¾ cup warm water. Puree until smooth and set aside in a large bowl. Then repeat with the remaining cauliflower.
+ Now it's time to make the roux, the secret weapon for all mac 'n' cheese recipes. Dry out your pot and place it on the stove over medium-low heat. Add the butter and once melted, slowly whisk in the flour. Keep whisking until all the flour is added and the mixture is bubbly smooth, 3 to 5 minutes. When the roux turns the color of caramel, add the coconut milk and continue whisking until it thickens, at least 5 minutes. Add the cauliflower puree, mace, garlic powder, and white pepper to the roux. Whisk until everything is combined and the sauce is smooth, about 5 minutes more. Remove from the heat and add it to the noodle and pea mixture.
+ Finally, pour the mac and peas mixture into an oven-proof 3½-quart casserole dish. Grate the nutmeg on top and sprinkle with paprika and chili powder, if using. Bake in the oven for 30 minutes, and just before you pull it out, turn the broiler to high to crisp the top layer of noodles, 2 to 3 minutes.
+ Serve immediately while piping hot. But I didn't need to tell you that.

+ sodium count:

Noodles: 0 to 10mg per serving depending on brand; Fresh peas: 5 mg per ½ cup; Frozen peas: 35mg per ½ cup depending on brand; Cauliflower: 16mg per ½ cup, 176mg per medium head; Canned coconut milk: 5 to 15mg per ¼ cup depending on brand

# RUGOSA BUTTERNUT SQUASH RAVIOLI

*Low-sodium guest: Chef Josip Martinovic, McCalls Catering & Events*

McCalls, a San Francisco–based catering company and their head team, are practically family to my family. They are accustomed to making hot, perfectly cooked dinners for hundreds of people at a time. They serve and expedite enormous orders of juicy lamb and fish fillets with as much care and attention as one would expect at a dinner party for twenty. They are talented, they are a well-oiled team, and they love to care for people with their food. But could they cook without salt? It was a question I asked them early on in my low-sodium days. And, of course, they replied with an enthusiastic yes. What that meant, though, was still new to all of us and together we had a lot of low-sodium learning to do.

Meals with McCall's started out simply, mainly consisting of steamed veggies and grilled meat. Soon, though, the food they were making got adventurous. Steaks were topped with cilantro chimichurri sauces. Fish rested over delicate purees. Potatoes and roasted vegetables were covered in herbs and olive oil. And they even read my blog for new ideas, fully embracing the concept of low-sodium substitutions for salty ingredients. It is an understatement to say that the team at McCall's took on the low-sodium challenge with as much determination as I had.

Below is a note from Josip, the chef de cuisine in their kitchen, in which he talks about the transformation of my low-sodium meals and, perhaps, the transformation of his approach to cooking as well. I hope you enjoy it as much as the squash ravioli he has created for you.

---

"From my past life experience in Venetian rule of the Adriatic salt control, I have believed that salt adds the proper amount of zest to bring food to its heightened flavor. While preparing food for Jess, I was asked to prepare foods using no salt. The initial response inside my head was there would not be enough flavor. I was challenged to alter the chemical complexities of the foods with herb and spices to highlight the cuisine. To supplement the different nuances of spice and herb to influence my style to create a grand result for the event. From the passion inside my eternal spirit, I thank you."

*—Josip Martinovic, Chef de Cuisine*

**Makes 24 to 32 ravioli**
**Effort Level: Got Time to Spare**

Butternut Squash Filling

- 1 butternut squash, halved
- 1 to 2 tablespoons olive oil
- 1 tablespoon light brown sugar
- 1 teaspoon ground cumin
- 1 dry ancho chile, seeded, stemmed, and soaked in hot water for 10 minutes, drained, and diced
- 1 tablespoon chopped fresh oregano (or 1 teaspoon dried oregano)
- 1 tablespoon chopped marjoram or thyme (or 1 teaspoon dried marjoram or thyme)
- 2 shallots, chopped
- 1 teaspoon cayenne pepper

Pasta Dough

- 1½ cups all-purpose flour
- 1½ cups semolina flour
- 2 tablespoons chopped thyme (or 2 teaspoons dried thyme)
- 3 large eggs
- 1 large egg yolk
- 2 tablespoons water
- 1 tablespoon olive oil
- Olive oil and leftover herbs. for serving (optional)
- Balsamic vinegar, for serving (optional)
- Saffron Lemon Broth, for serving (optional; recipe follows)

+ Preheat the oven to 375°F.
+ Peel the squash with a potato peeler or a knife, cut it in half lenghtwise and remove the seeds and any stringy fiber. Cut the pulp into cubes, place in a baking pan and sprinkle with olive oil, the brown sugar and cumin. Roast until the squash is very tender, 45 minutes or so, turning them halfway through the baking time.
+ While the squash is roasting, make the pasta dough. Put both the flours and the thyme in a large mixing bowl and make a well in the center. Add the wet ingredients to the well and work the flour in with your hands, slowly mixing the dry and wet ingredients together. Add a bit more water or flour as needed until you can make a ball of dough. Add more flour if it is too sticky to get off your hands. Then knead the dough on a clean, flat surface by pressing down on the ball with the bottom of your palms, pushing it away from you, and folding the dough over itself. Turn it a quarter-turn and repeat. Knead until the dough is soft and smooth, about 5 minutes. It should feel springy and a bit elastic.
+ Cut the ball into fourths and remove one of the pieces. Wrap the remaining pieces in plastic wrap so they don't dry out, and set aside. Roll the ball out using a pasta maker until it has gone through the thinnest setting. The sheet of pasta should be about 5 inches wide and a little over 2 feet. Cut into two 12 by 5-inch sheets. If you don't have a pasta roller, you can roll it by hand with a rolling pin. Lightly flour a clean surface and roll the dough into a 12 by 10-inch sheets and then measure out and cut into two 12 by 5-inch sheets.

+ When the squash is soft, place it in a food processor. You may need to do this in two batches. Add the ancho chile, oregano, marjoram, shallots, and cayenne to the squash. Pulse until it is mixed together and then set the filling aside to cool down before using.
+ On one of the 12 by 5-inch pasta sheets, place 1 teaspoon of the filling at least ½ inch from the edge. Continue to add teaspoons of filling, staggering them 1 inch from each other. Cover the filled pasta sheet with the second 12 by 5-inch sheet, and carefully press down on the sheets, removing any big air pockets where the filling is. Use your fingers to press and seal the edges and, using a pizza cutter or a 2½-inch ring mold, cut out the ravioli. Place the finished ravioli on a baking sheet, sprinkle with cornmeal, and refrigerate until you are ready to cook. Repeat this process with the other 3 portions of pasta dough. And if you have leftover dough or finished ravioli you'd like to save, sprinkle it with cornmeal, cover in plastic wrap, or put in a plastic bag, and refrigerate or freeze until your next ravioli party.
+ Fill a pot with water and bring it to a boil. Take the ravioli out of the refrigerator and check to make sure all of the edges are sealed. Taking a handful of ravioli at a time, slip them in the water to cook, 3 to 4 minutes per batch. Check one to see if you like the texture, and if you do, remove them from the pot with a slotted spoon. Place the cooked pasta in bowls and drizzle with olive oil and leftover herbs, balsamic vinegar, or saffron lemon broth.

# SAFFRON LEMON BROTH

2 cups salt-free vegetable stock
Pinch of saffron
Grated zest of 2 lemons

Place all of the ingredients into a small pot and bring to a boil. Remove from the heat and add to your bowl of ravioli.

### + sodium count:

Egg yolks: 8mg per large egg;
Egg: 71mg sodium per large egg

# PAD THAI

Pad Thai is a wonderful dish with noodles, proteins, crispy veggies, and a delicate sauce. And it is that last component—the sauce—that not only lends an explosion of flavor, but a bomb of salt. It is traditionally made with tamarind paste (the sour), palm sugar (the sweet), chili powder (the spice), and fish sauce (the savory), which is basically made from salted fish that is allowed to ferment for a very long time.

To get around the fish sauce dilemma, however, I focused less on its salty properties and more on its umami flavor. I think you know where I'm going with this. I simply mixed my umami broth with the rest of the traditional ingredients and let it simmer and reduce. And if you want to really accentuate the fishy flavor in the original sauce, you can always add a few clams or fish bones to the pot when making your umami broth. Or you can simply rely on the fish that is in the dish to bring out the briny essence.

But before you do anything, take a breath. This recipe takes time. Not just because you have to make the umami broth and then the pad Thai sauce before you even get to your wok, but also because pad Thai is best made in batches. If you throw everything in at once, the noodles will get gummy and the wok will lose its heat. If you have everything set up around you and prepped, though, the cooking process will go smoothly and your room full of guests will be wildly entertained as you fry up their dinner to order. Just like on the streets of Bangkok.

**Serves 4 to 6**
**Effort Level: Got Time to Spare**

- 2 cups Umami Broth (page 140)
- 6 garlic cloves, minced (about 2 teaspoons)
- 1 cup packed dark brown sugar
- 1½ tablespoon granulated white sugar
- 2 tablespoons molasses
- 1 tablespoon unseasoned rice vinegar
- 2 teaspoons tamarind paste (or 1 teaspoon pomegranate molasses)
- Sesame oil, for frying
- ¼ pound ground pork
- ⅛ teaspoon paprika

+ In a small pot, add the umami broth, garlic, brown and white sugars, molasses, and rice vinegar. Mix the tamarind paste with 1 cup of water and add it to the pot. Bring the whole thing to a boil and then immediately reduce the heat to a gentle simmer. Cover the pot and cook for 30 minutes, stirring every so often.
+ As the sauce cooks, prep the other ingredients. In a large skillet or wok, heat 1 teaspoon of sesame oil over medium-high heat. Add the ground pork and cook, stirring, for 2 to 3 minutes. Add the paprika and pepper and continue to stir until the pork is no longer pink, is broken up into little bits, and nicely browned, another 2 to 3 minutes. Turn off the heat, transfer the pork to a bowl, and set aside. Using the same pan, heat another teaspoon of sesame oil over medium-high heat. Add the fish and cook until the meat turns opaque, 3 to 5 minutes. Turn off the heat, add the fish to the bowl with the pork, and set aside. Wipe out the pan or wok with a cloth or paper towel.
+ Check on the pad Thai sauce to make sure it is not reducing too much. If it is, lower the heat or turn it off all together and keep the pot covered. You want at least 1 cup of sauce to make your noodles. This is not a thick sauce—it's silky, not sticky—so don't be alarmed if it is on the runny side.
+ Fill another medium pot with water and bring to a boil. Add the noodles and cook

for 4 to 5 minutes (or a few minutes less than the directions on the package)—ideally pad Thai noodles will still be slightly firm. When ready, drain them in a colander and rinse with cold water. Using kitchen shears or a knife, cut the noodle clumps in half and set aside.

+ Make sure all of your pad Thai accoutrements are ready to go. Have the cooked pork and fish, noodles, bean sprouts, carrot, cabbage, jalapeño, peanuts, cilantro, eggs, and noodles prepped and in bowls near your stove, because we're about to move quickly. Remember, it is best to make the pad Thai one serving at a time. But, of course, if the portions look large or you have extra mouths to feed, you can always split servings in half. Either way, repeat the steps below for each batch (a total of 4) and divvy up ingredients accordingly.
+ In the same large skillet or wok you used before, heat 1 to 2 teaspoons of sesame oil over medium-high heat. Add a few spoonfuls of cooked pork, a few spoonfuls of fish, and a few tablespoons of the pad Thai sauce. Mix until everything is coated. Then, push the meat to the side of the wok and crack 1 egg into the center. Let it set for a few seconds and then, using a wooden spoon or spatula, break it up and toss it with the rest of the ingredients. Add the bean sprouts, carrot, cabbage, and jalapeño, and mix them together, cooking and stirring for another 2 minutes. Taste a bit of the pad Thai and add more sauce if it needs extra kick. Then add a fistful of noodles and stir for a final 2 minutes.
+ Turn off the heat and serve the pad Thai to the first guests. Offer peanuts, cilantro, a lime wedge, and hot sauce for garnish. And before making another round, wipe the skillet or wok clean with a cloth or paper towel. Keep going, you're doing great, and make sure to save a serving for yourself.

⅛ teaspoon freshly ground black pepper
2 filets of rockfish or tilapia (about 1 pound), cut into bite-sized cubes (about 1-inch)
4 large eggs
½ of an 8-ounce package no-salt-added rice noodles (use your judgment to decide how many noodles you want to eat)
1 cup bean sprouts
1 medium carrot, cut into thin matchsticks (about 1 cup if you buy preshredded)
1 cup thinly sliced Savoy or Napa cabbage
1 jalapeño pepper, finely diced
1 cup unsalted peanuts, for garnish
½ cup chopped fresh cilantro, for garnish
1 lime, cut into wedges
Sodium-free hot sauce, for serving

### + sodium count:

Tamarind Paste: 20mg per ounce; Ground pork: 63mg per ¼ pound; Rockfish: 63mg per 3 ounces; Tilapia: 44mg per 3 ounces; Eggs: 71mg per large egg; Carrot: 42mg per medium carrot; Savoy cabbage: 20mg per cup shredded; Cabbage (general variety): 13mg per cup shredded

# CAST-IRON HERB PIZZA CRUST

While writing this book, I happened to be perusing some blogs (i.e., procrastinating) and I caught an ingenious recipe for cast-iron skillet deep-dish pizza. Lightbulb! Ovens on.

But let's back up a bit. A popular deep-dish pizza chain had just opened up across the street, and while I have made plenty of salt-free pizza dough before, I had never even considered trying the Chicago style 'za. The skillet idea is not only superfun (your guests will be impressed), but it also allows you to bring the deep dish (deeply salty) to your low-sodium table.

You can layer this basic dough with anything you want: veggies, low-sodium ricotta cheese, sun-dried tomatoes, you name it. I decided to go with my personal favorite toppings of red sauce, zucchini, mushrooms, and homemade sausage. And while I didn't use any cheese, I did want there to be a hint of Parmesan. So I used nutritional yeast in the dough, which is a yellow-colored powder made from deactivated yeast. It has a cheesy, savory taste, and it is popular with vegans as a parmesan substitute so I'm not talking crazy talk here. It tastes great on popcorn too and you can find it in bulk food aisles and natural food stores. Just make sure it is salt- and MSG-free.

**Makes one 12-inch cast-iron pie**
**(or two 6-inch skillets)**
**Effort Level: Got Time to Spare**

Crust

- 1 cup warm water
- 1 (1¼-ounce) package dry yeast
- 1 tablespoon granulated white sugar
- 1 tablespoon nutritional yeast
- 1 teaspoon garlic powder
- 1 teaspoon dried basil
- 1 teaspoon freshly ground black pepper
- 2½ cups bread flour (plus extra if dough looks too wet)
- 1 teaspoon olive oil
- Cornmeal, for the skillet

Toppings

- 1 to 2 teaspoons olive oil
- ½ pound white button mushrooms, sliced
- ½ red onion, diced
- 1 medium zucchini, sliced into thin rounds
- Chunky Red Tomato Sauce (page 108)
- Cooked Homemade Chorizo, cooked (page 67; see note)

+ In a stand mixer fitted with the dough hook attachment, combine the water, dry yeast, and sugar. Stir and let it rest for 5 minutes. The mixture will become foamy; this means that the yeast is alive and ready.
+ Add the nutritional yeast, garlic powder, basil, and pepper to the bowl and mix on medium speed until combined. Add 1 cup of the flour and mix at medium speed until combined. Then add the remaining flour, ¼ cup at a time, until the dough comes together in a ball, about 5 minutes. You may need to use your hands to knead the dough on a clean surface a couple of times to incorporate all of the flour and crumbs. Then take the bowl off the stand mixer and use your hands to spread the teaspoon of olive oil all over the dough. Cover the bowl with plastic wrap or a clean kitchen towel and allow it to rise for 1 hour. This is a great time to make your Smoky Red Tomato Sauce and Chorizo Sausage if it wasn't previously prepared. Otherwise, do a few sun salutations while you wait.
+ Once it has doubled in size, turn the dough out of the bowl and knead it by hand a few times. Place it back into the bowl and cover again with the plastic wrap or towel. Allow it to rise for 1 more hour.

+ If you plan on using vegetables that tend to leach out liquid when they cook—like the mushrooms, onions, and zucchini suggested here—it is best to cook them in a skillet first. And this is the perfect time to do that. Heat 1 teaspoon of olive oil in a skillet over medium-high heat. Add the mushrooms and cook, stirring, until they have softened and browned, about 5 minutes. Transfer them to a paper towel–lined plate to drain. Repeat to cook the red onions and the zucchini. Now they won't sog up your pizza.
+ When the dough is ready, preheat the oven to 425°F.
+ With a rolling pin, roll out the dough on a lightly floured surface until it is ½ inch larger than your cast-iron skillet and about ¼ inch thick. If you are using two smaller skillets, separate the dough into two even balls and roll out as described.
+ Rub olive oil over the skillet and sprinkle some cornmeal on the bottom. This will keep the dough from sticking to the pan and will give the crust some crunch. Place the dough in the skillet, pressing it flat against the bottom and sides. You will most likely have dough hanging over the side, so fold this extra bit under itself, pressing it down against the edge of the pan.
+ To get the skillet and dough hot, put it on the stove top over medium-low heat and cook until the crust starts to get crispy, about 5 minutes. Remove the skillet from the heat and fill it with layers of sauce, vegetables, more sauce, and cooked chorizo. Place the skillet into the oven and bake for 20 minutes.
+ When the toppings are bubbling and the crust is golden brown, remove the skillet from the oven and let the pizza cool for 5 minutes before cutting and serving. Carefully lift the pizza out of the skillet, slice, and serve.

### + sodium count:

Zucchini: 16mg per medium zucchini; Tomatoes: 6mg per medium tomato; Canned tomato puree: 15mg per ½ cup depending on brand; Carrots: 42mg per medium carrot; Portabella Mushroom: 8mg per 1 cup diced; Pork: 63mg for 4 ounces

## + note

Pizza dough can be rolled out more if you prefer thin-crust pizza. I won't judge. And for a Wolfgang-Puck-esque twist, use ingredients from the Chicken Wraps with Plum Sauce recipe (page 212) for your spread and toppings.

# CHAPTER 8

It was a game-changing moment when I realized I could eat fish. I had cut it from my diet because I determined it was not low-sodium friendly. It came from the sea, which equaled saltwater. Which meant it was high in sodium, right?

After flipping through the *Pocket Guide to Low Sodium Foods*, however, I discovered that not only was fish safe for me to eat, but it was actually low in natural sodium. With this knowledge in hand, the types of foods I cooked at home quickly expanded. I was frying halibut fillets in browned butter, roasting whole trout on the grill, stewing flaky chunks of cod in a curry-flavored broth, and filling tacos with lime-poached snapper. And most surprisingly, with seafood on my side, my dining options increased as well. Fish is one of the easiest things to order off a menu as it is rarely preseasoned and is often cooked to order. Just be aware of descriptors like cured, smoked, and breaded, which mean that fish may meet some sodium before it hits your plate.

Of course, not all seafaring friends are equal and there are some that you may need to avoid depending on your restrictions. I personally skip crab (251mg for 3 ounces), lobsters (150 to 360mg for 3 ounces), mussels (243mg for 3 ounces), scallops (333mg for 3 ounces), and some oysters (Eastern farmed are 151mg for 3 ounces). But dishes that use these ingredients don't need to get the axe. I've found ways of using other fish to mimic the feel and taste of saltier seafood. Just wait until you see the solutions that are in store!

And while following the recipes, only use a few types of fish—remember that there are many more to choose from, each with its own unique flavor and texture. Play with monkfish (15mg for 3 ounces), branzino or sea bass (58mg for 3 ounces), catfish (37mg for 3 ounces), and sardines or herring (around 70mg per 3 ounces). Or more exotic types like skate, mahimahi, or ono, which you might find on restaurant menus. With so many choices, you'll never fall into a protein rut. So it's time to dive into these recipes. The water's fine and surprisingly low-sodium.

## + note

To find the current list of sustainable fish, check out Monterey Bay Aquarium's Seafood Watch program online. And for more information on types of fish, nutritional information, and cooking methods, use Internet resources (like the Whole Foods website) or ask your local butcher or seafood monger for advice.

# SNAPPY ASIAN BAKED FISH

It is true that the easiest way to lower your sodium is to cut the prepared, packaged items from your diet. But it is false that home-cooked meal, have to be costly and time-consuming. Or that they can't come in a package.

Perhaps you have heard of the French cooking technique *en papillote*. If not, it sounds fancy, but simply means "in parchment," and that's exactly how you make it. The protein to be cooked is package in parchment paper (or foil), with a little oil (or water, wine, or stock), surrounded by vegetables, and then heated over a grill or in the oven. And since you can serve it directly in the package it makes for an impressive presentation. And even easier cleanup.

**Makes 4 hot pockets**

1 medium zucchini, cut into thin matchsticks or grated
2 cups or 2 big handfuls wild mushrooms (like shimeji, maitake, enoki, oyster)
4 garlic cloves, diced
1 (½-inch) piece fresh ginger, peeled and roughly chopped
1 (8-ounce) can water chestnuts, drained and diced
2 green onions, white and green parts separated, thinly sliced
½ teaspoon freshly ground black pepper
1 teaspoon garlic powder
1½ pounds snapper or halibut fillets, skin and bones removed, cut into 4 pieces
Sesame oil
Sodium-free mirin or sake
1 red bell pepper, stemmed and seeded and diced
Lemon or small orange cut into 4 equal wedges

+ Preheat the oven to 400°F.
+ Lay out 4 pieces of 10 by 12-inch pieces of aluminum foil. Fold each in half and then reopen.
+ Divide the zucchini, mushrooms, garlic, ginger, water chestnuts, and the white parts of the green onions into 4 equal-size portions, keeping the ingredients separate. Then, in a small bowl, mix the pepper and garlic powder. Now you are prepped for some hot pocket action.
+ Place a single portion of the zucchini and mushrooms in the middle of each piece of foil. Place 1 fish fillet on top and sprinkle it all with ½ teaspoon of the pepper and garlic powder mix. Place a single portion of the garlic, ginger, water chestnuts, and white parts of the green onion on each of the fish. Drizzle each fillet with 1 teaspoon of the sesame oil and ½ to 1 teaspoon of the mirin or sake.
+ Fold the foil over the fish and crimp the sides of the foil tightly together to make a package. Repeat the procedure for the other 3 pieces of fish.
+ Place the foil packets on a baking sheet and put into the oven. Cook for 20 to 25 minutes. The foil will puff up as the fish steams.
+ Remove the package from the oven and allow them to rest for 3 to 5 minutes. To serve, carefully open the foil packages—carefully as the steam is very hot—and slide the contents onto a plate. Sprinkle each plate with the remaining sliced green onion tops and the diced bell pepper. Serve with a single citrus wedge per guest.

### + sodium count:

Zucchini: 6mg per medium zucchini; Snapper: 54mg per 3 ounces; Halibut: 58mg per 3 ounces; Water chestnuts: 5 to 25mg per serving depending on brand

## + note

Experiment with other vegetables and flavors. But if you are using foil for your packages, steer clear of tomatoes and vinegar as the acid can create an upleasant, tinny taste.

# BAKED + BREADED FISH STICKS

Until I made these, I had not eaten fish sticks since I was six. And those came from a box, totaling around 120mg of sodium per stick. But when I was making dinner for my cousin and her adorable little boy, the memories of flaky fish meat covered in a crusty coating came back to me, and I had to give this childhood favorite a mature, low-sodium makeover.

To make a salt-free, kid-friendly, parent-pleasing version, I tossed out the frozen fish, the deep fryer, and the seasoned breadcrumbs. I opted for fresh catfish (or snapper), the oven, and a spicy cornmeal coating. I also added celery seed to the mix, an uncommon ingredient but one that lends a unique savory taste. Remember that celery has some natural sodium in it.

The result is a clean, crisp fish stick with a sneaky spice that slowly creeps up on your palate. Pair them with a cool yogurt dill sauce to balance the heat.

**Makes 20 to 24 fish sticks**

- 2 large eggs
- 1 cup yellow cornmeal
- ½ cup all-purpose flour
- 1 tablespoon paprika
- 1 tablespoon garlic powder
- 1 tablespoon onion powder
- 2 teaspoons freshly ground black pepper, plus more as needed
- 2 teaspoons celery seed
- 2 teaspoons dried thyme
- 2 teaspoons ground turmeric
- 2 teaspoons chili powder
- 1½ pounds catfish or snapper fillets
- Nonstick oil spray or 3 tablespoons olive oil
- 1 (6-ounce) container plain soy or low-sodium plain Greek yogurt
- 2 tablespoons chopped fresh dill
- Lemon slices (optional)

+ Preheat the oven to 450°F and cover a baking sheet with parchment paper.
+ Put the eggs in a medium bowl and beat well. In a second bowl, mix the next 10 ingredients (cornmeal to chili powder). Set aside.
+ Cut each filet in half horizontally and slice into 1-inch fish sticks.
+ Sprinkle additional black pepper over the fish pieces to season them and then, with one hand, take a couple of pieces of fish and dredge them in the egg. Shake off any extra egg and drop the fish in the cornmeal mixture. Using your other, clean hand, cover and toss the fish pieces in the cornmeal. Shake to remove excess cornmeal and set them on the parchment paper–lined baking sheet. Repeat this process, using one hand for the egg drench and the other for the cornmeal coating, until all the fish sticks have been breaded.
+ Spray the fish sticks with a quick mist of nonstick oil spray or olive oil (you don't want them to get soggy, just slightly wet so they brown) and place them into the oven. Cook until crispy, 12 to 15 minutes, then flip the fish sticks with a spatula. If they look dry, give them another misting of oil spray and cook 12 to 15 minutes more to brown the opposite sides.
+ When the fish is in its final minutes of cooking, mix the yogurt and dill in a small bowl.
+ Remove the fish sticks from the oven and serve immediately with the dill sauce.

## + sodium count:

Egg: 71mg per large egg; Catfish: 37mg per 3 ounces; Snapper: 54mg per 3 ounces; Plain soy yogurt: 15mg per 6-ounce container depending on brand; Plain Greek yogurt: 60mg per 6-ounce depending on brand

# LOBSTER-LESS CORN CHOWDER

There isn't much that can top the succulent, buttery-sweet taste of the ocean's prized gem, the lobster. But it turns out that there exists not just one, but three low-sodium lobster substitutes that can stand in for the original: halibut (58mg of sodium per 3 ounces), monkfish (15mg of sodium per 3 ounces), and crayfish (53mg of sodium per 3 ounces).

For this particular recipe, I decided to use halibut and I coarsely chopped it into chunks to look like pieces of lobster meat. Because it is a firm fish, the halibut held up well in the thick broth and stayed meaty even when I reheated it a day later. The corn lends its milky sweetness to the dish, helping further mimic the natural nectar of the lobster. And the potato thickens the soup and adds extra texture, guaranteeing you something to chew on with each bite.

**Serves 4**

- 4 ears fresh corn, shucked
- 6 cups water
- 1 leek
- 3 tablespoons unsalted butter
- ¼ cup all-purpose flour
- 1 Yukon Gold potato, peeled and cut into ½- to 1-inch chunks
- ¼ cup half-and-half (or plain soy yogurt or unsweetened coconut milk)
- 1 to 2 teaspoons ground white pepper
- ¾ pound halibut fillet, cut into 1½-inch chunks (or monkfish or crayfish)
- 2 tablespoons roughly chopped fresh flat-leaf parsley or chopped fresh dill
- Red chili pepper flakes

+ Remove the corn from the cob by standing each ear up in a bowl and using a knife to scrape off the kernels.
+ Put the corncobs and water in a large stock pot with a lid over medium-high heat. Bring to a boil and then lower the heat so that the water bubbles gently. Cover and cook for 30 minutes. This is your broth.
+ While the broth is simmering, let's work with that leek. To properly wash the leek, cut the roots off the leek and then cut the leek in half lengthwise. Run each half under cold running water and separating the layers with your fingers, to ensure no grit ends up in your food. Once cleaned, set both leek halves on their flat sides, next to each other, and cut the white and green parts into thin half circles. Set aside.
+ Melt the butter in a second large stockpot over medium-high heat. Add the leeks and cook, stirring, until softened, about 5 minutes. Lower the heat to medium and whisk in the flour until it is completely incorporated, 2 to 3 minutes. Add 3 cups of the corncob broth and increase the heat to medium-high. Continue whisking until the mixture is smooth and starts to thicken, 2 to 3 minutes. Add the potato cubes to the pot, lower the heat to a gentle simmer, and cover. Be sure to check the soup occasionally and stir so that the potatoes don't stick to the bottom of the pot.
+ In a blender, puree half of the corn kernels with one cup of the corncob broth until smooth. Then add the puree and the remaining corn kernels to the pot, increase the heat, and bring the soup to a boil. Cook for 5 minutes with roaring bubbles and then lower the heat back down to a gentle simmer. Continue to cook, covered, for 15 minutes more.
+ Just before serving, add the half-and-half (or yogurt or coconut milk), white pepper, and halibut pieces. Remove the lid and cook until the soup has reduced by a third, 15 to 20 minutes.
+ To serve, pour the soup into large soup bowls or mugs and sprinkle with parsley (or dill) and chili pepper flakes for a splash of color.

### + sodium count:

Leek: 18mg per leek; Potatoes: 13mg per medium potato; Half-and-half: 15mg per 2 tablespoons; Halibut: 58mg per 3 ounces

# MANHATTAN CLAM CHOWDER

Almost two years ago, I discovered canned baby clams in my local supermarket that only had 70mg of sodium for the whole can. That's when the wheels began to turn and the idea of low-sodium clam chowder attached itself to my mind, like a barnacle to the bottom of a boat.

But almost 770 days passed until I actually attempted the dish. And it wasn't until good friends taught me how to make salt-free sourdough that I was really motivated to try. I figured if I, the hapless baker, could make a fresh loaf of sourdough, then I had to master clam chowder as well. The dish is very easy to put together and, even without the bread, it is a perfect meal for a cold day or night. If you have the time, roast the tomatoes first. The smoky flavor adds a lot of depth to the soup.

**Serves 4 to 6**

- 1 teaspoon olive oil
- 1 fennel bulb, core and outer layer removed, diced
- 2 garlic cloves, diced
- 2 cups cherry tomatoes
- 2 large Yukon gold potatoes, peeled and cut into ½-inch cubes
- 1⅓ cups white wine
- 2 cups water
- Juice from 1 orange
- 1 small can low-sodium baby clams (or 20 fresh clams steamed open and meat removed)
- ⅛ teaspoon freshly ground black pepper
- ⅛ teaspoon paprika
- 2 tablespoons chopped fresh flat-leaf parsley
- ¼ cup crème fraîche

+ In a medium pot, warm the olive oil over medium heat. Add the fennel and garlic and cook, stirring, until softened, 3 to 5 minutes. Add the tomatoes and the potatoes, and cook, stirring occasionally, until the potatoes begin to get soft as well, 15 minutes more.
+ Raise the heat to medium-high and add the white wine, orange juice, and water. Bring to a boil, then lower to a gentle simmer. Cover with a lid and cook for another 15 minutes.
+ When the potatoes have completely softened, scoop half of the soup from the pot (veggies included!) and pour into the jar of a blender. Wait a bit for the liquid to cool and then puree the ingredients until smooth. Return the mixture to the pot and warm over medium heat.
+ As the soup continues cooking, separate the canned clams from the clam juice in two separate bowls. Or if you are using fresh clams, this is the perfect time to dig the meat out of the shell. Place half of the clam meat on a cutting board and give it a rough chop. Then add the chopped clams, the remaining whole clams, and a quarter to half of the reserved clam juice (or 1 cup of hot water) to the pot. Stir in the pepper, paprika, and half of the parsley and cook the chowder on low, letting it reduce a bit, for a final 20 minutes.
+ Just before serving, stir in the remaining parsley and the crème fraîche. Ladle hefty portions into soup or chowder bowls and top with dollops of more crème fraîche, if desired.

### + sodium count:

Fennel: 45mg chopped, 122mg per bulb; Cherry tomatoes: 7mg per 1 cup; Potatoes: 13mg per medium potato; Canned baby clams: 70mg per can depending on brand; Crème fraîche: 10mg per 2 tablespoons

# PISTACHIO + BROCCOLI PESTO–CRUSTED SALMON

This dish is simple yet special. It is totally guest-worthy and the elegant layers of pink salmon and green pesto take only minutes to make. Top layer of pistachio crumbs adds a pleasing crunch.

To heighten the flavor, I swapped basil pesto for one made with broccoli. I think it adds a woodsier taste and is more interesting. Have you ever made broccoli pesto? I hadn't. Of course, you can always stick to the traditional basil or try any other green for your pesto base, like chard, kale, tarragon, or even arugula. They all work and they all offer a slightly different pesto flavor. And if you don't like salmon, you can also make this recipe with another firm fish or even chicken breasts, in which case you would cook it for 25 minutes at the same temperature.

Oh, and did I mention it is simple? This is crazy simple to make. Serve on top of cooked noodles, like fettuccine or spaghetti, or your grain of choice, or just on its own. Ready, set, go eat.

**Serves 4**

- 1½ cups unsalted pistachios, shelled
- 1 garlic clove
- ⅔ cup broccoli florets, stems trimmed
- 1 cup fresh basil leaves
- ¼ cup olive oil
- 2 tablespoons pine nuts
- 4 salmon fillets, pinbones removed

+ Preheat the oven to 375°F.
+ Place the pistachios in a food processor and pulse until chopped. Pour into a bowl and set aside.
+ Add the garlic, broccoli, basil, olive oil, pine nuts, and 1 teaspoon of water to the food processor and pulse until you make a thick, chunky puree. This is your pesto. Believe it or not, the hard work is now done and the fun can begin.
+ Line a baking sheet with parchment paper and line up the salmon fillets in a single row, skin side down. With a spatula or knife, spread the pesto sauce over the top of each piece of salmon and then press a good helping of the chopped pistachios on top with your hands.
+ Place the baking sheet in the oven and bake the fish for 10 to 12 minutes. Perfectly cooked salmon will turn a light coral-pink color.
+ Remove the sheet from the oven and serve the pesto-crusted salmon over pasta or your grain of choice, if desired.

**+ sodium count:**

Broccoli: 30mg per 1 cup; Salmon: 40mg per 3 ounces (farmed Coho), 65mg per 3 ounces (pink)

# CIOPPINO

San Francisco is famous for a few things: foggy summers, twisty streets, cable cars, and cioppino, or fisherman's stew. The dish is traditionally made from the "catch of the day," which typically includes a meaty mix of crab, shrimp, scallops, mussels, and flaky fish. Combine those elements with a wine sauce, tomatoes, herbs, and some crusty bread and you've got a warm soup that will fight off even that stubborn sea mist.

To keep the seafood flavors and lose the salt, I removed the crab, shrimp, scallops, and mussels from the recipe and piled it high with clams, halibut, and cod instead. I also replaced the typical white wine with some sake, a liquor with a slightly edgier taste. And to add extra texture, I roasted some fresh corn, using the kernels as garnish and the cob to add a milky flavor to the stew.

Before you get cooking, just a quick note about clams: If you buy them fresh, make sure to clean them thoroughly to remove the dirt and grit on the shell. This can be done by putting the clams in a strainer and scrubbing them with a brush or sponge. Also, sometimes you can get a bad clam in the bunch that is full of sand. So if you want to be extra careful, cook the clams in a separate pot with ½ cup water and ½ cup sake. When the clams have opened, add them to the soup at the very end of the cooking process.

**Serves 4 as a main; 6 as a side**

- 3 tomatoes, cored
- 4 tomatillos, outer husks removed
- 1 poblano pepper, stemmed seeded
- 2 red bell peppers, stemmed seeded
- 1 ear of corn, shucked
- 2 teaspoons olive oil
- 1½ cups cleaned and sliced leeks, everything but the bulb
- 2 garlic cloves, minced
- ½ cup no-salt-added tomato paste
- ½ cup dry, filtered sake
- 2½ cups water
- ½ cup chopped fresh flat-leaf parsley
- ½ pound halibut, skin and bones removed, cut into bite-sized chunks
- ½ pound cod, skin and bones removed, cut into bite-sized chunks
- 20 littleneck clams, scrubbed

+ Turn the oven broiler to high.
+ Place the tomatoes, tomatillos, poblano pepper, bell peppers, and corn on a baking sheet and put them into the oven on the middle rack. Roast until the corn kernels begin to brown and the skins on the tomatoes, tomatillos, and peppers bubble and turn black, about 5 minutes. With tongs, turn the vegetables a quarter turn and roast them for another 5 minutes. Repeat until every side of the tomatoes, tomatillos, and peppers has been roasted and charred and the corn is soft and slightly browned. Remove the vegetables from the oven. Transfer the peppers to a paper bag, close the top, and let them steam for 15 minutes. Set the tomatoes, tomatillos, corn, and their roasting juices aside.
+ When cool to the touch, rub the blackened skin off of the peppers. Dice the tomatoes, tomatillos, and peppers into small, ½- to 1-inch chunks and set aside. Remove the kernels from the corn by standing it on one end and cutting downward with a sharp knife. Continue to rotate the cob and cut until all the kernels are removed. Set the kernels aside and save the cob for the soup.
+ In a large stockpot or 5-quart Dutch oven, warm the olive oil over medium high heat. Add the leeks and garlic and cook, stirring, until softened, 2 to 3 minutes. Add the tomatoes, tomatillos, the peppers, and their juices. Cook for 10 minutes more. Add the tomato paste, sake, and water. Bring the soup to a boil and cook for another 10 minutes. Add ¼ cup of the parsley as well as the corncob, and

lower the heat to a gentle simmer. Cover the pot and cook for 40 minutes. If it seems like the cioppino is evaporates too quickly, add a bit more water to the pot. Although this is technically a stew, you definitely want to develop a rich broth.

+ Right before serving, add the fish and clams to the pot. Raise the heat to medium and cover with the lid. Cook until the clams have all opened, about 15 minutes.
+ Remove the corncob from the pot and ladle the cioppino into bowls. Sprinkle each with the remaining ½ cup parsley and the roasted corn kernels. Enjoy.

### + sodium count:

Leek: 18mg per leek; Tomato paste: 10mg per 2 tablespoons; Halibut: 58mg per 3 ounces; Cod: 46mg per 3 ounces; Clams: 95 to 511mg per 3 ounces depending on treatment

## + note

Recently, the USDA National Nutrient Database for Standard Reference updated the sodium information for clams. While they once weighed in at a mere 48mg per 3 ounces, they are now listed as a whopping 511mg per 3 ounces. Yikes. Thankfully, Dr. Jacob Wexler came to the rescue again to explain that, indeed, clams (like shrimp and other shellfish and finfish) may be stored in sodium-rich solutions before they hit the market. Which means more moisture retention as well as sodium absorption by the fish flesh.

So here's the deal: if you can find non-treated clams or go digging for your own (what an adventure!), feel free to use the shelled guys in this recipe. They should land somewhere between 90 and 300mg per 3 ounces according to the latest data for raw clams.

But if you don't have the afternoon to go clam digging, then use frozen clams or canned clams—with a nutrition label—to guarantee your shellfish is as low in sodium as possible. Or if you can handle the extra sodium, go ahead and swap back in some frozen, low-sodium shrimp.

San Francisco is famous for a few things: foggy summers, twisty streets, cable cars, and cioppino, or fisherman's stew.

# ZUCCHINI-WRAPPED HALIBUT "SCALLOPS"

Between the bacon (around 200mg of sodium per slice) and the scallops (over 330mg per 3 ounces), the classic dish is too salty for me to enjoy. But when the bacon is replaced with smoky zucchini ribbons and the scallops are swapped out for halibut rounds, you have a whimsical reinterpretation that actually tastes equally thrilling.

I used smoked paprika and cumin to mimic the smoky flavor of bacon and I decided to glaze the halibut rounds in honey and sugar to mimic the natural sweetness of scallops. The curry is purely for color and to balance the sweetness of the fish, and the spinach pasta lends a rich backdrop for the yellow-tinted "scallops."

**Serves 4**

Zucchini Rub

- 1 teaspoon smoked paprika
- 1 teaspoon ground cumin

Scallop Rub

- 2 teaspoons curry powder
- ½ teaspoon ground white pepper
- ½ teaspoon onion powder

Glaze

- 1 tablespoon honey
- 1 teaspoon water
- 1 teaspoon dark brown sugar

The Main Meat

- 1 large zucchini
- 1 pound halibut, fillets cut into 1-inch cubes (see note page 204)
- Toothpicks

+ To prep, mix the ingredients for the two rubs and the glaze in 3 separate bowls. Then, using a vegetable peeler, start peeling along the length of the zucchini, beginning with the green outer layer, creating ½-inch-thick ribbons. Rotate the zucchini a quarter-turn after each peel in order to make somewhat even-sized ribbons. Make as many as possible and stop when you get to the seeds. Lay the ribbons out on a plate and sprinkle the zucchini rub on both sides, spreading gently it with your hands until all of the pieces are covered. It doesn't have to be an even coating, but you want every ribbon to have some color and spice.
+ Bring a large pot of water to a boil.
+ Dip the halibut chunks into the scallop rub, making sure they are coated on all sides. Tightly wrap a zucchini ribbon around a halibut cube like a belt, so that the ends overlap. Use a toothpick to secure the zucchini and push it through to the other side. Place the wrapped halibut on a plate and repeat the procedure with the remaining fish and zucchini ribbons.
+ Now it's time to start on your sauce. Add the spinach to the boiling pot of water and cook for 1 minute. Immediately remove the spinach from the water with a slotted spoon, reserving the cooking liquid, and transfer the spinach to a colander to drain. Rinse with cold water and when cool to the touch, use your hands to tightly squeeze the spinach and wring out the liquid. Do this 4 to 5 times until no water remains. Finely chop the spinach into little green bits and set aside.

+ In a saucepan, melt the butter over medium heat. Add the shallot and cook for 2 minutes. Then add the flour and whisk until combined, 2 to 3 minutes. Add the cream and whisk until the sauce begins to thicken, about 5 minutes. Add the wine and the chopped spinach and continue to cook for 5 more minutes. The sauce will look thick, like creamed spinach. Reduce the heat to the lowest setting to keep the sauce warm.

+ Reheat the water you used to cook the spinach, and bring to a boil. Make sure you have your halibut rounds, the glaze, a plate, a large sheet of foil, and your serving bowl ready to go, because you are about to be moving around your kitchen quickly.

+ Add the pasta to the boiling water and cook for 10 minutes or according to the instructions on the package. While the pasta is cooking, heat 1 teaspoon of vegetable oil over medium heat in a large skillet (nonstick if possible). When the oil starts to hiss and sizzle, place the halibut pieces in the pan in a single layer and cook for 2 minutes. Evenly spread the glaze on the top of the fish and then flip the halibut rounds, cooking the other side for 2 minutes more. Spread more glaze on the top side again, flip, and cook for a final 1 to 2 minutes. The halibut will have a crisp, brown sear on both sides. Put the cooked fish on a clean plate and cover it with foil to keep warm. If you had to split the fish into two batches, repeat until all the halibut rounds are cooked.

+ Finally, drain the pasta and put it into a large bowl with a drizzle of olive oil so the noodles don't stick together. Add the warm spinach sauce to the pasta and toss.

+ To serve, make a nest of the sauced noodles on a plate and top with 4 or 5 "scallops" per guest. Remove the toothpicks and dig in.

Noodles and Sauce

1 pound spinach (I use the whole thing, stems and leaves, because I'm lazy)
2 tablespoons unsalted butter
1 shallot, finely diced
2 teaspoons all-purpose flour
½ cup heavy cream
¼ cup dry white wine
1 pound dry fettuccine
Vegetable oil
Olive oil, for drizzling

### + sodium count:

Zucchini: 26mg per large zucchini; Halibut: 58mg per 3 ounces; Spinach: 24mg per 1 cup; Heavy cream: 5mg per 1 tablespoon; Noodles: 0 to 10mg, per 4 ounces dry depending on brand

## + note

If you really want to fool your guests, it is easy to make your halibut cubes look more like scallops. Using a tablespoon as your stencil, press down slightly on the halibut and then trace around it with a sharp knife. If you cut your cubes small enough, you can just press them into the tablespoon to form a ball shape without having to cut the fish. But if you do have leftover fish scraps, don't throw them away. Cook them in a skillet with leftover rice, peas, and other vegetables to make a quick fried rice dinner the next night.

## + note

If you don't have time to make the noodles and sauce, here's an easy swap. Use your zucchini to make noodles instead of fake bacon. Skip the spinach sauce and the zucchini wrap, and simply serve the scallops over a healthy bed of zucchini pasta noodles.

# FAUX MISO-MARINATED COD

One of my proudest achievements as a low-sodium cook is my recipe for Faux Miso-Marinated Cod. If you haven't experienced the real thing, a two-day miso, sake, and mirin bath gives this already fatty fish a sweet, silky taste that melts in your mouth. It is an utterly decadent dish and incredibly easy to cook.

The problem? Miso paste contains over 700mg of sodium per tablespoon. But I wasn't going to let that stop me from enjoying it. I was determined to find a way to mimic the taste of the miso without the salt. So I created an America's Test Kitchen of my very own.

On one side of the counter there was a 3-ounce cut of cod that I soaked in the original salt-filled mixture. And in the other corner, I prepared a second 3-ounce cut that waded in a bath of sake, sugar, and mirin. The miso-free piece of fish looked quite pale in comparison and I anxiously surveyed the gaggle of sauces I had to see if there was anything that could add color to my bland protein. And then, a moment of olfactory déjà vu. I caught a whiff of the miso paste and it had a familiar aroma. Sweet and musky, I knew I recognized it, but from what? I gazed back at my collection of sauces and there it was. Molasses. Dark, syrupy, and bittersweet. It was the perfect substitute.

Serve on top of rice with greens, mushrooms, or anything earthy to compliment the umami flavors of the cod.

**Serves 4**
**Effort Level: Plan Ahead**

¼ cup dry, filtered sake
6 tablespoons mirin (or more sake)
¾ cup molasses
½ cup dark brown sugar
1¼ pounds boneless cod or sablefish fillet
Cooked rice; for serving

+ Begin this recipe a day (or two) before you plan on serving the meal because the fish needs a long soak to sponge up all the flavors.
+ To make the marinade, put the sake, mirin, molasses, and brown sugar in a double boiler (or in a pot or bowl set over a larger pot with water in it). Whisk the mixture until it is well combined. Over medium heat, bring the water in the lower pot to a strong simmer. Cook the mixture, stirring occasionally and adjusting the heat to keep it at a simmer until the sugar completely melts and the mixture is glossy and smooth, about 20 minutes. Remove from the heat and cool.
+ Place the whole fillet in a shallow dish or large baking pan, large enough that the fish can lie flat. Pour the cooled marinade over the fish, cover with plastic wrap, and refrigerate for 24 to 48 hours, turning the fillet twice so that each side gets an even coating.
+ When you're ready to cook, preheat the oven to 400°F.
+ Remove the fish from the marinade and lay it flat on a greased baking sheet. Bake the fish in the oven for 10 minutes. Then turn the oven off, turn the broiler to high, and caramelize the top of the fish, about 3 minutes. You'll know the fish is done when it flakes easily with a tug of a fork and the tops are browned.
+ Seriously. That's the whole recipe. Amazing, right? Now cut the fillet into four evenly-sized servings, pour yourself a bevy, and admire your work. Serve the cod with rice and steamed bok choy or a mixture of exotic mushrooms.

**+ sodium count:**
Molasses: 10mg per 1 tablespoon; Cod: 46mg per 3 ounces; Sablefish: 48mg per 3 ounces

# Poultry

CHAPTER 9

Over the past year, I have really gotten to know my birds. I've become accustomed to buying whole fryer chickens—which is much cheaper and more sustainable than purchasing the packaged bits and pieces—and I've learned to butcher them (no feather plucking, yet) and use every last bit, from the limbs to the giblets to the bones for my meals and for developing flavors. I've discovered that every inch of every type of fowl has a unique taste unto itself, and that by using the whole bird I can make the most of my pennies and my time. I can earn major bragging points with friends, too.

But a quick word about our feathered friends: Poultry ranges in sodium content depending on the type of meat (light or dark), part of the bird (leg, wing, liver, or breast), and most importantly, how it is treated before it gets to your butcher or supermarket. Beware of plumping! A lot of meat producers fill their turkeys and chickens with water or brine solutions that contain salt to keep the meat moist. Check packaging carefully, talk to your butcher, and look for meat that is free of salt-water solutions. Often, if a label reads "air chilled," it is a good indicator that it has not been plumped.

*I can make the most of my pennies and my time.*

# JOOK, CHINESE BREAKFAST (OR ANYTIME) PORRIDGE

Let's talk about chicken noodle soup. It is exactly what you want to eat when you are down and out with the sniffles. The rich broth, silky noodles, steam, and slurpiness are all magical ingredients that, even if only for a moment, clear your fogged head and drippy nose.

All this is not impossible to re-create without sodium. But here's the issue: the whole point of chicken noodle soup is that it is easy to make. Just open a can of the packaged stuff and heat. On a low-sodium diet, though, you'd have to labor over a homemade broth and this doesn't sound too appealing if you're fighting off a fever.

So when it comes to a comforting, easy dish for those under-the-weather or cold weather days, make this jook instead. Also called Chinese breakfast porridge, it only requires throwing a few ingredients into a pot and letting them boil. All while you sit on the couch and recuperate. This comfort food has rich chicken flavor, hearty rice, and lots of steam and slurping, hitting all the high notes of the original chicken noodle soup without the salt.

**Serves 4 to 6**

- 12 cups (3 quarts) water
- 1 chicken backbone or any other leftover chicken bones you have, no meat or skin
- 2 skinless, bone-in chicken legs
- 2 skinless, bone-in chicken thighs
- 6 fresh shiitake mushrooms, stemmed sliced
- 1¼ cups white jasmine rice
- 6 garlic cloves
- 3 teaspoons sesame oil, plus extra for garnish
- ½ cup shimeji or oyster mushrooms (or more shiitake if you can't find the other kinds)
- (1-inch) piece fresh ginger, peeled
- 2 green onions, thinly sliced (everything but the bulb)
- Unsalted peanuts, diced water chestnuts, and salt-free chili oil, for garnish
- Poached or fried egg, for garnish (optional)

+ Place the water, chicken bones, chicken legs, chicken thighs, and shiitake mushrooms in a large pot. Cover and bring to a boil over medium-high heat. Cook for 5 minutes and then lower the heat so the liquid simmers gently. Add the rice and cook, covered, for 40 minutes.
+ Meanwhile, prep the garnishes—if you have the energy for it! First, cut the garlic lengthwise to make thin, almond-shaped slices. In a small pan, warm 1 teaspoon of the sesame oil over high heat and when it starts to hiss and sizzle, add the garlic. Reduce the heat down to medium and cook the garlic until it turns golden brown and crispy, 2 to 3 minutes per side. Transfer the garlic to a paper towels to drain excess oil.
+ In the same pan, heat another teaspoon of the sesame oil. Add the shimeji or oyster mushrooms and cook, undisturbed, over medium-high heat until they turn golden brown, about 5 minutes. Flip them to the opposite sides and cook for 5 minutes more. Remove the mushrooms and set them aside with the garlic. Cut the ginger lengthwise into thin matchsticks, then cut them all in half. Heat the remaining 1 teaspoon of sesame in the pan and add the

ginger sticks. Cook until they are toasted and turn a light brown color, about 5 minutes. Set them aside with the other garnishes.

+ When rice is done, take the cover off the pot. At this point, your chicken meat will be falling off the bone. Using tongs, carefully transfer the chicken bones to another bowl and pick off what's left of the meat. Discard the bones and leave the meat in the pot. Continue to cook for a final 15 minutes.
+ Your jook is ready when it looks like a thick porridge. I tend to like mine when the rice has soaked up the majority of the juices (like oatmeal when it is cooked), but others (cue: husband) love it with a broth-like consistency. So play with how much you cook out or leave in the liquid.
+ To serve, ladle the jook into bowls and let diners top their porridge with the crispy garlic, browned mushrooms, toasted ginger, green onions, peanuts, diced water chestnuts, chili oil, and a poached or fried egg, if desired. And then try and tell me this is not better than chicken soup. It's pretty difficult when your mouth is full.

### + sodium count:

Chicken leg (with skin): 95mg per ¼ pound; Chicken thigh (with skin): 87mg per ¼ pound; Water chestnuts: 5 to 25mg per serving depending on brand; Eggs: 71mg per large egg

## + note

To really cut back on sodium, replace the chicken with more sliced shiitake mushrooms, dried or fresh. Their natural umami will provide a savory broth without the salt.

# MAMA'S ENCHILADAS CASSEROLE

Last year, I received the following letter from one of my blog readers:

> Dear Sodium Girl,
> I'm on a low-sodium diet to prevent complications from migraines. I've been on it for over a year now and have found a whole new world of food and flavor that I ignored back when I could just grab a burger at the closest drive-through. What I miss the most, though, is my Mom's famous enchiladas. I'm half Mexican and we would make these at least once a week. Now it's been over a year since I've had them. But here's the catch: not only am I not allowed high salt, I can't eat dairy or onions either. Thankfully I can still have green onions.
> I've seen your skill with recipes. Can you help me out? Or am I stuck never eating Mom's delicious enchiladas again?

Of course, I had to come to her rescue and show her that, yes, she could enjoy her mama's enchiladas again. They were just going to be a little different. And to take on the enchilada challenge, I started by examining the original ingredient list of the reader's recipe:

1 large can of red enchilada sauce
2 small cans chicken or turkey gravy
Crushed red chili pepper flakes
1 large onion, white or yellow (chopped)
1 large block cheddar cheese (shredded)
2 packages small corn tortillas

Other than the onion, red chili pepper flakes, and tortillas, everything else contained a high amount of sodium and needed to be replaced. Taking creative liberties, I decided to skip the cheese, the gravy, and the red sauce. But I kept to traditional Mexican flavors and I set my sights on creating a recipe that required as little effort and cleanup as possible, so that my dear reader could have her enchiladas not only once a week, but every night of the week, if she wished.

Normally, I would have reached for crème fraîche or ricotta to mimic the cheese, but because of the reader's dairy sensitivity, I needed to think of another way to provide a milky texture to the dish. The answer was corn. I pureed 2 cups of corn kernels with a medium avocado and this thick, silky spread replicated that melted cheese texture while also providing an unexpected sweet flavor. As for the sauce, I made a salsa verde from tomatillos, a poblano pepper, a serrano pepper, and some cilantro, that, with an immersion blender in hand, only took minutes to whip up.

For the meat filling, I wanted to be extra certain that my chicken was infused with flavors, but I also wanted to cook it quickly. So I poached the thighs in a pot full of Tecate beer and the juice of a lime. In thirty minutes, my chicken was drunk and tender enough to be shredded.

Finally, because salt-free corn tortillas tend to fall apart easily, I chose to layer the ingredients like a Mexican lasagna rather than roll them individually. Again, I was taking liberties with the classic preparation, but I think the alteration works well, and you still achieve the crispy hug of tortillas wrapped around the ingredients. If you want to roll each tortilla, though, just heat them in a microwave or hot pan first to make them more pliable.

Fifteen minutes in the oven and Mama's Enchiladas were done. Crunchy, creamy, and spicy, the meal was familiar and flavorful. And according to the reader, "they are FANTASTIC! And seriously cured a little piece of homesickness."

For extra color, serve with Roasted Pepper and Tomato Salsa, diced tomato, or green onions sprinkled on top.

---

**Serves 4**

- 4 tomatillos, husks removed, washed
- 1 poblano pepper, stemmed and seeded
- 1 serrano pepper, stemmed and seeded
- 1 (12-ounce) can pale ale
- Juice of 1 lime
- 4 cups water
- 5 boneless, skinless chicken thighs
- 1 tablespoon olive oil
- 6 garlic cloves, roughly chopped
- 1 cup roughly chopped fresh cilantro
- Kernels from 2 ears of corn or 2 cups frozen corn kernels
- 1 ripe avocado
- 1 package corn tortillas
- Roasted Pepper and Tomato Salsa (page 99) or 2 cups diced tomato
- 2 green onions, thinly sliced (everything but the bulb)

+ Preheat the oven to 400°F and prep your vegetables by cutting the tomatillos, poblano pepper, and serrano pepper into large cubes. No need to be exact. They are going to be pureed.
+ In a medium pot, bring the beer, lime juice, and 2 cups of the water to a boil. Add the chicken thighs and cook for 5 minutes at a strong bubble. Reduce the heat to medium and allow the chicken to simmer for another 20 minutes. Set your timer! When it is done, take the poached chicken off the stove and out of the pot. The chicken should be white all the way through and tender enough to shred into pieces with two forks. Set aside.
+ In a separate pot, heat the olive oil over medium heat and cook the garlic until slightly browned and soft, 2 to 3 minutes. Add the tomatillos and 1½ cups of the water. Bring to a boil and cook until the tomatillos have softened, about 10 minutes. Add both peppers and the cilantro, and cook on low heat until softened, stirring occasionally, 10 minutes.
+ Transfer the ingredients to a blender. Puree until the combo has the texture of a salsa and set aside in another pot or bowl. This is your salsa verde.
+ To the same blender, add the corn kernels, avocado, and remaining ½ cup water. Puree until the ingredients are well combined and the mixture has a hummus-like consistency. This is your avocado spread.
+ Now for the fun part: in an 8 by 8-inch oven-proof dish, begin to layer the ingredients. Start by drizzling a little bit of the salsa verde on the bottom of the dish and spread it into an even layer with the back of a spoon. Cover the sauce with a single layer of tortillas, tearing them in half to cover the bottom. About 2½ tortillas should do the trick. Next, cover the tortillas with half of the shredded chicken, half the avocado spread, and about ¾ cups of the salsa verde. Repeat with a second layer of tortillas, avocado spread, and the remaining salsa verde. Bake in the oven for 15 minutes.
+ The enchiladas will not brown in the oven, but if you want to give the top layer crunch, broil for 2 to 3 minutes at the very end.
+ Remove the casserole from the oven and scoop big portions onto plates. Top with Roasted Pepper and Tomato Salsa or fresh tomatoes and a sprinkle of sliced green onions. Enjoy.

### + sodium count:

Chicken thigh (with skin): 87mg per ¼ pound; Fresh corn: 11mg per ½ cup; Frozen corn: 0mg depending on brand; Avocado: 14mg per avocado; Corn tortillas: 0 to 15mg per tortilla depending on brand

# CHICKEN WRAPS WITH PLUM SAUCE

Plum sauce was one of my first low-sodium cooking coups. The kind you buy in the store often has 140mg of sodium per tablespoon. But I thought, maybe, if I mixed plum jam with ginger and unseasoned rice vinegar, I could make a passable substitute. Somehow, it worked. And if you cannot find plum jam, you can use any dark berry jam in its place.

The whole meal is very simple to put together and the deep purple sauce against the orange carrot sticks and bright green lettuce cups is pleasing to the eye as well as to the palate. This is a great family-style dish that cooks up quickly and will wow your guests too. Leftovers are great cold the next day for lunch; just reheat the sauce.

**Serves 4**

- 6 garlic cloves, smashed in a garlic press
- 2½ tablespoons (2 to 2½-inch piece) peeled and diced fresh ginger
- 3 teaspoons sesame oil
- 1 cup plum or dark berry jam
- ¼ cup packed dark brown sugar
- 3 tablespoons unseasoned rice vinegar
- 2 green onions, white and green parts separated, thinly sliced
- 1½ pounds ground chicken meat (I like using half thigh, half breast meat)
- ½ teaspoon dry mustard powder
- ¼ teaspoon ground white pepper
- ⅛ teaspoon ground cloves
- Red chili pepper flakes
- 1 (8-ounce) can water chestnuts, drained and diced
- 1 carrot, cut into thin matchsticks
- 2 heads butter lettuce, washed

+ In a small saucepan over medium heat, add three-quarters of the smashed garlic, 1½ tablespoons of the ginger, and 1 teaspoon of the sesame oil and cook, stirring, for 2 to 3 minutes. Add the jam, brown sugar, and rice vinegar. Whisk until smooth and then cook, covered, over very low heat for 20 minutes. Remove the lid and continue cooking, reducing the liquid, for 10 minutes. Then cover the saucepan and reduce the heat to very low, to keep the sauce warm while you prepare the rest of the ingredients.
+ In a wok or large skillet, heat the remaining 2 teaspoons sesame oil over medium-high heat. Add the remaining ginger and garlic, and the white parts of the green onions. Cook, stirring, until the ginger takes on a golden brown hue, about 5 minutes. Then add the chicken and cook, using your spoon to break the meat apart, until it turns white, about 10 minutes. Add the mustard powder, white pepper, cloves, and chili flakes to taste and cook for 5 minutes. Add the water chestnuts, carrots, and the sliced green tops of the green onion, and stir a few times to combine. Remove from the heat and toss with a third of the sauce.
+ Serve the chicken warm or cold, scooping it into the leaves of the butter lettuce and topping with extra dollops of the plum sauce. After that, it's a wrap.

### + sodium count:

Ground chicken: 67mg per 4 ounces; Water chestnuts: 5 to 25mg per serving depending on brand; Carrot: 42mg per medium carrot; Lettuce: 9mg per 4 ounces

# CHICKEN CACCIATORE

Cacciatore means "hunter" in Italian and the dish of the same name is made by slowly braising chicken (English for "lots of flavor, little work") in a hunter-style sauce of tomatoes, onions, mushrooms, herbs, and wine—all the things you'd find while out shooting game, I'd imagine.

The cacciatore that my mother lovingly remembers from her childhood, however, wasn't made from freshly foraged vegetables and meat. It was made with canned tomatoes, canned cream of mushroom soup, salt, and other ingredients that are not low-sodium friendly. But creating a salt-free version was not out of the question; nor did it require archery lessons.

To make the dish, I went back to the basics and focused on the technique (see: slow braising) rather than using bottled spices and soup to develop flavor. I let the chicken, the hunter sauce, and the herbs do the hard work, releasing their own juices while I attended to other things. And the result was a pot of bright vegetables, fall-off-the-bone chicken, and a flavorful sauce. Serve the cacciatore on its own or over a bed of soft polenta, risotto, or pasta noodles.

**Serves 4 to 6**

- 1 whole fryer chicken, cut into 8 pieces with skin on, bone-in (save back and neck bones to make broth)
- ½ cup all-purpose flour
- 2 tablespoons plus 1 teaspoon vegetable oil
- 1 yellow onion, halved and sliced
- 3 garlic cloves, diced
- 3 red bell peppers, stemmed, seeded and sliced lengthwise into 1-inch-thick strips
- Leaves from 10 to 12 sprigs fresh thyme or 1 teaspoon dried thyme
- 1 teaspoon freshly ground black pepper
- 1 teaspoon ground turmeric
- Red chili pepper flakes
- 1 cup white wine
- 1 cup no-salt-added tomato puree
- 1 tablespoon red wine vinegar
- 4 plump tomatoes, chopped into big chunks
- ¼ cup chopped fresh basil leaves

+ Preheat the oven to 350°F.
+ Place the chicken pieces and flour in a large mixing bowl. With your hands, mix so all the chicken pieces are evenly coated in the flour. Set aside and wash your hands.
+ Put 1 tablespoon of the vegetable oil in a 7-quart Dutch oven and heat over medium-high heat. When the oil is spitting hot, tap any excess flour from the chicken pieces and place them in the pot in a single layer, about four at a time. You want to hear those skins crackling. Cook until both sides have turned golden brown and crispy, about 5 minutes per side. Transfer them to a plate and then add another tablespoon of the vegetable oil, the second batch of chicken, and repeat.
+ When the chicken is cooked, lower the heat to medium and add an extra teaspoon of vegetable oil to the pan if it is dry. Scrape all the browned chicken bits into the oil. This is flavor! Add the onion and garlic to the pot and cook, stirring, until softened, 3 to 5 minutes. Add the bell peppers, thyme, black pepper, turmeric, and red chili pepper flakes to taste. Stir and sizzle, 3 to 5 minutes. Deglaze the pot with the wine, scraping up the brown bits again. Then add the tomato puree, vinegar, and chopped tomatoes. Raise the heat until the liquid bubbles gently. Return the chicken pieces to the pan and adjust them

so that they are a little more than three-quarters of the way submerged in the sauce. Place the pot, covered, into the oven and cook for 40 minutes. Then kick up the heat to 375°F, move the lid slightly to the side so that some of the steam can escape, and cook for 15 minutes more.

+ To serve, you can simply scoop some chicken and sauce onto a plate or over a soft bed of polenta, risotto, or pasta. Or, for a really special presentation, transfer the chicken to a clean plate. With a slotted spoon, transfer the stewed tomatoes, onion, and pepper bits to another clean bowl. Place the pot back on the stove and bring the remaining liquid to a boil. Cook until it reaches your desired thickness. Then layer the stewed veggies, with a chicken piece or two on top, and a drizzle of the cacciatore gravy over it to finish. Tear the basil into small pieces and sprinkle them over the dish for some color and fresh flavor.

**+ sodium count:**

Chicken leg (with skin): 95mg per ¼ pound; Chicken breast (with skin): 71mg per ¼ pound; Chicken thigh (with skin): 87mg per ¼ pound; Chicken wing (with skin): 82mg per ¼ pound; Canned tomato puree: 15mg per ½ cup, depending on brand

*But creating a salt-free version was not out of the question; nor did it require archery lessons.*

# PUMPKIN TURKEY PASTA

You can't have a cookbook without a good pasta and meat sauce recipe. Everyone adores the smack of chunky sauce and noodles, and I can't deny you that. But I didn't want to simply make beef and red sauce. It's been done. I wanted to use another meat, namely turkey, and I wanted to create a unique sauce that had tomatoes but wasn't red.

So I brainstormed. What goes with turkey: Cranberries? Mashed potatoes? Pumpkin? Yes, pumpkin! And pumpkin also goes well with tomato. It's orange and dances that thin line between savory and sweet. It is the perfect sauce combination. And it's lip-smacking delicious.

**Serves 4 to 6**

- 3 teaspoons olive oil
- 5 garlic cloves, diced
- ¼ white onion, diced
- 1 (15-ounce) can pureed pumpkin
- 3 fresh tomatoes, seeds removed and chopped
- 1 cup no-salt-added tomato puree
- 2 teaspoons no-salt-added tomato paste
- ½ teaspoon ground cinnamon
- ½ teaspoon ground white pepper
- ¼ teaspoon red chili pepper flakes
- 1 pound ground turkey thigh meat
- 3 tablespoons roughly chopped fresh sage (or basil or thyme)
- ½ pound pappardelle pasta

+ In a medium pot or saucepan, warm 1 teaspoon of the olive oil over medium heat. Add the garlic and onion and cook, stirring, until softened, 2 to 3 minutes. Add the next 7 ingredients (pumpkin to chili pepper flakes) and cook, stirring occasionally, for 10 minutes.
+ While the sauce is developing, add the remaining 2 teaspoons olive oil to a skillet and warm over medium-high heat. Add the turkey meat to the skillet and cook, stirring, until the meat has turned from pink to brown, 8 to 10 minutes. Remove the skillet from the heat, add the meat to the sauce, and reserve the turkey fat in the skillet. Cover the sauce and cook for 15 to 20 minutes more.
+ Meanwhile, cover a plate with a paper towel and place it next to the stove. Reheat the skillet with the leftover turkey fat over high heat. When the skillet is sizzling hot, add the sage and fry for 5 minutes. When it is crispy, transfer it to the paper towel to drain and cool.
+ Just before the turkey pumpkin sauce is done, fill a large pot with water and bring to a boil. Add the pasta noodles and cook until they are done to your liking, 5 to 8 minutes or according to the package directions. Drain the pasta in a colander and rinse with cold water.
+ To serve, put the noodles into individual serving bowls and top with a healthy portion of the sauce. Sprinkle the fried sage on top of each and enjoy.

**+ sodium count:**

Canned tomato puree: 15mg per ½ cup or lower depending on brand; Tomato paste: 10mg per 2 tablespoons depending on brand; Turkey meat, ground: 78mg per ¼ pound; Noodles: 0 to 10mg per 4 ounces depending on brand

You can't have a cookbook without a good pasta and meat sauce recipe.

# CREAMY CHICKEN CURRY

This curry is a far cry from the lovingly labored-over recipes of true Indian cooks. But in following lessons from authentic curry makers, I learned that the key to flavor is in taking the time to toast the spices. The aromas in the mustard seed, cardamom pods, black peppercorns, fresh garlic cloves, fresh ginger, and the cinnamon stick all blossom with a little bit of heat.

**Serves 4 to 6**

- 2 cups jasmine or other kind of rice
- 1 tablespoon vegetable or sesame oil
- 1 medium white onion, peeled and cut lengthwise into ¼-inch thick slices
- 5 garlic cloves, diced
- 2 tablespoons peeled and diced fresh ginger
- 5 cardamom pods
- 1 cinnamon stick
- ¼ teaspoon whole black peppercorn
- ⅛ teaspoon whole yellow mustard seed
- 3 large tomatoes, diced
- 1½ pounds skinless, bone-in chicken legs, thighs, and breast
- 2 tablespoons curry powder, or more as needed
- 1 cup water
- 1 (6-ounce) carton plain soy or coconut yogurt
- 2 tablespoons minced fresh cilantro leaves, for garnish
- Red chili pepper flakes

+ Cook the rice according to the package directions or according to the instructions for your rice cooker.
+ Heat the oil in a large saucepan over medium-high heat. Add the onion, garlic, and ginger and cook, stirring occasionally, until the onion begins to soften, about 5 minutes.
+ Meanwhile, crack the cardamom pods by placing the flat side of a knife over a pod and then smashing down with your hand, releasing the little black seeds. (Note: You can use both pod and seeds in the dish for flavor as long as you don't mind eating around the pod, which I do all the time. Otherwise, just use the small seeds that have now been freed.)
+ When the pods are cracked, push the onion, garlic, and ginger mixture to the side of the saucepan, creating a well in the middle. Add the popped cardamom pods and seeds (or just the seeds), cinnamon stick, peppercorns, and mustard seed. Toast the spices without stirring for 3 to 5 minutes, then add the tomatoes. Cook, stirring, until the tomatoes start to release their juices, another 5 minutes.
+ Push the ingredients to the side again and add the chicken pieces and a little more oil if pan is too dry. Increase the heat to medium-high and cook the chicken until the skin browns, 6 to 8 minutes per side. Stir in the curry powder and water. Bring the mixture to a boil and cook for 5 minutes. Reduce the heat to medium, cover the pan, and cook for 25 minutes.
+ Just before serving, turn the heat to low and wait a few minutes for the broth to cool. Then add the yogurt, and stir and cook for a final 3 minutes.
+ Remove the cinnamon stick, scoop some rice into each bowl, and ladle the chicken curry over each. Garnish with the cilantro and chili pepper flakes to taste. Serve and savor.

### + sodium count:

Tomato: 9mg per large tomato; Chicken leg (with skin): 95mg per ¼ lb; Chicken breast (with skin): 71mg per ¼ lb; Chicken thigh (with skin): 87mg per ¼ lb; Plain soy yogurt: 15mg per 6-ounce container depending on brand; Plain coconut yogurt: 10mg per 6-ounce container depending on brand

# Meat

When I first began dining out, steak saved me. Unless it had been braised, seasoned, or marinated, a prime cut was usually a safe low-sodium choice. It allowed me to eat out with others. And once my taste buds adjusted to my diet, I also began to really appreciate the natural flavors in meat—often sending plates back to the kitchen as I couldn't believe no other spices, or salt, were used.

Back at home I began to experiment with other meat options, playing with the flavors of pork (the white and more delicate choice), lamb (earthier in taste), and buffalo (gamy and awesome). I found that adding even little bits of meat to a recipe added robust flavor and various levels of savory notes, making it a perfect substitute for salt. It also turns out that the less common the meat, the lower the sodium, most likely because (for now) they are less processed and not enhanced with brine or other salty solutions. Rabbit has only 42mg per 3 ounces; deer (venison) prances in at 42mg per 3 ounces; buffalo or bison has 56mg per 3 ounces; and elk stands at 48mg per 3 ounces. The same is true for poultry, like duck (63mg per 3 ounces) and goose (73mg per 3 ounces).

Now, you may not eat beef, pork, lamb, or game by any other name for a host of reasons. But don't pass on this chapter. Simply adjust these recipes according to your individual needs. Use the same flavor combinations to spice up meat-free meals and trade the cow, pig, or lamb for fowl, fish, tofu, or more veggies. This book is all about finding freedom in your diet and taking inspiration from unexpected resources, so use this chapter to help flex those creative muscles.

*This book is all about finding freedom in your diet.*

# BEEF TAQUITOS

Here's where the story begins: I'm eight, I'm hungry, and all I want to eat is a small taco filled with spicy meat, crispy shreds of lettuce, cheese, and sour cream. Fast-forward twenty years and not much has changed. Except that I'm taller. By a little bit. Now that I live in San Francisco, my love for tacos and taquitos has only increased. I am surrounded by even more authentic Mexican spots and I really cannot walk half a mile without being blanketed by the spicy smells of chorizo, roasting peppers, or carne asada. And like most quick take-out food, salt is as innate to this cuisine as chili powder and masa.

But there's no need to deny your cravings. If you want taquitos, then grab some ground beef, smoky spices, and corn tortillas (which have less sodium than the flour kind), and get to work. Of course, this recipe has a few personal alterations from traditional versions. To avoid unnecessary messes, I skipped the whole frying process and baked them instead—the result being equally crispy and a smidge healthier. And to imitate the texture of cheese, I added shreds of cooked zucchini and avocado cream, giving each bite something stringy and smooth.

Although these taquitos are larger than the traditional version, these low-sodium tacos have bite, they have spice, they have moments of silky sauce. And most importantly, they take just as much time to make as it would take to walk to your favorite taqueria.

**Makes 8 to 10 taquitos**

- 2 teaspoons vegetable, grapeseed, or avocado oil
- 1 pound ground beef
- 2 teaspoons dried oregano
- ½ red onion, diced
- 1 teaspoon freshly ground black pepper
- ¼ teaspoon chili powder
- 2 medium zucchini, cut into thin matchsticks or grated
- 1½ avocados
- 1 tablespoon diced jalapeño (approximately ½ jalapeño pepper)
- 3 tablespoons crème fraîche
- 12 small corn tortillas (good to have extras in case some break)

+ In a medium skillet, warm the oil over medium heat. Add the ground beef and brown, stirring occasionally, for 3 to 5 minutes. Add the oregano, onion, pepper, and chili powder and cook, mixing with the meat, for an additional 10 to 12 minutes. Transfer the meat to a bowl.
+ In the same pan, which now has all those lovely meat juices, add the zucchini. Cook over medium-high heat, stirring occasionally, for 5 to 8 minutes. The zucchini is ready when it has browned a bit and is very soft. Turn off the heat and set aside.
+ In another small bowl, mash the avocado flesh and with a fork. Add the jalapeño and crème fraîche, and stir to combined into a smooth spread.
+ Now it is taquito-making time, so preheat the oven to 375°F.
+ Heat another clean skillet over medium-high heat. Place one tortilla in the skillet and allow it to soften, 1 to 2 minutes. Remove the tortilla from the skillet and spread with 1 tablespoon of the avocado mixture all over the tortilla. Place a little less than 1 tablespoon of the beef mixture in a line on the very left side of the tortilla. Top with some of the wilted zucchini and begin to fold the tortilla tightly around itself. Place the rolled taquito on a baking sheet with the seam side down. Repeat until all the taquitos filling is used up.
+ Place the taquitos in the oven and bake for 15 to 20 minutes. The tortillas will be golden and crisp when ready. Serve with Roasted Pepper and Tomato Salsa (page 99) and some crème fraîche, if desired.

+ sodium count:

Lean ground beef: 56mg per 3 ounces; Zucchini: 16mg per medium zucchini; Avocado: 14mg per avocado; Crème fraîche: 10mg per 2 tablespoon ; Corn tortillas: 0 to 10mg per tortilla depending on brand

+ sodium count:

Tomato paste: 20mg per 2 tablespoons depending on brand; Molasses: 10mg per 1 tablespoon; Strip steak: 44mg per 3 ounces, 59mg per ¼ pound; Egg whites: 55mg per 1 large egg; Broccoli rabe: 13 mg per 1 cup chopped

# BEEF + BROCCOLI WITH SZECHUAN ORANGE SAUCE

Szechuan peppers are one of the traditional ingredients found in Chinese five-spice powder. They also happen to be the star of the fiery sauce in this classic take-out dish, which can cost you 200mg of sodium per 1 teaspoon. Which is why we're going to make it from scratch.

If you have trouble finding Szechuan peppers, replace them with red chili pepper flakes. They will not have that tongue-tingling, lemony sensation of the Szechuan, but they will still have the kick your palate expects. If you want the real deal, however, check out spice shops, like Penzey's, to buy true Szechuan peppercorns. And remember, once they are on your spice rack, they don't have to be a one-trick pony. Use them with meat rubs, noodles, or even sugar cookies for an extra bite.

**Serves 2 to 4**

- 2 tablespoons plus 1 teaspoon sesame oil
- 4 garlic cloves, minced
- 1 (11-ounce) can mandarin oranges, drained, or 1 cup fresh slices
- 2 tablespoons no-salt-added tomato paste
- 1 teaspoon honey
- 1 teaspoon dark brown sugar
- 2 teaspoons unseasoned rice vinegar
- 1 teaspoon molasses
- ½ teaspoon whole Szechuan peppercorns (or 5 dried chile de árbol or ¼ teaspoon red chili pepper flakes)
- ½ teaspoon ground white pepper
- 3 large egg whites
- ¼ cup cornstarch
- ½ cup all-purpose flour
- ½ pound strip steak or top round, sliced into ½- to 1-inch strips
- 1 bundle broccoli rabe, chopped into ½-inch pieces
- 1 (1½ inch) piece fresh ginger, peeled and thinly sliced

+ Heat 1 teaspoon of the sesame oil in a saucepan or pot over medium heat. Add the garlic and cook, stirring, until browned, 2 to 3 minutes. Add the mandarin oranges, tomato paste, honey, brown sugar, rice vinegar, molasses, Szechuan peppercorns, and white pepper. Bring to a boil, stirring often so the mixture doesn't burn and cook for about 5 minutes. Reduce to the lowest heat setting and simmer until the sauce thickens and reduces by one third, 10 to 15 minutes more.
+ When the sauce becomes viscous, remove it from the heat and set aside.
+ Place the egg whites in a small bowl, and mix together the cornstarch and flour in a second bowl. Using one hand, dip a sirloin piece into the egg whites and then place it into the cornstarch and flour coating. With the other hand, tap off any excess coating from the beef and set it aside on a plate. Repeat until all the beef is coated.
+ In a high-sided skillet or wok, heat the remaining 2 tablespoons sesame oil over medium-high heat. Test a small piece of meat and when the oil spits and sizzles, add the rest of the meat pieces to the pan, being careful not to overcrowd, and cooking in two batches if necessary. Fry the meat for 3 to 5 minutes per side. When ready, it will be crispy and brown. Transfer the meat to a clean plate and let it rest. Repeat until all the meat is cooked.
+ Add the broccoli rabe and sliced ginger to the pan and cook, stirring, for 3 to 5 minutes. Add the meat and the sauce and cook for a final 2 minutes: the broccoli should still be crunchy. Serve warm on top of rice or with noodles. High five. This is a take-out takeover.

# PORK + FENNEL MEAT LOAF

There are a couple of ways to elevate a dish: spend time expertly plating the final components or use unexpected ingredients to surprise your palate. In order to improve and unsalt a standard meat loaf, I went for option two. And like a good magic trick, the addition of unusual components distracts the eater so much that he or she never notices the lack of salt.

In place of celery, I used fennel. Instead of white or red onions, I used the more mild and buttery leek. For a common potato, I subbed in the less common and slightly peppery turnip. And to mix up a typical herb blend, I added fennel seed, which provides interesting crunch as well as a mild hint of licorice flavor. With a heavy slathering of homemade ketchup, all of the ingredients literally melt together in a bread pan until you have a succulent loaf of juicy meat.

**Makes 1 meat loaf; serves 6 to 8**

- 1½ cups Salt-Free Ketchup (page 106)
- 5 slices no-salt-added bread
- 1 teaspoon olive oil
- ½ cup diced leek
- ½ cup diced red bell pepper
- ¾ cup diced turnip
- ½ cup diced portabella mushroom, brown gills and stem removed
- 1 pound ground beef
- ½ pound ground pork
- 2 large eggs, beaten
- 1½ teaspoons fennel seed
- ½ teaspoon dried thyme
- ½ teaspoon dried oregano
- ½ teaspoon freshly ground black pepper
- ½ teaspoon paprika
- Pinch of cayenne pepper

+ Preheat the oven to 350°F and make the Salt-Free Ketchup, if not already prepared.
+ Cut the no-salt-added bread into squares. Place on a cookie sheet and bake in the oven until dark brown and crisp, 10 minutes. Remove the bread squares from the oven, cool and pulse in a food processor until you form fine bread crumbs.
+ In a small pot or saucepan, warm the olive oil over medium heat. Add the leek and cook, stirring, until softened, about 5 minutes. Add the bell pepper, turnip, and mushroom and continue to cook, stirring, until they begin to soften, about 10 minutes more. Add ¾ cup of the ketchup and cook for 5 minutes more. Remove the saucepan from the heat and set aside to cool.
+ Mix the meat with the bread crumbs, eggs, herbs, spices, and the sauce. Use your hands or a spoon to combine the ingredients, and once completely mixed, put into a greased bread pan. Place the loaf in the oven and bake for 1 hour, basting with the remaining ketchup every 20 minutes.
+ After an hour, take it out and use a meat thermometer to check the internal temperature of the meat loaf. It should be 155° to 165°F. If you do not have a meat thermometer, cut a small piece and look to see that the meat is no longer pink. Serve warm and be sure to save leftovers.

### + sodium count:

Canned tomato puree: 15mg per ½ cup depending on brand; No-salt-added bread: 10mg per slice depending on brand; Turnip: 44mg per ½ cup; Portabella mushroom: 8mg per 1 cup diced; Lean ground beef: 56mg per 3 ounces;; Ground pork: 63mg per 4 ounces; Leek: 18mg per leek; Eggs: 71mg per large egg

# WHISKEY ORANGE PULLED PORK

Pork. Orange juice. Whiskey. A few hours in a pot. Magic.

Serve the shredded pork meat over soft polenta or a red cabbage salad. Or make some fresh Murray Circle Butter Rolls (page 56) and stuff them to make pulled pork sandwiches.

**Serves 4**

**Effort Level: Got Time to Spare**

Spice Rub

- 1 tablespoon dark brown sugar
- 2 teaspoons ground cumin
- 2 teaspoons freshly ground black pepper
- 2 teaspoons smoked paprika
- 1½ teaspoons garlic powder
- ¼ teaspoon chili powder
- ¼ teaspoon ground coriander

Pulled Pork

- 3 pounds boneless pork butt (also called shoulder)
- 1 tablespoon vegetable oil
- ¼ white onion, thinly sliced into crescent-shaped strips
- 3 garlic cloves, diced
- Juice of 2 blood oranges (or other oranges)
- 1½ cups no-salt-added tomato puree
- ¼ cup whiskey or (bourbon)
- ¼ cup apple cider vinegar
- 1 tablespoon molasses
- 1 tablespoon honey

+ Preheat the oven to 300°F.
+ In a small bowl mix together the spice rub ingredients. Use your hands to pat it on the pork butt, front and back and both ends, until it is completely coated. Reserve any leftover spice rub.
+ Warm the oil in a 5-quart Dutch oven over medium heat. Add the onion and garlic and cook, stirring, until softened, 2 to 3 minutes. Add the pork butt and let it brown for 3 to 5 minutes per side. Whisk together the remaining ingredients and any leftover rub and add it to the Dutch oven. Scrape any browned bits at the bottom of the pot into the liquid, bring the mixture to a boil, and cook for 10 minutes. Turn off the heat, cover the pot, and put it in the oven. Cook until the meat falls easily from the bone, 2½ to 3 hours, checking the pot every hour to make sure nothing is sticking or burning.
+ Before serving, transfer the meat to a plate or bowl. Cover with aluminum foil to keep warm. Then reheat the Dutch oven and cooking juices on the stove top over a medium-high heat and bring the liquid to a rolling boil. Cook until the liquid is as thick as gravy. While it is reducing, use two forks to pull the delicate pork into shreds.
+ To serve, spoon generous helpings of pork over polenta or a cabbage salad and top with gravy.

### + sodium count:

Pork shoulder: 55mg per 3 ounces, 74mg per ¼ pound; Molasses: 10mg per 1 tablespoon; Canned tomato puree: 15mg per ½ cup, depending on brand

# CHAR SUI SPARE RIBS

I have always been jealous of the impossibly aromatic Chinese char sui meat that my husband buys at the local Asian market. The pink chunks of juicy ribs smell of spice and smoke and always make me drool. But alas, because the red dye comes from fermented tofu and the flavor comes from a generous helping of soy sauce and hoisin, this low-sodium girl and her delicate kidneys have to pass on the original. But that doesn't mean we can't make the dish at home, without the salt.

To lower the high-sodium content but keep the flavor, I swapped a mixture of honey, molasses, and Chinese five-spice for the soy and hoisin. I added a bit of orange juice and chili powder for a sweet-and-sour spice. I reduced the marinade into a thick glaze. And then I baked the ribs until the meat fell right off the bone. Sure, it isn't traditional char sui, but it has all the same mouthwatering, meat-melting taste—and the sticky hands—without any of the salt.

**Serves 2 to 4**

**Effort Level: Plan Ahead**

- ¼ cup packed dark brown sugar
- ¼ cup molasses
- 3 teaspoons honey
- 2 teaspoons Chinese five-spice powder
- ½ teaspoon garlic powder
- 2 tablespoons sherry or red wine vinegar
- 1 cup apple or orange juice
- 2 teaspoons chili powder
- 1½ pounds pork spareribs

+ In a plastic container with a lid, mix the first 8 ingredients (everything but the meat) until well combined. Add the spareribs and using your hands, make sure all of the meat is covered in the marinade. Put on the lid, close tightly, and give it a couple of strong shimmy shakes. Place the container in the refrigerator and marinate for 2 to 24 hours, turning the meat over at the halfway point. The longer it marinates, the stronger the flavor development.
+ Just before cooking, preheat the oven to 325°F. While the temperature is climbing, take the meat from the refrigerator and let it warm to room temperature, 15 to 20 minutes. Place the ribs in an oven-proof pan or baking sheet, and reserve the marinade. Cover the pan with aluminum foil, place the ribs on the middle rack of the oven, and cook for 30 minutes.
+ As the ribs are getting juicy, pour the reserved marinade into a small pot and bring to a boil over medium-high heat. Cook for 10 minutes and then reduce the heat to low so that the liquid is gently simmering. Cook, uncovered, until the liquid thickens and reduces by half, 15 to 20 minutes. Remove the glaze from heat and set aside.
+ Remove the ribs from the oven, take off the foil, and baste the meat with the glaze. Return the ribs to the oven without the foil and cook until the meat is tender enough to fall off the bone, 30 to 40 minutes.
+ Serve warm and be sure to top it off with a drizzle of glaze if there is any left over.

**+ sodium count:**

Molasses: 10mg per 1 tablespoon; Pork spareribs: 69mg per 3 ounces, 92mg per ¼ pound

# HONEY-BAKED PORK CHOP

Honey-baked ham, by definition, is cured in salt, forming that crusty, fatty layer on top and the flaky, brined skin underneath. So making a salt-free version was going to be a tough challenge, and since November of 2010, I have tested multiple versions. Which means not only a lot of work, but also a lot of pork. No complaints there.

The first attempt was a real fail. I covered an entire pork butt (the cut of meat often used for ham) in sugar and molasses. And the giant chunk of meat took so long to cook that by the time I could safely slice into it, the pork was dry, dry, dry. The cut of meat was just too thick. So I changed my game plan and swapped a butt for a chop. But this second attempt was just too boring. It had a tasty sugar coating, but it wasn't crisp or caramelized. And once again, the meat was just too dry. Finally, I switched to an even thinner chop and I used a glaze instead of a sugar rub. I basted, I roasted, I broiled, I smothered that chop with gooey love. And the result? A chop dripping with sweet succulence that looks nothing like ham, but has the sugary crunch you crave.

**Serves 2 to 4**

- 2½ teaspoons dark brown sugar
- 2 teaspoons ground cumin
- ¼ teaspoon dry mustard powder
- ⅛ teaspoon chili powder (if you like spice)
- 4 center-cut, 1-inch-thick pork chops
- 1½ tablespoons molasses
- ½ cup orange juice
- ¼ cup apple cider vinegar
- 1½ tablespoons maple syrup
- 1 tablespoon honey
- 1 tablespoon vegetable oil

+ Preheat the oven to 375°F
+ In a small bowl, mix 2 teaspoons of the brown sugar, the cumin, mustard powder, and chili powder. With your hands, rub this dry rub all over the pork chops, reserving any leftover spices that do not stick to the meat.
+ In a small pot, mix the molasses, orange juice, apple cider vinegar, maple syrup, honey, and any remaining spice rub. Bring the mixture to a boil then lower to a simmer, and slowly reduce the liquid by one-third.
+ In a large, oven-proof skillet, warm the oil over medium-high heat. Add the pork chops in a single layer so that they all touch the bottom of the skillet. Sear them and cook for 2 minutes per side. Remove the skillet from the heat and cover the chops with one-third of the molasses mixture. Place the skillet in the oven and cook for 5 minutes.
+ Carefully remove the skillet from the oven—remember the handle is hot, hot, hot!—and turn the chops, and baste the other side with another one-third of the molasses mixture. Return the pan to the oven and cook the chops for 5 minutes more.
+ Pull out the skillet again, turn the chops, baste with the remaining molasses mixture, and sprinkle with the remaining ½ teaspoon brown sugar. Place the pork on the lowest rack in the oven, put the broiler on low, and broil for 2 to 3 minutes more.
+ Take the pork out of the oven and let the chops rest on a cutting board so they don't lose any of their juices, 2 to 3 minutes. While the chops take a breather, put the now porkless skillet on the stovetop over medium heat and reduce the cooking liquid until the juice reaches your desired thickness, 3 to 5 minutes. This is your gravy.
+ To serve, transfer the pork chops onto plates and drizzle with the reduced meat gravy.

**+ sodium count:**

Pork chops (loin, center rib chop): 48mg per 3 ounces, 64mg per ¼ pound; Molasses: 10mg per 1 tablespoon

# PORK + PEACHES

*Low-sodium guest: Chef Scott Youkilis, Maverick and Hog and Rocks*

Chef Scott Youkilis has played a very large part in the evolution of my low-sodium diet. His restaurant was one of the first places where I received a salt-free meal that was cooked with as much care and flair as all the other plates coming from the kitchen. From the start, Chef Youkilis treated me like every other diner, and he was determined not only to offer me food with color, flavor, and thoughtful presentation, but to provide options as well, varying the meals every time I returned.

This book could not be written without a recipe from him. And, of course, in the Chef Youkilis way, he didn't come up with just one idea, but five, from escabeche to Spanish mackerel to the gorgeous dish you'll find below. He is a master at layering flavors and using whole ingredients, spices, and unexpected combinations to heighten the experience of eating food—with or without salt.

**Serves 4 to 6**

**Effort Level: Plan Ahead**

- 1 tablespoon whole coriander seed
- 1 teaspoon smoked paprika
- Freshly ground black pepper
- 4 to 6 pork shoulder steaks (or loin chops), each ½ to 1 inch thick
- Extra-virgin olive oil
- ¼ cup red wine vinegar
- 2 tablespoons tequila
- 6 yellow peaches, almost ripe (if not in season, use pears)
- 3 large spring onions (or green onions)
- 1 fennel bulb, core and outer layers removed
- 1 jalapeño pepper
- 2 tablespoons dark brown sugar
- ½ cup salt-free chicken stock
- 2 (15-ounce) cans no-salt-added cannellini beans
- ½ cup basil, chopped

+ Toast the coriander seed in a skillet over medium heat for 2 to 3 minutes. Transfer them to a spice grinder or mortar and pestle and grind them. (Note: You can also use 1 teaspoon of ground coriander if you do not have a grinder or mortar and pestle.) Mix with the paprika and pepper. Rub the pork steaks with the spice mix and then pour about 2 tablespoons of olive oil, the red wine vinegar, and the tequila over them. Rub down again and let the steaks marinate, covered, for 4 hours or overnight in the refrigerator.
+ Preheat the oven to 400°F.
+ Split the peaches in half, use a knife to remove the outer skin, and take out the stone. Slice the onion, fennel, and jalapeño into thin strips, reserving the fennel fronds for later. Set aside the sliced vegetables, separate from the peaches.
+ Heat a skillet over medium-high heat. Rub a little oil on the peaches and sear them quickly in the pan, giving them a bit of color, but not necessarily cooking them through. Remove the peaches from the skillet and let them cool. Cut each peach half into 4 pieces and sprinkle with brown sugar. Wipe the skillet out with a damp cloth.
+ Add a few more tablespoons of olive oil to the skillet and add the pork steaks, cooking in two batches, if necessary in order not to crowd the pan. Cook until the steaks have

browned on the bottom, about 5 minutes, and adding more oil if the spices start burning slightly. Flip the steaks and brown the opposite sides, about 5 minutes. Repeat until all the steaks have been done, setting them aside when cooked. Add a few more tablespoons of olive oil to the pan, add the sliced vegetables, and cook, stirring, to caramelize them, 2 to 3 minutes. Remove from the heat and place the vegetables on the bottom of a shallow roasting pan. Pour the chicken stock over the vegetables, place the steaks over the vegetables, place the peaches on top of the pork, and put the whole thing in the oven. Cook until the pork is tender, 10 to 12 minutes.

+ Meanwhile, heat the beans in a small pot or saucepan and season with pepper. Chop the reserved fennel fronds and add them to the beans along with the basil. Cook until warm, about 15 minutes.
+ Transfer the pork out to a large platter, layering the vegetables and peaches over the pork. Serve with a side of the beans. Mix any leftover roasting juices into the beans before serving.

### + sodium count:

Pork loin chop: 59mg per 3 ounces, 78mg per ¼ pound; Fennel: 45mg per 1 cup, 122mg per bulb; No-salt-added cannellini beans: 40mg per ½ cup depending on brand

*Chef Youkilis treated me like every other diner, and he was determined not only to offer me food with color, flavor, and thoughtful presentation, but to provide options as well.*

# AWESOME BUCO

This dish is all about the marrow, which is the buttery, fatty, super-tasty filling stuffed inside the lamb shank bones. It is the real flavor powerhouse in the recipe, and the additional bite of whole herbs and black peppercorns helps round out its richness.

As for the meat itself, this tough cut gets slowly braised in an earthy brew of red wine and vegetables. And for this version, instead of the traditional veal shanks, I opted to use lamb because it is (a) cheaper, (b) has slightly less sodium, and (c) is a more flavorful meat in my opinion. You can serve this over couscous, polenta, noodles, or anything else that will soak up the gravy.

**Serves 4**

- ½ cup all-purpose flour
- 2½ teaspoons freshly ground black pepper
- 1 teaspoon paprika
- 4 large lamb shanks, cut into 1½- to 2-inch-long osso buco–style pieces
- 4 teaspoons vegetable oil
- 2 garlic cloves, diced
- 1 yellow onion, sliced
- 2 medium carrots, roughly chopped
- 1 medium fennel bulb, roughly chopped, core and outer layer discarded
- ½ cup no-salt-added tomato paste
- 2 cups water
- 2 cups hearty red wine
- 5 fresh sage leaves
- 5 sprigs fresh thyme
- 2 bay leaves
- 2 tablespoons whole black peppercorns

+ In a bowl, mix the flour with 1½ teaspoons of pepper and ½ teaspoon of the paprika. Add the lamb shanks and coat them completely with the flour-spice mixture.
+ Heat a 7-quart Dutch oven large pan or a over medium-high heat. Add 2 teaspoons of the vegetable oil.
+ One by one, tap the shanks to remove excess flour and add half of them to the pot so that one side of the exposed bone is touching the pan. It takes a little maneuvering to balance them and you may need to hold them upright with tongs. But this step, although slightly acrobatic, is essential to sealing in the tasty marrow juices. Allow the shanks to brown, 3 to 5 minutes. Then, using the tongs, flip the shanks to the opposite side, putting the exposed bone directly onto the pot again. Brown for 3 to 5 minutes. Finally, lay the shanks on their sides and cook and rotate until the rest of the meat has browned, 6 to 8 minutes more. When done, transfer the shanks to a plate and set aside. Repeat to cook the remaining batch. Great work.
+ Add the remaining 2 teaspoons vegetable oil to the pot and scrape all the brown bits from the lamb shanks into the oil. Lower the heat to medium and add the garlic, onion, carrots, and fennel to the pot. Cook, stirring until softened, about 5 minutes. Add the tomato paste, water, red wine, sage leaves, thyme, bay leaves, and peppercorns. Bring the whole mixture to a boil and reduce for 10 minutes, stirring occasionally.
+ Lower the heat until the liquid simmers gently and return the shanks to the pot. You want them to be covered at least three-quarters of the way in liquid, so add more water if you need to. Cover the pot with a lid and cook until the meat is tender and falling off the bone, about 2 hours. You are now free to do other tasks around the house. Just continue to check in on the osso buco, stirring occasionally, to make sure that nothing sticks or burns on the bottom of the pot and that the liquid has not evaporated too much. While you're stirring, also spoon the roasting liquid over the tops of the shanks. You want to keep that meat moist.

+ When the shanks are done, transfer them to a clean plate or platter and set aside. Strain the juices in the pan through a sieve, separating the liquid from the vegetables and herbs. Discard the solids, and pour the liquid in a small saucepan, bring to a boil. Cook for 5 minutes and then reduce the heat to a low simmer. Cook, uncovered, until the gravy is reduced by two-thirds, about 15 minutes. Note: If you want less fat in the gravy, simply put the liquid in a covered container in the freezer for 15 minutes. When it is cool, the fat will form a hard layer on top and you can use a spoon to scrape it off.
+ Before serving, return the shanks to the pot along with the gravy and warm over low heat. Depending on the preferences of your guests, you can serve the meat on or off the bone, layered over your choice of grain—couscous, polenta, or pasta noodles—and covered with the gravy. Either way, it will look like moist cuts of lamb covered in a dark, luscious sauce. Garnish with leftover slices of fennel and fresh thyme for a bit of color.

## + sodium count:

Lamb shanks: 66mg per ¼ pound; Carrots: 42mg per medium carrot; Fennel: 45mg per 1 cup, 122mg per bulb; Tomato paste: 10mg per 2 tablespoons depending on brand

*This dish is all about the marrow, which is the buttery, fatty, super-tasty flavor powerhouse.*

# LAMBURGERS + CURRY KETCHUP

I love hamburgers, but I hate manning the barbecue. Actually, true confession, I hardly know how to turn one on. I'm sure it's simple, but the whole deal with the gas and the coal and the cleanup afterwards . . . it's just too much for me to handle. So for those nights when no one else offers to man the barbie and I'm craving a succulent bite of summer, I take my meat to the stove.

This recipe for panfried lamburger packs ginger, garlic, and a flurry of fresh herbs directly into the patty. A topping of tomato, curried ketchup, crème fraîche, and caramelized onions finishes off the bite. For a salt-free bun, I use sturdy pieces of cabbage, which hold up well to the moisture from the meat. This curried lamburger is a great dish for one, two, or ten, and can be easily cooked to order any time of the year. Rain or shine.

**Makes 4 to 6 burgers**

- 1 tablespoon plus 1 teaspoon vegetable oil
- 10 garlic cloves, diced
- 2 pounds ground lamb
- 2 tablespoons chopped fresh mint
- 1 tablespoon chopped fresh cilantro
- 1 tablespoon chopped fresh chives
- 1 teaspoon freshly ground black pepper
- 1 teaspoon ground cumin
- 1 teaspoon ground ginger
- ½ cup Salt-Free Ketchup (page 106)
- 1 tablespoon curry powder
- ½ red onion, sliced
- Murray Circle Butter Rolls (page 56), burger buns, or cabbage leaves for serving
- 1 large tomato, sliced
- Crème fraîche

+ In a skillet, warm 1 teaspoon of the vegetable oil over medium-high heat. When the oil is hot, add the garlic and cook, stirring, until it turns golden brown, 3 to 5 minutes. Remove from heat and let it cool, about 5 minutes.
+ Place the ground lamb in a mixing bowl and add the cooked garlic along with the mint, cilantro, chives, black pepper, cumin, and ginger. Using your hands, mix all the ingredients together and form 4 to 6 patties, depending on your serving size.
+ Heat the remaining tablespoon oil in a skillet over medium-high heat. When hot, add your patties. Make sure the pan is big enough so that all the patties are laying flat. Cook for 8 to 10 minutes on each side. If you prefer your meat well done, cook the patties longer.
+ While the burgers get a nice sear, mix the ketchup and curry together in a separate bowl.
+ Once the patties have cooked on both sides, transfer them to a plate to rest. Drain most of the meat juices from the skillet and add the onions to the leftover oil, cooking over medium-high heat until they soften and turn a delicious caramel-brown color, about 5 minutes.
+ To plate, place the patties in toasted buns or cabbage leaves and layer with toppings in the following order: tomato slices, the curried ketchup, crème fraîche, and onions. Dig in and let the curried juices flow!

### + sodium count:

Ground lamb: 67mg per 4 ounces or ¼ pound; Canned tomato puree: 15mg per ½ cup depending on the brand; Tomato: 9mg per large tomato; Crème fraîche: 10mg per 2 tablespoons

# MOROCCAN LAMB STEW

There are three ingredients that I find crucial to creating lip-smacking, seconds-please Moroccan stew: dried fruit (mainly apricots), freshly diced tomatoes, and lamb chops on the bone.

**Serves 4 to 6**

**Effort Level: Got Time to Spare**

- 1 large zucchini
- 1 large carrot, peeled
- 1 red bell pepper, stemmed and seeded
- 2 large tomatoes
- 2½ teaspoons olive oil
- 2 pounds cubed lamb shoulder blade or lamb stew meat with bone in
- 2 garlic cloves, diced
- 1 cup roughly chopped dried apricots
- Zest and juice of 1 orange
- 1 cinnamon stick or ½ teaspoon ground cinnamon
- 1½ teaspoons paprika
- 1 teaspoon ground cumin
- ½ teaspoon freshly ground black pepper
- ¼ teaspoon peeled and grated fresh ginger
- Sprinkle of red chili pepper flakes
- 2 cups water
- 1¼ cups couscous
- 1 (15-ounce) can no-salt-added chickpeas (garbanzo beans), rinsed
- 1 medium head cauliflower, cored and broken into florets
- 2 tablespoons chopped fresh flat-leaf parsley
- 2 tablespoons chopped fresh mint (optional)

+ Prep your zucchini, carrot, bell pepper, and tomatoes by dicing them into ¼-inch cubes. Set aside.
+ Heat 1 teaspoon of the olive oil in a large pot or 5-quart Dutch oven over medium heat. Add the lamb and brown, about 5 minutes per side. Remove the meat and set aside.
+ Add another ½ teaspoon of the olive oil to the pot, scraping the browned bits into the oil. Add the garlic and cook, stirring, over medium heat until softened, 2 to 3 minutes. Add the carrot and brown, without stirring, 2 to 3 minutes. Return the lamb to the pot and add the bell peppers, tomatoes, and dried apricots and cook another 10 minutes. Isn't it starting to smell great?
+ Add the water, orange zest and juice, and spices (cinnamon through chili pepper flakes).Bring to a boil and cook for 5 minutes. Lower to a simmer and cook, covered, until the lamb is tender, 1 to 1½ hours. Add more water and lower heat, if necessary, to keep the stew moist.
+ Meanwhile, in another pot, bring 2 cups water to a boil. Add the remaining 1 teaspoon olive oil and the couscous. Stir, lower heat, cover the pot, and cook, about 5 minutes. When the water is absorbed, remove from the heat and let rest.
+ Now back to the stew. When the lamb is tender, add the zucchini, chickpeas, and cauliflower. Cook until they are just tender, but not mushy, 15 to 20 minutes. Stir in half of the parsley and mint and remove from the heat.
+ It's show time. Remove the lamb bones from the pot. Fill bowls with couscous and ladle a hefty portion of the stew on top. Sprinkle with the remaining parsley and mint, if using, and enjoy.

## + sodium count:

Zucchini: 26mg per large zucchini; Carrots: 50mg per large carrot; Tomatoes: 9mg per large tomato; Lamb shoulder blade: 71mg per ¼ pound; Lamb stew meat (leg and shoulder): 74mg per ¼ pound; No-salt-added chickpeas: 10mg per ½ cup depending on brand; Cauliflower: 16mg per ½ cup, 176mg per medium head

# Sweets

# CHAPTER 11

I'm not a baker.

But Jacques Torres, that guy who makes buildings out of sugar and chocolate, sure is. And a wonderful chef whom you'll meet later in this chapter is a professional as well.

But me? No, I'm not a baker.

I'm an experimenter, an adventurer, a thrower-inner. I am a confident low-sodium cook. And when it comes to the exact science of baking, I take shortcuts, I am messy, and I am always surprised that my cookies turn out looking like piles of melting lava and that my floor is covered in flour and broken measuring cups.

This book forced me to overcome my fear of making desserts and made me dig deeper into the challenges of baking without salt. It also reminded me what it was like to try a recipe with extra scoops of intimidation and anxiety. But I'll tell you what I told myself time and time again as my kitchen and I got splattered in batter and dough: the more you make these recipes, the more comfortable you will be. And soon, these sweet treats will be no big thing.

*I'm an experimenter, an adventurer, a thrower-inner.*

# QUINOA CHOCOLATE TRUFFLES

Lately, I've been craving the crispy pop of that famous crunchy chocolate candy bar filled with puffed rice. And in a search for a low-sodium alternative, I happened upon quinoa chocolate bars. I also happened to have bags of dark chocolate and quinoa at home. And suddenly, one plus one equaled a dessert that was completely guilt-free, dreamy, and as simple to make as a box of premixed brownies. This treat has trace amounts of sodium and is packed with protein and antioxidants. So go ahead, eat a couple of them. They're undoubtedly good for you.

**Makes 8 mini truffles**

½ cup white quinoa
¾ cup water
¾ cup dark chocolate (or semi-sweet) baking chips
Juice of 1 orange

+ Add the quinoa and water to a pot and bring to a boil. Then lower the heat so the water is gently simmering and cover the pot. Cook until the liquid is completely absorbed and the quinoa is a bit dry, 12 to 15 minutes. Remove the pot from the heat, fluff the quinoa with a fork, and set aside to cool.
+ Meanwhile, set up your treat-making station by laying out 10 mini silicone or paper cupcake liners. In a double boiler (or a microwave), melt together the chocolate and orange juice. Stir constantly to make sure that the chocolate doesn't burn.
+ Add the cooled quinoa to the chocolate, stirring so all the quinoa pearls are evenly mixed in. Scoop about 2 tablespoons of the chocolate quinoa into each liner and place them in the freezer for 15 minutes to harden.
+ When ready to eat, pry the treats out of the cups and serve immediately so they melt in your mouth and not on your hands or carpet.

### + sodium count:

Quinoa: 0 to 10mg per 1 cup depending on brand; Dark chocolate: 0 to 10mg per ounce depending on brand

# COCONUT DREAM BARS

This recipe for Dream Bars is from my wonderful grandmother, who I am sure pickpocketed it from someone else. But for the sake of legacy and honor, we will just go ahead and give her full credit.

These brookies (brownie cookies) are good. Really good. They are dense and insanely sweet, and the real surprise comes from the crunchy brown sugar crust (who knew you could make a crust from sugar?) and sweetened, sugar-soaked coconut (who knew coconut could get even tastier?). This is what makes them really addictive. So don't be embarrassed when you find yourself picking at the caramelized pieces of dream bars that stick to the side of the pan. I do it, too, every time I make them.

This dessert is superchewy and it holds up well when given a deep dunk in a glass of coconut milk. To make them, you need only a few bowls, one pan, and 40 minutes of your precious time. So bake up a batch whenever you have a sweet-tooth craving and an hour to spare. And make sure to grab a few for yourself before daring to share with others.

To jazz them up, pair the bars with fresh strawberries or raspberries, or even a drizzle of melted dark chocolate on the top, because who says no to melted chocolate? These are sweet dreams come true.

**Makes 12 to 16 bars**

- ½ cup unsweetened shredded coconut
- 1 cup sugar water (1 cup water plus 1 cup granulated white sugar)
- 1 cup plus 2 tablespoons all-purpose flour
- 8 tablespoons (1 stick) unsalted butter, cut into small chunks and softened at room temperature
- 1½ cups packed dark brown sugar
- 2 large eggs, beaten
- 2 teaspoons vanilla extract
- ½ teaspoons sodium-free baking powder
- Powdered sugar

+ Preheat the oven to 350°F.
+ Place the coconut into a small bowl, and in a small saucepan, bring the sugar water to a simmer over a medium-low heat. When it begins bubbling, pour the sugar water over the coconut and let it soak for 30 minutes. Drain the coconut from the sugar water.
+ In a separate small bowl, using your fingers to mix 1 cup of the flour, the softened butter cubes, and ½ cup of the brown sugar until it forms a crumbly dough. This is your crust.
+ Spread the dough evenly along the bottom of a greased 8 by 8-inch baking pan, using your fingers to press the dough onto the bottom and sides of the pan. Your crust should be about ½ inch thick. Place the pan in the oven and bake until the crust is lightly browned, 15 minutes. Remove the pan from the oven and let the crust cool for about 10 minutes.
+ Meanwhile, mix the remaining 1 cup brown sugar, the eggs, vanilla extract, remaining 2 tablespoons flour, the baking powder, and the drained coconut. Pour the mixture evenly over the crust.
+ Place the dream bars in the oven and bake for 25 minutes. When the top has turned a caramel-brown color and has hardened, remove the bars from the oven, sprinkle with powdered sugar, and serve warm.

**+ sodium count:**

Raw coconut: 0 to 15mg per 1 cup depending on brand; Eggs: 71mg per large egg

# CARROT CUPCAKES + FAKE CREAM CHEESE FROSTING

Carrot cupcakes were not difficult to re-create without sodium. But the frosting posed the real challenge. Cream cheese frosting has tang and bite along with sweet undertones. It also has about 46mg of sodium per 2 tablespoons, which is not horrible, but it can add up quickly. So I decided to look for an alternative. I found three. Both kefir and Greek yogurt have a sour punch and, when mixed with powdered sugar, a thick frosting texture. And if you want to stick with cream cheese, look for Nancy's brand cream cheese. It only has 35mg of sodium per 2 tablespoons.

**Makes 18 cupcakes**

Cupcakes

- 2 cups all-purpose flour
- 3 teaspoons no-sodium baking soda
- 1½ teaspoons ground cinnamon
- 4 large eggs
- 1 cup granulated white sugar
- 1 cup safflower, corn, or canola oil
- 2 cups peeled and grated raw carrots, about 3 large carrots
- ½ cup unsweetened shredded coconut
- ½ cup chopped and toasted salt-free pumpkin seeds
- 1 cup raisins or currants

Frosting

- 3 cups powdered sugar
- ½ cup low-sodium plain Greek yogurt, kefir cheese, or low-sodium cream cheese

+ Preheat the oven to 350°F. Line a cupcake pan with paper liners.
+ In a medium bowl, mix together the flour, baking soda, and cinnamon. In a separate large bowl, using an electric mixer, beat the eggs, sugar, and oil until it has a thick, paste-like consistency.
+ Using a spoon, slowly add the flour mixture and stir until well combined. Fold in the grated carrots, coconut, pumpkin seeds, and raisins. Your batter is ready to go.
+ Gently pour the batter into each cupcake well, distributing it equally and filling it to just below the edge. Place the cupcakes in the oven, on the middle rack, and bake for 20 to 25 minutes. To check if they are done, insert a toothpick into a cupcake's center. If it comes out clean and dry, they are done. Remove the cupcakes from the oven and transfer to a wire rack, to cool for 15 to 20 minutes.
+ While you're waiting, make the frosting. In a large bowl, using an electric mixer, beat the Greek yogurt (kefir cheese or cream cheese) and powdered sugar on high speed until it is thick and smooth, about 2 minutes. Your frosting may look a little chunky before getting creamy, so be patient. With a knife or small spatula, spread the frosting on top of each cooled cupcake. Cover the cupcakes until it is serving time.

### + sodium count:

Eggs: 71mg per large egg; Carrots: 42mg per medium carrot; Raw coconut: 0 to 15mg per 1 cup depending on brand; Pumpkin seeds: 5mg per ¼ cup; Raisins: 16mg per cup; Plain Greek yogurt: 60mg per 6-ounce container depending on brand; Kefir cheese: 20mg per 2 tablespoons depending on brand; Low-sodium cream cheese: 35mg per 2 tablespoons

# SWEET MATZO CRACKER PIE CRUST

One thing stands between low-sodium eaters and pie: the graham cracker crust. But this past Passover, with cupboards full of salt-free matzo, I began to wonder if this unleavened cracker could successfully replace the higher-sodium cookie crust. And then I thought, if Moses could part the Red Sea, then I could certainly give this a try.

Here's the best news. It worked. It totally, deliciously, crunchily, sweetly, crackingly worked. It was a Passover miracle. On this past year's particularly holy night, I chose to fill my crust with a standard lemon chiffon. But with this graham cracker–like crust, you could go in multiple pie directions. My friend made a key lime pie. A s'mores version, with a chocolate filling and marshmallow or meringue topping, would be delicious. And you could even skip the pie altogether and simply use the batter to make sodium-free graham cracker cookies instead. The possibilities are now endless. Thou shalt eat pie.

**Makes one 9-inch pie crust**

1¼ cups no-salt-added matzo meal or 5 matzo crackers ground into crumbs
½ cup packed dark brown sugar
4 tablespoons (½ stick) cold unsalted butter, cubed
5 to 6 tablespoons ice cold water
2 teaspoons orange marmalade

+ Preheat the oven to 325°F.
+ Put the ground matzo crumbs, brown sugar, and butter into a food processor and pulse until all the butter chunks are completely blended with the matzo cracker crumbs and sugar.
+ One tablespoon at a time, add the water as you continue to mix the dough. Add the orange marmalade and continue to mix until the dough forms a ball on its own. Remove the dough from the food processor, cover in plastic wrap, and place it in the refrigerator for 30 minutes to chill.
+ Just like a graham cracker crust, this dough requires no rolling. Yipee! So when you're ready to get your pie on, simply put two-thirds of the dough into your greased pie pan. Then, using your hands and fingertips, pat the dough evenly on the bottom of the pan to form a crust. Add the remaining dough as necessary to cover the pie dish and form a ½-inch-thick crust.
+ Place the pie pan into the oven and bake for 15 to 20 minutes. The crust will still be slightly soft to the touch when you remove it from the oven, but it will harden as it cools. Wait at least 20 minutes before filling with your chosen pie custard and then cook according to your chosen recipe's directions. Gorgeous!

**+ sodium count:**
Practically sodium-free.

**+ sodium count**

Egg white: 55mg per large egg;
White chocolate: 25mg per ounce, depending on brand;
Dark chocolate: 0 to 10mg per ounce, depending on brand

# ANGEL FOOD CAKE

*Low-sodium guest: Chef Alan Carter, Mission Beach Cafe*

There is no better lunch date than someone who can talk endlessly about butter, sugar, and chocolate. And that's why I happily said yes (more like, YES!) to an afternoon meal with Chef Alan Carter, owner and pastry chef at the Mission Beach Cafe, a local restaurant that continuously accommodates my health needs with savory dinners and even French fries.

But dessert—that was a subject we had not yet explored. And when Chef Carter heard about this book and the opportunity to bake for you, he was eager to get started. That's because Chef Carter is a huge advocate of healthy food that can still be decadent. He's no stranger to creative substitutions and has been known to use avocados to provide creaminess in chocolate tortes and spinach to color his frostings, staying far away from anything processed. As such, overcoming low-sodium challenges came easily to him. That afternoon, over lunch, we brainstormed ways to keep the texture, rise, and taste in his cakes while losing the salt. The answers lay in egg whites for air and lemon juice for kick and the result was the weightless chocolate angel food cake you see opposite.

**Makes 1 cake**

- 1½ cups large egg whites, room temperature (about 8 large eggs)
- ½ teaspoon cream of tartar
- 1½ cups (12 ounces) granulated white sugar
- ½ cup (4 ounces) cake flour
- 1 teaspoon vanilla extract
- 1 teaspoon fresh lemon juice
- ½ cup (2 ounces) grated white chocolate
- 1 cup (4 ounces) grated 76% dark chocolate

+ Preheat the oven to 350°F.
+ Rinse an angel food cake or Bundt pan with hot water and leave it wet. Then measure out all of the ingredients and have them ready (including grating your chocolate) because this cake needs to come together quickly before putting it in the oven.
+ Using an electric or standing mixer filled with the whisk attachment, whip the egg whites on medium speed until frothy. Add the cream of tartar and beat on high until they form very soft peaks. Slowly add half of the sugar to the egg whites while beating until they form stiff peaks when the mixer whisk is lifted. Remove the bowl from the mixer and set aside.
+ Sift the flour and mix with the remaining sugar. Fold it into the egg mixture one-third at a time. Add the vanilla and lemon juice and fold lightly (about 4 turns). Add the white and dark chocolate, mixing very little. Do not overmix! There will be pieces of unmixed ingredients in the batter and that's okay.
+ Pour the mixture into the wet, ungreased angel food cake pan and then immediately put it in the oven and bake for 45 minutes. When the cake is done, turn it upside down (if the pan has feet) or on the neck of a glass bottle to cool completely.

# QUICK CHAI TEA COOKIES

Sometimes, at the end of a day, you just crave a cookie fix without the effort. You want to dip your hand into a box of goodies, nibble on a couple of chocolate treats, and call it a night, without having to stir, whisk, or clean a single pan. But most premade cookies and cookie dough are high in sodium, and so sweet-tooth emergencies require making batter from scratch.

Don't panic, though, because I've come up with a recipe that is quick to make and salt-free. It requires minimal mixing and measuring, and you will have a batch of spicy treats ready before you even have time to change into your evening comfies.

Now, I have to confess: these cookies were supposed to be meringues. But I could never get the egg whites to peak right, and I kept opening my oven to find puddles of sugar, not swirls of crisp meringues. So I moved to macaroons, which brought about an equal set of mishaps and misshapen mounds of coconut. Finally, my good friend (thanks, Kat) taught me how to make foolproof coconut cookies that cook up in a flash. I added some chai tea and pumpkin seeds, and with some help from another good pal, parchment paper, we had gooey, crunchy, aromatic cookie clusters that even I could bake. The parchment paper also keeps cleanup to a minimum. And if your first batch does end up crumbling, don't throw those cookies away. Use them as a topper for low-sodium, soy, or coconut ice cream.

**Makes 12 cookies**

- ½ cup unsweetened shredded coconut
- ½ cup packed dark brown sugar
- ½ cup no-salt-added pumpkin seeds
- 1 large egg white, beaten
- 1 teaspoon chai tea (or 1 tea bag)
- 1 teaspoon vanilla extract

+ Preheat the oven to 350°F. Cover a baking sheet with parchment paper.
+ Place all the ingredients in a mixing bowl and mix together with your hands, making sure it is well combined. Take small handfuls of your cookie mix and squeeze to remove as much of the egg liquid as possible. Add an extra ¼ cup of pumpkin seeds and ¼ cup of coconut if it seems too runny. Place the cookies in mounds on the parchment-lined baking sheet. Repeat until all the cookie mix is used. Each cookie should be about 1 teaspoon of the batter. Bake the cookies until they turn a toasted brown color and are firm to the touch, 12 to 15 minutes. Remove the baking sheet from the oven and allow the cookies to cool on the sheet. When they are hard enough that you can peel them from the parchment, snack away.

**+ sodium count:**
Raw coconut: 0 to 15mg 1 per cup depending on brand; Pumpkin seeds: 5mg per ¼ cup; Egg white: 55mg per large egg

# INDEX

D



E



F